OCCULT
THE
CONSPIRACY

MICHAEL HOWARD

MJF BOOKS
NEW YORK

Published by MJF Books
Fine Communications
Two Lincoln Square
60 West 66th Street
New York, NY 10023

Library of Congress Catalog Card Number 97-72753
ISBN 1-56731-225-X

The Occult Conspiracy
Copyright © 1989 by Michael Howard

This edition published by arrangement with Inner Traditions International, Ltd.

Manufactured in the United States of America on acid-free paper

MJF Books and the MJF colophon are trademarks of Fine Creative Media, Inc.

10 9 8 7 6 5 4 3 2

CONTENTS

Dedicated to the memory

of

the Archduke Franz Ferdinand

and

the Archduchess Sophia

von Habsburg

Iuncti coniugo fatis iungunter eisdem.

Rumour is not always wrong

Tacitus

The world is governed by very different
personages from what is imagined by
those who are not behind the scenes.

Benjamin Disraeli

It is a strange desire to seek power and to
lose liberty or to seek power over others
and to lose power over a man's self

Francis Bacon

PREFACE

It is the generally accepted view among those who have very little knowledge of the matters discussed in this book that occultism is the province of a minority of deluded individuals. Those who study or practise the occult are generally dismissed by the public, usually on the basis of sensational media stories, as cranks, charlatans, sexual deviants or lunatics. Anyone involved in the twilight world of the occultist must, so the argument goes, be weird or unusual because occultism in the popular imagination conjures up visions of incense filled temples, naked virgins on altars, bizarre rituals, secret initiations and, if Christian propaganda can be believed, the worship of the Powers of Darkness.

The rational intellectual who is the leading critic of occultism will therefore be surprised to learn that the word 'occult' can be simply defined as 'hidden'. It is used in that sense in astronomy to describe a planet which is occulted or hidden from view by another planet. Occultism is therefore the study of the hidden which makes it sound far less sensational and mysterious. In practice those who follow the occult path are heirs to an ancient tradition of esoteric knowledge which is thousands of years old. Experienced occultists who have probed the inner mysteries of this arcane tradition are the guardians of an Ancient Wisdom which is the secret teaching behind all established religions. While occultism, like all religious systems, has its fair share of eccentrics it also boasts members who are respectable people of high social standing.

A dyed-in-the-wool materialist who dismisses the occult as pure fantasy will be even more shocked by the central thesis of this book. It will prove, offering evidence gathered from both orthodox and unorthodox sources, that many of the famous historical personalities of the last 2,000 years, including statesmen, politicians, religious leaders and royalty, were actively involved in the occult, mysticism and magical practices. In addition it will show that many of the major historical events of the period have a hidden significance which can only be explained in terms of an occult conspiracy. The revealing of this conspiracy is integral to any true understanding of world history and the development of Western civilization because of its wide-ranging and far-reaching influence.

To the average citizen the political system of the country they live in involves the mundane. Politics is generally concerned with economics, education, social welfare, the defence of the nation, the legal system and the daily governance of the country. International politics, on the other hand, touches upon larger issues, including treaties between nations, global economic structures, and the awesome responsibility of preserving world peace in the face of an escalating arms race. When we see the smiling faces of international statesmen and religious leaders on the television or in the newspapers it is difficult to imagine that behind the diplomatic facade exists a very different world; a world of secret societies and occult fraternities peopled by shadowy figures who have often been obsessed with the pursuit of power. Since the days of the Pharoahs in ancient Egypt the occult has entangled the black arts of espionage, subversion and revolution in its web. Today the occult conspiracy still affects politics, although there are few who are aware of its influence even though those who control it are often well known faces and household names.

The purpose of this book is not sensationalism for its own sake, although many who are not conversant with the hidden world of secret societies and parapolitics may criticize it on those grounds. In presenting the facts about the influence of occultism on politics we have tried to avoid falling into the trap of over-dramatizing certain historical events. However once you step from the well worn path which the conventional historian treads and examine the real motives which engineered key situations in Europe during the last 2,000 years, you enter the realm of a 'secret history'; an alternative history which has seldom been chronicled and remains the study of a few dedicated researchers of the arcane and the esoteric. It is this secret history, melodramatic as it may appear to the outside world, which is only dimly aware of its existence, which is the subject matter of this book. It is the background upon which the participants in the occult conspiracy play their games with the lives of millions of ordinary men and women.

In many cases the influence of the occult puppetmasters can be recognized as benevolent and the pattern which emerges is one which has been instrumental in the progress of human civilization. However, as the historical story unfolds, it becomes clear that the pursuit and exercise of power, especially absolute power, can become a corrupting force leading astray those who have high ideals and the purest of aspirations. History is littered with the remnants of grand plans which crumbled to dust because of human frailty. The road to Utopia is too often paved with the bones of the common man martyred in the cause of freedom.

Occult knowledge is a double-edged sword and those who seek to unravel its secrets and discover its mysteries should be aware of the grave responsibility which comes with that task. Unfortunately in these pages you will meet those who have not been worthy of the quest and the task they were given by higher authority. But you will also discover that through the acquisition of the Ancient Wisdom it is possible that the aspirations of humanity can be fulfilled, providing those who guide the destiny of our nations are not diverted from the narrow path they tread by the lure of temporal power at the expense of spiritual integrity.

I would like to thank the following for their help during the writing of this book; the staff of the British Library reading room at the British Museum, the Westminster Public Reference Library, the Folklore Society Library, the librarians of the British Federation of International Co-Freemasonry, the Theosophical Society (UK), and Robin Ramsey of *Lobster* magazine.

1

THE ANCIENT MYSTERIES

In order to understand the origins of the occult conspiracy as it first openly manifested in medieval Europe through the secret societies of the period it is advisable to examine their ancient roots which can be traced back to ancient Egypt and the classical civilizations of Rome and Greece. During the Middle Ages several secret societies based on occult doctrines emerged which claimed antecedents dating back almost to the beginning of human history. The mystical ideas which they espoused had their origin in the earliest religious beliefs known to mankind. These pagan beliefs survived the formation of the major world faiths of Judaism, Christianity, and Islam by adopting the outward form of these religions and operating within them as a heretical, secret and esoteric tradition.

With the persecution of alternative spiritual beliefs in medieval Christian Europe, the guardians of this ancient wisdom went underground forming secret societies to preserve their pagan ideals. The two major secret societies which were formed in this period, although they only revealed themselves in a public form in the sixteenth and seventeenth centuries, were Freemasonry and the Order of the Rosy Cross. The beliefs and practices of those two clandestine fraternities provide an insight into the workings of the occult conspiracy and the socio-political vision which exists at its heart.

While the Order of the Rosy Cross or the Rosicrucians is still a secret society which has received very little publicity in modern times, considerable public attention has been drawn to Freemasonry recently. Freemasonry has been singled out as a potentially corrupting influence because its membership includes businessmen, judges, and police officers whose Masonic oaths and activities are regarded as the ideal cover for nepotism. To the outside world Masonry is depicted as a superior working mens' club for the professional person who wants to progress in his career through membership of an élite social group. Favours are allegedly shown by Masons to each other in business deals and job applications, while the prominence of legal officers in Masonic lodges indicates to the suspicious that the course of justice could be perverted by rich men gathering in darkened lodge rooms.

The Masons have responded to these allegations by denying that membership of their lodges offers any special rewards in the business or professional worlds. They have attempted to present a respectable image to the outside world using the argument that their Craft is not a secret society but a society with secrets. However, despite this public relations exercise, the popular image of Freemasonry is a group of middle-aged businessmen meeting once a month wearing fancy dress and performing mumbo-jumbo schoolboy rituals. In many cases the activities of the modern Masonic lodge may be just this eccentric pantomime but if Masonry is so laughable why, over the centuries, has it attracted some of the most brilliant minds; leading scientists, prominent politicians, writers, intellectuals, artists, financiers and even royalty? The answer must lie in the inner teachings of Freemasonry which are seldom discussed in public.

At a recent Church of England synod a report on Freemasonry was presented to the assembled clerics and lay people for debate. Several speakers denounced Masonry as contrary to the teachings of Christianity and condemned Christians, especially clerics, who might be members. One speaker even went so far as to attack Masonry as 'blasphemous' because he claimed its central initiation ritual, which involves a symbolic death and rebirth enactment, was a travesty of the Christian belief in the crucifixion and resurrection of Jesus of Nazareth. Since its inception Freemasonry has been the target of Christian wrath, although later in this book it will be revealed that the Catholic Church has been infiltrated by agents of the secret societies.

Why should Christians be so critical of Freemasonry, apart from the obvious reason that the Church is opposed to any alternative belief system which might threaten its spiritual monopoly? Again the answer to this question lies in the 'secrets' of Freemasonry. If these secrets were readily available to the general public it is doubtful if their meaning would be understood to those who were not versed in the doctrines of occultism and ancient religion. In fact it is doubtful if many of the ordinary lodge members understand what its secrets represent. In the inner circle of Masonry, among those who have obtained higher degrees of initiation, there are Masons who understand that they are the inheritors of an ancient and pre-Christian tradition handed down from pagan times. The medieval Masons inherited this secret tradition in the form of symbolic teachings which expressed spiritual truths. These teachings originated in the pagan Mysteries which were followed widely in the ancient world.

To understand these secret teachings, and by doing so place the involvement of the medieval secret societies in international politics into a spiritual context, it is necessary to examine the alleged origins of Freemasonry in the pre-Christian period. The information about these origins are preserved in the writings of Masonic historians, in the theories put forward by occultists who have investigated the symbolism of Freemasonry and in the academic accounts of the pagan religions which influenced the medieval occult tradition.

Historically it is known that speculative Freemasonry developed from the early medieval guilds of masons who built the Gothic cathedrals of Europe. They formed themselves into guilds which operated as mutual self-help groups similar to modern trade unions. These guilds used secret symbols – the so-called masons' marks found in old churches – and passwords and a special handshake so they could recognize each other. It is generally believed in occult circles that these medieval masons had inherited esoteric knowledge from their pagan antecedents and this knowledge was incorporated into the sacred architecture of the cathedrals. When the lodges of speculative, as opposed to operative, Freemasonry were founded in the seventeenth and eighteenth centuries this knowledge was transformed into the symbolism which today forms the basis of Masonic ritual.

Medieval associations of masons could involve up to 700 members who made contracts with the Church to build cathedrals and monasteries. It is believed that one particular masonic building association originated in Cologne in the thirteenth century which utilized initiation ceremonies when it granted entry to its members who were called 'free masons'. Eventually these operative masonic lodges accepted outsiders, provided they could prove themselves to be men of learning or those who held high social position. By the end of the sixteenth century the lodges of working masons had largely dispersed and were replaced by speculative Freemasonry with its emphasis on the esoteric symbolism of the Craft as a metaphor for spiritual progress and enlightenment.

Although the medieval masons could be regarded as down-to-earth artisans they also possessed a mythical framework to explain the origins of their trade. The operative masons also divided all available knowledge into seven liberal arts and sciences. These were classified as grammar or correct speech, rhetoric or the application of grammar, dialectics or distinguishing truth from falsehood, arithmetic or accurate reckoning, geometry or the measurement of the Earth, music and astronomy. Of all these arts and sciences the masons regarded geometry as the most important.

According to their beliefs, geometry had been taught by a pre-Flood patriarch called Lamech who had three sons. One invented geometry, another was the first mason and the third was a blacksmith who was the first human to work with precious metals. In common with Noah, Lamech was warned by Jehovah of the impending flood caused by the wickedness of humanity and the interference of the Fallen Angels in world affairs. Lamech and his sons decided to preserve their knowledge in two stone pillars so that future generations would discover it.

One of these pillars was discovered by Hermes Trismegistus or Thrice Greatest, known to the Greeks as the god Hermes and to the Ancient Egyptians as the ibis-headed scribe of the gods Thoth (pronounced Tehuti). The so-called Emerald Tablet of Hermes is said to contain the essence of the lost wisdom from before the days of the biblical Flood. According to occult sources, this tablet was discovered in a cave by the mystic Apollonius of Tyana who was regarded by the early Church as a rival to Jesus. The first published version of the Emerald Tablet dates from an Arabic source of the eighth century CE and it was not translated into Latin in Europe until the thirteenth century.

However the myth of the Hermetic wisdom had a profound effect on the Gnostics who were heretical Christians in direct conflict with the early Christian Church for attempting to fuse paganism with the new faith. They also claimed to possess the secret teachings of Jesus which he only divulged to his inner circle of disciples. These teachings had been censored from the authorized version of the New Testament approved by the Church councils who met to decide the structure and dogma of early Christianity. The Gnostic philosophy emerged in a different form in medieval Europe in the rise of the heretical Christian movement of the Cathars and the chivalric Order of the Knights Templar. The Hermetic tradition provided the spiritual inspiration for many secret societies in the Middle Ages and its influence can be discerned in both speculative Freemasonry and Rosicrucianism.

In the Masonic tradition it is said that masons were first organized into a corporate body during the building of the Tower of Babel. The concept of this tower was to reach up to heaven and contact God according to *Genesis* 11:4-6. The fall of the Tower of Babel destroyed the common language spoken by humanity and ended the second Golden Age which followed the Flood. The architect of the tower was King Nimrod of Babylon who was a mason. He provided his cousin, the king of Ninevah, with sixty masons to assist in the construction of his cities. The masons were told on their departure to remain steadfastly true to each other, avoid dissensions at any cost, live in harmony and serve their lord as their master on Earth. According to popular belief the Hebrews received their knowledge of masonry from the Babylonians and introduced it to Egypt when they were taken into slavery. In Egypt this knowledge was influenced by the Mysteries and the occult traditions of the pyramid builders who were versed in the techniques of sacred geometry.

The key to the pagan origins of Freemasonry lies in the symbolic story related to candidates for initiation into the three degrees of Masonry, known as Entered Apprentice, Fellow Craftsman and Master Mason. In Masonic lore the basis of this legend is the semi-mythical story of the construction of King Solomon's temple in Jerusalem. This building was regarded as the repository of ancient occult wisdom and symbolism by both the Freemasons and the Knights Templar.

King David initiated the building of the temple at Jerusalem and after his death his son Solomon completed the task. To build the edifice Solomon imported masons, artists and craftsmen from neighbouring countries. Specifically he sent a message to the king of Tyre asking if he could hire the services of the king's master builder, Hiram Abiff, who was skilled in geometry. Hiram was a widow's son who had trained as a craftsman working in brass. Because of his artistic talents Solomon appointed Hiram as the chief architect and master mason of the temple to be built in Jerusalem.

Hiram completed the temple in a period of seven years (this number is especially significant in occult tradition and Masonry) but this achievement was overshadowed by his mysterious and violent death. At noon one day, as the other masons were resting in their midday break, Hiram visited the temple to check on the progress of the work which was nearly finished. As he entered the porch of the temple, passing through the entrance flanked by the two pillars at the gateway, Hiram was approached by one of his fellow masons who demanded from him the secret of the Master Mason's word. Hiram refused to provide this secret information, telling the worker that he would receive it in good time once he had progressed further in his career. The mason was not satisfied with this answer and struck Hiram a blow which made him stumble, dazed and bleeding, to the second gate of the temple. There he was accosted by a second mason who asked the same question and when no answer was forthcoming hit him. Hiram staggered to the third (western) entrance to the temple where another mason lay in wait. The process was repeated and this time the chief architect died from the third blow.

The three renegade masons carried Hiram's body from the temple to the top of a nearby hill where they dug a shallow grave and buried him. They marked the grave with an acacia tree and returned to work as normal in the afternoon. When Hiram was found to be missing a search party was organized but it was fifteen days before his corpse was discovered. Solomon was informed and ordered that Hiram's body should be exhumed and reburied with a full religious ceremony and the honours due to a craftsman of his rank. The three assassins were eventually exposed, tried and put to death for their crime.

If this legend is examined in relation to the religious situation in the reign of Solomon some interesting facts arise which provide insights into the hidden pagan symbolism of Freemasonry. Firstly, Tyre, during the time Solomon was on the throne of Israel, was renowned as a centre of Goddess worship. Although Solomon is regarded as a leading devotee of Yahweh (or Jehovah) he had a lengthy correspondence with the pagan king of Tyre and requested that he send his master builder, who must have been engaged in erecting temples dedicated to the worship of the Great Goddess, to help him design and build his temple to Yahweh.

A careful reading of the Old Testament reveals that when the Hebrews resettled in Canaan after their escape from slavery in Egypt the worship of their tribal god, Yahweh, was strongly resisted by the indigenous inhabitants who revered the fertility goddess Aserah or Astarte and her male consort. The situation when the worship of Jehovah was introduced into Canaan can be compared with the early medieval period in Europe when the Roman missionaries tried to convert the heathen tribes and to nineteenth-century Africa when white settlers forced Christianity on the natives. It is also obvious from discrepancies in the Hebrew creation myth recorded in *Genesis* that early Judaism was heavily influenced by the pagan beliefs of the nomadic tribes who were the ancestors of the Israelites. In establishing the religion of Yahweh the Old Testament patriarchs drew upon the rich structure of mythology which existed in neighbouring countries, including Sumeria and Babylon. In particular the myths of the Garden of Eden and the Flood can be identified as foreign imports grafted onto the Judaic belief system.

Yahwehism became the dominant religion of ancient Israel only through the militant campaigns of a small élite of patriarchal priests who, for the most part but not always, were supported by the monarchy and the ruling class. It was resisted bravely by the common people supported by heretic members of the Establishment. The conflict which this caused can still be detected in orthodox Judaism where the Supreme Creator is represented as neither male nor female. One medieval Jewish philosopher stated 'God is not a body nor can bodily attributes be ascribed to him (sic) and He has no likeness at all.' Despite this attempt to present Divinity as an abstract entity, the majority of Jewish rabbis regarded Yahweh as masculine in nature. His alternative title of Adonai which is translated as 'Lord' confirms this belief.

It is only in the secret, occult teachings of the mystical system known as the Cabbala, which is the esoteric doctrine of the Judaic religion, that the ancient concept of an androgynous deity survived in the feminine image of the Shekinah or Bride of God. In Jewish synagogues the Shekinah is welcomed at sunset on a Friday evening in prayers to celebrate the beginning of the Sabbath. In these prayers the Shekinah is welcomed as the Bride of God and the Cabbalists teach that only through her can creation be manifested. This idea is reinforced by the folk belief that the Shekinah materializes unseen over the marriage bed on the wedding night which suggests a relic of ancient fertility rites performed in honour of a goddess.

Ancient memories of Goddess worship also survive in the Jewish myth of the she-demon Lilith who inspired sexual desires in men by sending them erotic dreams. In Cabbalistic teachings Lilith was the first wife of Adam before Eve and taught him the arts of magical enchantment. From their illicit union was spawned the elemental realm of elves, fairies and gnomes according to occult lore. Lilith was not originally a demonic figure but can be traced back to a Sumerian goddess with the title of the Lady of Beasts who was depicted in the form of an owl. Lilith symbolizes the dark aspect of the Great Goddess of the pagan old religion in her *femme fatale* or enchantress form. This aspect of the feminine has always been rejected by patriarchal cultures whose sexual puritanism transformed it into a demonic symbol because they were incapable of handling the potent erotic energies associated with it.

Initially the worship of the fertility deities of Canaan was an integral part of Judaic religion. The goddess Aserah or Ashtoreth, her consort El and their son Baal – meaning Lord – were widely venerated. Effigies of the Goddess were erected all over Israel as described in the Old Testament books of *Kings, Chronicles, Judges, Deuteronomy, Exodus* and *Micah*. Gideon is recorded as having destroyed an altar to Baal on the command of an angel (*Judges* 6: 25-31) and there are references to the worship of the fertility god and goddess at altars erected in the temple at Jerusalem.

How does Solomon feature in this tradition of Goddess worship? During the Middle Ages the Hebrew king gained an infamous reputation as a master magician who could raise elemental spirits and several grimoires or magical workbooks were either named after him (e.g. *The Key of Solomon*) or credited to his authorship. He was generally regarded as a powerful magus, healer and exorcist and today some born-again Christians denounce him as a devil-worshipper who led the Israelites away from the true God. In the apocryphal *Book of Wisdom*, written in the first century BCE, Solomon is quoted as saying, 'God gave me true knowledge of things as they are; an understanding of the structure of the world and the way in which the elements work, the beginning and the end of eras and what lies between . . . the cycles of the year and the constellations . . . the thoughts of men . . . the power of spirits . . . the virtues of roots . . . I learnt it all, secret and manifest.'

In addition to his magical attributes and occult powers Solomon is regarded by some authorities as a secret worshipper of the Goddess. Solomon's conversion to paganism and his worship of strange gods is blamed on his marriages to foreign princesses who introduced their religious customs to his court (I *Kings* 11:1-8). There is also speculation that the legendary Queen of Sheba introduced the heretic king to the occult doctrines of her land (situated either in Africa or Arabia). She not only brought camels loaded with spices, gold and precious stones when she visited Solomon but included in her entourage priests who initiated the Jewish monarch into the mysteries of the pagan old religion.

In the Old Testament it is said of Solomon that 'he sacrificed and burnt incense in high places', (I *Kings* 3:3) which were the sites of shrines dedicated to the worship of the Great Goddess. The available evidence suggests that during the 370-year history of the original temple at Jerusalem it was wholly or partly used for Goddess worship for 200 years of that period. When one of Yahweh's prophets denounced Solomon's waywardness in favour of a young man called Jeroboam who became the new king (I *Kings* 11:29-40), the worship of pagan gods briefly abated. In I *Kings* 23: 4-7 it is recorded that the high priest Hilkaih destroyed the shrines to the goddess Ashtoreth which Solomon had erected all over Israel.

Unfortunately for the Yahwehists the choice of Jeroboam to be the new religious leader of Israel was a miscalculation. The young man soon reverted to the worship of the pagan bull god (I *Kings* 12:33) and was disgraced. The cult of Goddess worship was further reinforced by the arrival in Israel of Princess Jezebel, the original 'scarlet woman' who was the daughter of the king of Sidon and a priestess of the pagan faith. Her image as a shameless hussy evidently stems from the explicit sexuality of the rites Jezebel performed to the Goddess, which horrified the puritanical priests of Yahweh. Under the influence of Jezebel her husband, King Ahab of Israel, built an altar to Baal and a sacred grove to the Goddess (I *Kings* 16: 30-33). It is said that 850 priests of Baal and Ashtoreth were entertained at a lavish banquet organized by the new queen. She worshipped Astarte and in the streets of Jerusalem sacred fires were lit, spiced honey cakes baked, libations of wine were poured on the ground and incense was burnt as a sacrifical offering to the fertility goddess. Jezebel was eventually overthrown by the worshippers of Yahweh because of her erotic excesses and she was killed. However Goddess worship survived for many years and when Josiah began his crusade to restore Yahwehism he first had to destroy the shrines and altars to the pagan gods erected by the common people. (II *Kings* 23: 4-15).

The Goddess-worshipping Solomon had sent to Tyre, a centre of pagan worship, for Hiram Abiff, the master builder to become his chief architect at the temple in Jerusalem. Hiram was murdered at the conclusion of the building work in the circumstances described earlier which suggested a ritual killing or human sacrifice. As Hiram was the designer of pagan temples it seems probable that he incorporated elements of paganism into the architecture of Solomon's temple. In fact the temple was built in a pagan style with a vestibule, a nave and an inner sanctuary with two pillars guarding its entrance.

The main entrance of the temple was of primary symbolic importance as this was flanked by two pillars, historically known as Jachin and Boaz. They formed the framework to the outer court or porch of the temple where, according to legend, the masons who built the edifice gathered to hold their meetings. It has been suggested that these two pillars were placed in position to imitate the obelisks which were erected at the

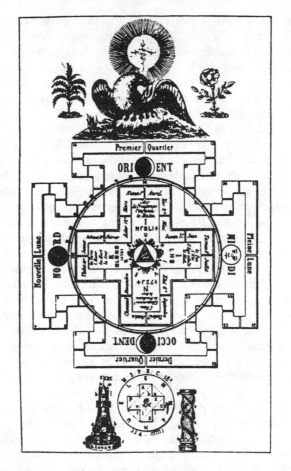

Solomon's Temple (a 19th Century illustration from a Rosicrucian source)

gateways of Egyptian temples. The most famous of these were erected on the orders of the Pharoah Thothmes III at Heliopolis or the City of the Sun in the fifteenth century BCE. These pillars, called for some unknown reason Cleopatra's Needles, can be found today on the Thames embankment in London and in Central Park in New York. Symbols on the base of the American obelisk have been tentatively identified as Masonic signs. Thothmes is regarded by some modern occultists as the legendary founder of the Order of the Rosy Cross.

The twin pillars in front of Solomon's temple also have similiarities to traditional Canaanite fertility symbols. The temples dedicated to the Goddess in Tyre are said to have featured stone pillars of phallic design at their entrances. These pillars were the focus of fertility rites performed in honour of Astarte at her special festivals. Connections have also been made between these pillars and the monoliths used by Lamech and his sons to preserve their ancient knowledge in the hieroglyphic symbols carved on their surfaces. Cabbalists have identified them as symbols of the masculine and feminine principles by which the Universe came into manifestation as expressed on the Tree of Life symbol. It is also agreed by both occultists and Masons that these two pillars represent the male and female energies which are the basis of creation. Their position on either side of the entrance to the temple which was dedicated to the Goddess suggests that this gateway may represent the female labia. In ancient religious belief the temples of the Goddess, whether as Astarte, Ishtar or Isis, were designed as symbols of her body and this was reflected in their sacred architecture.

The most sacred part of Solomon's temple was the inner sanctum or Holy of Holies which symbolized the womb of the Goddess and was the repository of the Ark of the Covenant which contained the sacred laws of the Hebrew race given to Moses on Mount Sinai by Yahweh. Only the high priests of Yahweh were allowed to enter the inner sanctum where the Ark, made of gold and shittim wood, was kept. The lid of the Ark was a gold plate on which knelt effigies of the mythical guardians of the Covenant known as the Cherubim. They faced each other and had large wings which arched over the Ark. This was the mercy seat upon which the God of Israel allegedly descended to communicate with His high priest.

According to Professor Raphael Ktav in his book *The Hebrew Goddess*, the Cherubim who guarded the Ark of the Covenant in the temple were in the shape of naked female figures with wings. The word Cherubim means 'messenger' and in Hebrew mythology it refers to an intermediary of divine origin who acts as a go-between for humanity and God. The two Cherubim in the Holy of Holies were described by the Jewish mystic Philo, writing in the first century CE, as symbols of the dual nature of God and the male and female principles of creation. Philo regarded the deity worshipped by the ancient Hebrews as androgynous having both male and female characteristics. According to one account one of the Cherubim was male and the other was female.

If Hiram Abiff was a pagan worshipper of the Goddess and was responsible for designing her temples in Tyre, what was the significance of his ritual murder at the hands of fellow masons in Jerusalem? In the ancient rites of the Goddess the ritual death or sacrifice of her consort, or a priest representing him, features prominently. This sacrificial element in Goddess worship was widespread in the Middle East and would have been well known to the Israelites. With this sacrificial aspect is also found the myth of the resurrection of the dying god which is found in the legend of Hiram Abiff in his burial and exhumation and the best-known example of which, in a pagan religious context, is the story of Isis and Osiris in ancient Egypt. The myth had a profound effect on the development of the pagan Mysteries in the classical world and also influenced early Christianity.

In Egyptian mythology Isis and Osiris are represented as the earliest rulers of the Nile delta in primeval times. During their reign Egypt flourished because the two deities civilized the land and its people who had previously been savage barbarians addicted to cannibalism and perverted sexual practices. Isis and Osiris introduced a legal code, agriculture, the arts and crafts, temples and the correct worship of the gods. Because of these deeds the Egyptian people adored their rulers and worshipped them as divine beings.

Osiris however had a rival and enemy, his twin brother Set (or Typhon meaning 'insolence' or 'pride' in Greek). Set wanted to rule the country and was constantly plotting against the Royal family. While Osiris was away abroad and Isis ruled alone, Set plotted with seventy-two fellow conspirators to kill the king. He had secretly measured Osiris' body and made a special chest which would fit the king perfectly. When Osiris returned he invited the king and the conspirators to a welcoming feast. Isis warned her husband not to go but Osiris laughed and said he had nothing to fear from his weak brother.

At the feast everyone present admired the jewelled chest made by Set, and he said that he would give it as a present to the person whose body fitted it. One after another the guests tried but they were the wrong size. Finally Osiris climbed into the chest and Set and his co-plotters slammed down the lid, nailed it shut and sealed it with molten lead. Then they threw the casket into the Nile.

When Isis heard the news of her husband's murder she was grief-stricken. In the beliefs of the Egyptians the body had to be buried with the correct funeral rites or the soul would wander the Earth for eternity. Isis set out on a quest to find the body of Osiris and travelled up and down the Nile asking everyone she met if they had seen the chest. Eventually some children told her they had seen the coffin at the mouth of the river floating out to sea. The queen discovered that it had been washed up on the shores of Byblos in Syria where it had become entangled in the branches of a tamarisk tree. The king of Byblos cut down the tree, not realizing that the coffin of Osiris was embedded in the trunk, and made a pillar from it to support the roof of his palace.

When Isis found out what had happened she sailed to Byblos and by deception became a nurse in the Royal household serving the queen of the land who was called Astarte. This, of course, was also the name of the fertility goddess worshipped at Tyre, Sidon and in Canaan by the Israelites. Through her friendship with the young queen Isis persuaded the king to cut open the tree releasing the body of Osiris. She took the corpse of her husband back to Egypt and the tamarisk tree pillar became an object of worship in Byblos.

On her return to Egypt, Isis left the chest in a safe place while she went off to find her son Horus. However Set had heard of her return and while out hunting he discovered where the chest was hidden. In his rage he dismembered the body of Osiris and scattered it into fourteen pieces all over Egypt. When Isis was told of this further outrage she travelled all over the land and every time she found a part of the body she erected a shrine to mark the place. Each of these sacred sites was on a hill and the burial spot was marked by a tree to signify that Osiris had risen from the dead. The fourteenth part of Osiris' body – his penis – was never found because it had been swallowed by a fish. Isis made a gold replica of her husband's penis and buried it at Mendes where there was a temple dedicated to the worship of a goat god. In medieval times the Devil was sometimes called the Goat of Mendes because at this temple in ancient Egypt bizarre rituals were performed involving naked priestesses performing the sex act with goats. In the medieval witch trials it was alleged that women had intercourse with the Devil who appeared in the shape of a ram or goat.

Osiris became the focus of the cult of resurrection in dynastic Egypt and his worshippers believed that by practising his rites they would attain eternal life after death. As Osiris had introduced barley and corn to Egypt and his major religious festival coincided with the gathering of the harvest, he has been recognized as a god of vegetation who died in the autumn and was reborn in the spring. His myth therefore has similarities with other Middle Eastern fertility gods such as Adonis, Attis, and Dionysius.

Osiris was credited with introducing the vine and grapes into Egypt and in the Greek Mysteries Dionysius or Bacchus was worshipped as the patron god of the vineyard. He was often simply depicted as a bearded face carved on a tree or his image was a pillar decorated with a bearded mask surrounded by leaves. These representations are similar to the foliate masks said to represent the English folklore character Jack-in-the-Green or the Green Man which can be seen in pre-Reformation churches. Compare these images also with the story of Osiris' body entangled in the branches of a tree which is later worshipped as a sacred object.

Dionysius and Osiris both have links with the cult of Adonis whose worship was widespread throughout the Middle East in ancient times. Adonis was revered by the Semitic peoples of Babylonia and Syria and was originally known as Tammuz. This name was changed to Adonis which means 'Lord' and his linguistic connections with the Jewish Adonai used to describe one of the aspects of Yahweh. Adonis or Tammuz was born at midnight on the 24th December and burst into life from the trunk of a tree. Both these events suggest parallels with Osiris and Jesus. Tammuz is the boy god who is the consort of the Babylonian goddess of love and war, Ishtar, who was revered by the Sumerians as Inanna and by the Canaanites as Astarte. Ishtar was identified with the Moon and the morning star Venus (the symbol associated with the rebel angel Lucifer in the Judeo-Christian Bible who was later misidentified as Satan or the Devil) and features in the Babylonian myth of the Flood which was borrowed by the Hebrews.

In the myth of Tammuz and Ishtar, the young God who is her lover is killed by a wild boar and transported to the Underworld. The Goddess, mourning her loss, travels to the land of shadows in an attempt to recover her lost consort. While she is away from Earth the crops fail, the cattle become sterile and men and women lose the ability to make love. At each of the seven gates of the Underworld the goddess is forced to remove an item of clothing until she finally enters the realm of the dead naked and defenceless. As a result of her plea to the rulers of the Underworld Tammuz is reborn, Ishtar returns to Earth and the fertility of the land is restored.

The pagan worship of the fertility god Tammuz in the vicinity of the temple in Jerusalem is mentioned by the Old Testament prophet Ezekiel. Describing a vision given to him by Yahweh the prophet says in *Ezekiel* 8:14, 'Then He brought me to the door of the gate of the Lord's house (Solomon's temple) which was towards the north; and behold there sat women weeping for Tammuz'. He then goes on to describe a group of men standing within the temple precincts facing the east and worshipping the Sun in the manner of the pagans.

In the myths of Osiris, Dionysius and Adonis/Tammuz are contained the key elements of death, rebirth and fertility. These elements, together with their role as consorts of the Mother Goddess, are central to any understanding of the legend of Hiram Abiff, the pagan origins of Freemasonry and the utopian vision which forms the political ideal of Masonically-derived occult fraternities. According to ancient myths, the ruler of Tyre was also called Hiram and was said to have been a priest king of the cult of Adonis. In accordance with the religious beliefs of the time this priest king was sacrificed to the Goddess when he became too old to represent Tammuz in the annual festival dedicated to the god. On his death his soul allegedly passed into the body of his son or the chosen replacement who ruled as priest king in his place. Is it possible that Hiram Abiff was the son of the priest king of Tammuz? He is certainly referred to as the son of the widow (the mourning goddess) and this title was adopted by medieval masons to describe themselves.

In the Cabbalistic traditions of the building of Solomon's temple it is said that the craftsmen who came from Tyre were paid in corn, wine and oil. These were the sacrificial offerings associated with the fertility cults of the dying gods such as Osiris and Adonis. The same traditions relate how Solomon carried King Hiram of Tyre off to Hell by evoking a demon. When the king returned he told Solomon all that he had seen and learnt in the infernal kingdom. The rabbis suggest this was the true source of Solomon's wisdom. It is possible that the Hebrew king became a pupil of Hiram and was instructed by him in the mysteries of the goddess Ishtar or Astarte and her descent into the underworld. There are references in the lengthy correspondence between the two kings, consisting of riddles which Solomon had to solve, which suggest that some secret information was being transferred to the Hebrew monarch in coded form.

Early Masonic historians regarded Hiram Abiff as a symbolic representative of Osiris, the Egyptian god of death and rebirth. He is slain at the west gate of the temple, which is where the Sun sets. In Egyptian mythology the Underworld or Halls of Amenti ruled by Osiris as the Lord of the Dead is situated beyond the western ocean. Osiris traditionally rises from the dead in the north which in Egyptian mythology is ruled astrologically by the Zodiac sign of Leo the Lion. In the third degree of Freemasonry the candidate, representing Hiram

Abiff, is raised from the dead by a special Masonic handshake known as the lion's grip.

In both Masonic and Egyptian Mysteries the resurrected 'god' is buried on a hill in a tomb marked by a tree. Osiris additionally was called the Lord of the Acacia Tree which was the same tree planted on the grave of Hiram Abiff by his three assassins. In Canaan the worship of the goddess Astarte involved trees and pillars erected in sacred groves and on hills as symbols of her divinity. In royal Arch Masonry the candidate for initiation is informed that the sacred name of God is really Jebalon. This name has been deciphered as a coded reference to the two major gods of the Middle Eastern fertility cultus – Osiris and Baal – combined with the Hebrew tribal god Jehovah. In Masonry God is also referred to as the Great Architect of the Universe, which signifies the importance of sacred geometry in the design of sacred buildings based on the Hermetic axiom of 'As above . . . so below'. This axiom teaches the ancient philosophy that the material plane of existence is a reflection of the spiritual realm.

The political aspirations of Freemasonry, revealed in their influence on the revolutionary movements and proto-socialism of eighteenth- and nineteenth-century Europe, can be traced back to the myth of the Golden Age in pre-dynastic Egypt during the reign of Osiris and Isis and, before the Flood, to the Babylonian and Hebrew myths of creation. In the legend of Osiris the god king is a civilizing influence in a land inhabited by primitive savages who had no concept of morality or law. The priesthood of Osiris were heirs to a political utopia expressed through spiritual symbols. It is this vision which was shared by the secret societies of medieval Europe who were associated with the rise of Freemasonry and the political doctrine which was at its centre.

Occult tradition alleges that Hiram Abiff was secretly a member of an ancient society known as the Dionysian Artificers who first appeared around 1,000 BCE when the temple at Jerusalem was being erected. They took their name from the Greek god and possessed secret signs and passwords by which they recognized each other, were divided into chapters or lodges ruled by a Master and were dedicated to helping the poor. They established lodges in all the Mediterranean lands and their influence spread as far east as India. With the rise of the Roman Empire lodges were founded in Central and Western Europe, including the British Isles.

The Artificers were connected with another secret society known as the Ionians. Members of this society had settled in Asia Minor and were dedicated to the spreading of civilization, especially in its Greek form, to what they regarded as the barbarian world. Allegedly the Ionians were responsible for the famous temple of the goddess Diana at Ephesus. Architects from this society together with members of the Dionysian Artificers travelled from Tyre to work on Solomon's temple. Later the Artificers called themselves the Sons of Solomon and used his magical seal – two interlaced triangles representing the union of the male and female energies – as their trademark. The Artificers who settled in Israel founded the Cassidens who were a guild of craftsmen skilled in the repair of religious buildings. This new sect were instrumental in the foundation of the mystical Jewish group known as the Essenes who became famous through the discovery of the Dead Sea Scrolls. In occult tradition, Jesus of Nazareth was an Essene and there are connections between this group and the medieval Knights Templar.

The Dionysian Artificers believed that the temples they built had to be constructed by the principles of sacred geometry which reflected the divine plan of God. By the use of symmetry, measurement and proportion the Artificers constructed religious buildings to represent the human body as a symbol of the universe. Their theory of architecture was based on the Hermetic philosophy and the pantheistic pagan belief in the unity between the universe and God. They also promoted the political ideal of Utopia on Earth which was expressed in symbolic form. Humanity was the crude block of stone which the master mason or Grand Architect (God) was constantly moulding and polishing to transform it into an object of perfection. The hammer and chisel of the mason became the cosmic forces which shaped the spiritual destiny of humankind. In eighteenth-century speculative Masonry the hammer or gavel was a symbol of divine power. It was used to measure the hallowed precincts of the lodge which was as far as the Grand Master could throw the hammer in any direction.

The Roman architect and master builder Vitrivius, who was born in the first century CE, was influenced by the Dionysian Artificers. His theories formed the basis for the architecture of the Roman Empire and, with the rediscovery of classical knowledge in the sixteenth century, also had an impact on the greatest architects of the Renaissance. Vitrivius' concept of the magical theatre representing the microcosmos of the world as a symbol of the macrocosmos of the universe was repeated in William Shakespeare's famous phrase 'All the world's a stage, and all the men and women merely players . . .' and the naming of his theatre The Globe. It is claimed that Shakespeare was a Rosicrucian initiate and as such would have been familiar with the ideas of Vitrivius and the Dionysian Artificers.

In Masonic tradition Caesar Augustus is named as the patron of the masons in ancient Rome and is said to have been Grand Master of the Roman College of Architects. This society was organized into guilds with symbols based on the tools of their trade such as the plumb line, the square, compasses and the level. The College had initiation rituals involving the pagan myth of death and rebirth which are familiar from the Egyptian Mysteries. A temple built and used by the College was unearthed at Pompeii which had been destroyed by the volcanic eruption of Mount Vesuvius in 71 CE. Among the symbols discovered in the temple were the double triangle of Solomon, the black and white tracing board (first used by the Dionysian Artificers), the skull, the plumb line, the pilgrim's staff and the ragged robe. These symbols later emerged in medieval masonry and speculative Freemasonry.

The traditions of the Roman College seem to have been passed onto the Order of Comacine Masters who flourished during the reign of the Emperors Constantine and Theodosius in the fourth century CE when Christianity was emerging as the dominant religion of the Roman Empire. According to legend the Order was founded by ex-members of the Roman College who were forced to flee from the barbarians. They set up their headquarters on the island of Comacini in Lake Como and in 643 CE were placed under the patronage of the king of Lombardy who gave the Order control over all the masons and architects in Italy. The Comacine Order was divided into lodges ruled by Grand Masters, wore white aprons and gloves and recognized each other by secret signs and passwords.

The Order was responsible for the Lombardic and Romanesque styles of architecture and can be seen as the link between the architects and masons who built the pagan temples and the master builders who erected the Gothic cathedrals of Western Europe in the Christian Middle Ages. There is evidence that the Comacini masons travelled all over Europe and, according to the historian Bede, even reached Anglo-Saxon England where they were responsible for building a church in Northumbria.

Although the masons who built the medieval churches and cathedrals were nominally Christian, the profusion of pagan symbols and images in these ancient buildings indicates many of them were still pagans at heart. Reference has been made earlier to the Green Man images found in old churches but other pagan symbols can also be found including the

Sheela-na-gig. These are crude representations of the naked female form in the shape of women with spreadeagled legs displaying their cunni. They have been identified as images of the pagan goddess of fertility worshipped in Celtic times. Other carvings found in medieval churches depict monks and priests in sexual poses with wanton young girls, performing homosexual acts or wearing the heads of animals.

Even stranger examples of pagan masonry can be found. While researching a book on witchcraft, the medieval survival of the pagan old religion, author Michael Harrison came across the work of the late Professor Gregory Webb of Cambridge University who in 1946 was the secretary of the Royal Commission on Historical Monuments. Webb was an authority on medieval architecture and at the end of the war was appointed by the Government to survey ancient churches in southern England which had been damaged by the German bombing. In one of the churches he surveyed, a Nazi bomb had dislodged the top of the altar revealing the interior for the first time since the fourteenth century.

Inside the damaged altar Webb and his team discovered a stone image of a phallus which had been carefully concealed within the hollowed interior. At first Webb thought this discovery was unique but he began to examine other churches for signs of paganism. In 90 per cent of all the pre-Reformation churches built before the outbreak of the bubonic plague at the end of the fourteenth century, when church building ceased for a long period, Webb discovered the altars hid fertility symbols which dedicated the Christian churches to the old pagan religion.

As well as their pagan religious beliefs the medieval masonic guilds also had political views which were advanced for their age and which they expressed freely and with some conviction. In common with their pagan antecedents the masons were promoters of a utopian vision of humanity's future. At a period when feudalism was just another name for slavery, the guilds of artisans had organized themselves into mutual self-help groups who were already preaching the virtues of democracy and the rights of the individual several hundred years before these political goals would be achieved by the common people.

This public image of protective associations using their powers to promote fair trading and business ethics concealed the fact that the medieval society of freemasons were a secret society with pagan origins who clandestinely promoted radical political opinions. In accordance with the esoteric doctrine concealed by the building of Solomon's temple, the masons believed it was their spiritual duty to perfect the temple of the human body as a symbol of the Divine. The occult initiates who were the real power behind the secret societies knew that to achieve their aim they had to use the political system and in the twelfth century they began to put their plan into operation.

THE CURSE OF THE TEMPLARS

To understand the rise of the medieval secret societies we first have to examine the background to the foundation of Christianity which formed the major religious influence on European politics in the Middle Ages. Orthodox histories of early Christianity give the false impression that the new faith replaced the degenerate pagan religions within the space of a few hundred years with only moderate resistance from the followers of the old gods. The deathbed conversion of the Emperor Constantine to the new religion and his acceptance of it as the faith of the Roman Empire, which was already in decline during his lifetime, certainly provided the early Christians with an established power base. However they still faced strong and often violent opposition from the adherents of the pagan belief system who were reluctant to accept the new teachings, or at least not in the form they were presented by the early Church which had effectively suppressed the authentic gospel of Jesus of Nazareth.

When Jesus was preaching his radical message to his fellow Jews in Judea, which was under Roman occupation, the pagan religion in the classical world had degenerated. The priesthood of the established pagan religions had become corrupt, power-crazed and addicted to paederasty. They were being challenged by the Mystery cults which offered initiation into secret societies preserving the Ancient Wisdom and teaching the occult path to spiritual enlightenment. These Mystery cults were based on the ancient motifs of death, rebirth and fertility, expressed through the inner symbolism of the pagan religions of Egypt, Chaldea, Babylon, and Greece.

The Mystery cults used elaborate initiation ceremonies, arcane symbolism and theatrical rituals to provide the initiate with the revelation of the spiritual reality hidden behind the illusion of the material world. During initiation, the neophyte was placed in a trance and experienced contact with the gods through a symbolic journey to the Underworld. Initiates symbolically died and were reborn as perfected souls. The purpose behind these rituals was to prove to the candidate that the body in which they incarnated on the physical plane was an illusory object, that spirit was the only true reality and that reincarnation on the Earth was a learning process for spiritual development. These pagan beliefs were to form the central mystery drama of the initiation rituals practised in the lodges of speculative Freemasonry.

Early Christianity was permeated by the influence of the Mystery cults. While the Church prohibited pagan doctrines such as reincarnation, which was condemned by the Council of Nicea in 325 CE, rededicated pagan temples to Christian worship, and transformed pagan gods into saints, it soon discovered that it was impossible to eradicate paganism totally. Goddess worship was prevalent in the ancient world and the Catholic Church's devotion to the Virgin Mary is one example of the feminine principle's influence on early Christian belief. The Virgin was given the title Queen of Heaven and is depicted wearing a blue robe decorated with stars and standing on a crescent Moon. This image is almost identical to pagan representations of the goddess of love Ishtar who was worshipped by the Babylonians. The statues of the Madonna holding the infant Jesus in her arms, which were erected in Catholic churches, are almost exact copies of the effigies of Isis suckling her baby son Horus, found in Egyptian temples.

During the period following the emergence of the Mystery cultus and the adoption of Christianity as the official religion of the Roman Empire a new mystical movement arose in the Middle East which attempted to synthesize the best elements of the decaying paganism with the new Christian beliefs. This movement was known as Gnosticism, from the Greek *gnosis* meaning 'knowledge', and the Gnostics believed, in common with the original disciples of Jesus, that direct contact could be made with God without the intercession of an established priesthood. They claimed to have preserved the real teachings of Jesus which had been suppressed by the ecclesiastical councils set up by the Church to produce a unified dogma for the new religion.

The Gnostics derived their spiritual inspiration from a variety of sources, including the Greek and Roman Mysteries, Ancient Egyptian mythology, the Hermetic tradition, the dualistic doctrines of Zoroastrianism, the Middle Eastern fertility cults, the Chaldean stellar religion and Esoteric Christianity. Gnosticism derived its central beliefs from the writings of the Persian spiritual teacher Zoroaster who had lived circa

1800 BCE. He was a priest of the Indo-Iranian religion which involved the worship of the elemental forces of water and fire. At the age of thirty Zoroaster had a vision during which one of the Iranian gods, Ahura Mazda or Ormazd, appeared to him and said he was the Supreme Being. From this moment Zoroasterebroke away from the established religion and taught his own philosophy based on the universe as a cosmic battleground between the opposing forces of light and darkness which were in eternal conflict. According to Zoroastrianism the enlightened person had to choose between one or other of these principles.

Initiation into the Zoroastrian religion took place at the age of fifteen when both sexes were admitted to its rites. The candidate for initiation was given a special cord which he or she wore as a girdle. It was passed three times around the waist and knotted in the front and at the back. Every day the initiate untied the cord and then replaced it while reciting prayers using it in the fashion of a Catholic rosary. There are similarities between this cord and the one worn by the Brahmin priests in India, especially as it was worn over a white cotton shirt or tunic which was a symbol of spiritual perfection.

In its later stages Zoroastrianism became associated with the Mystery cult of the bull god Mithras which originated in Persia as an offshoot of the Zoroastrian religion but swiftly spread westwards where it made many converts among the soldiers of Imperial Rome who were attracted by its masculine image. Mithras was a scholar god of light who, in common with Jesus, was born in a cave surrounded by animals and shepherds at the Winter Solstice in December. A famous statue of Mithras, which can be seen in the British Museum, depicts him sitting astride a bull and plunging a dagger into its throat. Blood pours from the wound and drips onto the earth to fertilize the land. Mithras wears a short tunic and cloak and on his head is the Phrygian cap which was also associated with Adonis and Attis. This distinctive headgear was adopted by both the medieval masons and the revolutionary guard during the French Revolution.

In Zoroastrianism and Gnosticism Mithras became the mediator between the cosmic opposites of Ormuzd and Ahriman, the gods who represented the powers of light and darkness. By understanding the role of Mithras, the Gnostics taught that his human devotees could learn how to reconcile the good and evil aspects of their own nature by realizing that evil was only the shadow image of good and both had to exist in an imperfect world. Mithras was also associated with another Gnostic deity known as Aion who represented endless time. The Zoroastrians viewed the universe as operating within a cyclic time scale and Aion was a god of both destruction and creation. He was symbolized in human form by a lion's head and a serpent entwined around his body. He is often ithyphallic and stands on a globe of the world surrounded by the circle of the Zodiac. A statue of Aion, unearthed from a Roman villa of the first century CE and now preserved in the Vatican, depicts him winged and naked except for a Masonic-type apron.

The candidate for initiation into the Mithraic Mysteries participated in a rite of death and rebirth which can be compared with Masonic ceremonial. He was told to lie on the ground and act as if he were dead. The high priest of the cult then grasped the 'dead' initiate by the right hand and raised him up in a symbolic act of rebirth. After the ritual the members of the cult shared a ritual meal of bread and wine. During this symbolic communion they believed they were eating the flesh of the young Sun god and drinking his blood.

As stated earlier, the Gnostics derived some of their lore from the stellar religion practised by the Chaldean astrologers. They adopted the seven planetary spirits or gods of their pagan pantheon which were also represented by the classical gods of Roman and Greek mythology – Mercury (Hermes), Venus (Aphrodite), Mars (Ares), Jupiter (Zeus), Saturn (Chronos), Sol and Luna. In Gnostic belief these gods were transformed into archangels who became the central focus of medieval magic and the Hermetic tradition.

The Gnostics attempted to unite both paganism and Christianity and they produced a hybrid version of the new faith based on the heretical texts which circulated after the death of Jesus. It is well known that the gospels were written many years after the crucifixion and their authors were not direct witnesses of the events they describe even though they used the names of the disciples of Jesus. The early councils of the Church decided which gospels were to be included in the authorized New Testament and rejected those which did not correspond to their version of the Christian faith.

In the orthodox version of the New Testament Jesus is alluded to as the offspring of the Royal house of David, which means he was descended from the magician Solomon who built a temple in Jerusalem for the worship of the Goddess. The Gnostics noted references in the heretical gospels to Jesus having brothers and also the fact that he was called the son of the widow because Joseph died before Jesus began his preaching crusade. The son of the widow was a symbolic title given to Hiram Abiff, the Egyptian god Horus and Mithras.

Gnostic belief stated that Jesus had been an ordinary man who had been overshadowed by the spirit of God and became the Christ – from the Greek *kristos* meaning 'anointed one'. The physical death of Jesus on the cross, the Gnostics argued, can only be truly explained if the Christ force left him before the crucifixion. Alternatively, Jesus survived death on the cross by substituting a scapegoat who died in his place, or he was taken down from the cross while still alive, revived and smuggled out of the country. If Jesus did not die on the cross, what happened to him? Various speculative theories have him leading a monastic life in an Essene community on the shores of the Dead Sea, dying of old age in Kashmir, being killed by the Romans at Masada during the Jewish revolt or travelling to Europe to sire the future French Royal dynasty.

Whatever they believed about the death of Jesus the majority of Gnostics rejected the symbol of the cross. They believed it was wrong to worship an instrument of death and torture. Other Gnostics adopted the more extreme view that the god of the Old Testament, Jehovah, was Satan and that the Supreme Creator of the universe had sent the Christ to incarnate in the body of Jesus to save humanity. The Romans and the Jewish priests acting as agents of Satan-Jehovah conspired to have Jesus murdered, so to honour the cross was to worship a symbol of Satanic evil.

The latter belief was also held by the Manicheans, who took their name from their founder Mani who was born in Persia in the third century CE. Mani had been converted to Gnosticism through the teachings of Zoroaster and preached the duality of the Universe which, in Judeo-Christian belief, was symbolically divided between God and Satan who were eternally battling for the souls of humankind in a cosmic chess game. The Manicheans had strict religious beliefs which included celibacy for their priesthood – both men and women – , a vegetarian diet and the prohibition of alcohol and drugs. The teachings of Mani spread rapidly through the Middle East and the Roman Empire and at one stage were seriously competing with the emergent Christian cultus for converts. It also spread eastwards from Persia and gained many converts in China and India during the early centuries of the Christian era.

Mani's heresy seems to have been a contributing factor in the rise of the Cathars or Albigensi in the eleventh and twelfth centuries CE. The origins of the Cathars are obscure but it is known that dualistic heretics had established groups in the Middle East and Eastern Europe in the tenth century. In Bulgaria one sect known as the Bogomils were ruthlessly persecuted by the Church who accused them of unnatural sexual practices. It is from this sect that we owe the origin of the modern slang word 'buggery' meaning anal intercourse, although there is no evidence that members of this cult ever indulged in this practice.

From Bulgaria and Yugoslavia the heretical doctrine of the Cathars (from the Greek *cathari* meaning 'pure ones') established communities in Northern Italy, the Alpine regions and Southern France. In common with most Gnostic philosophies, the Cathars taught the dualistic belief in the opposing powers of light and darkness. However, they also taught the pagan belief of reincarnation and identified the material world as the plane of illusion. The Cathars believed that humankind could be saved by leading a moral life and, in common with the Gnostics, they rejected the cross as an evil symbol. They refused to accept the Catholic Church as the true guardians of the teachings of Jesus, taught that all men and women were equal and founded hospitals and schools for the poor. The Cathars had an inner circle within the priesthood with seven degrees of initiation, representing the stages to spiritual perfection. Ceremonies were performed out of doors in caves and woods and the Cathar initiates wore white tunics tied with a cord.

Faced with the Cathar threat the Church reacted in its traditional manner. It charged the heretics with devil worship, human sacrifice, cannibalism, incest, homosexuality and celebrating the Black Mass. The last charge was based on the Cathar practice of the *agape* or love feast which had been inherited from the pagan Mysteries. In 1209 the Church launched a crusade against the Cathars and thousands were killed. The knight who led the crusade, when asked by his men who they should put to the sword and who they should spare in the towns they attacked, replied with the immortal words, 'Kill them all. God will know His own.'

The Cathars did not accept their persecution by the Church meekly but fought back with all the resources at their disposal. Final defeat came, however, at Montsegur in the foothills of the Pyrenees when in March 1244 more than 200 Cathar priests were massacred by Christian forces. Shortly before the stronghold was overwhelmed by the crusaders it is claimed that a secret treasure was removed from the castle and hidden somewhere in the surrounding countryside. Speculation has been rife over the centuries as to the nature of this treasure. Some occultists have even claimed that the Cathars were the guardians of the Holy Grail – the cup used by Jesus at the last supper – which they did not want captured by the Roman Church which the Cathars regarded as the puppet of Satan. Other theories claim the mysterious treasure was a hoard of esoteric writings which revealed the hidden teachings of the Cathars from their pagan origins. This does seem more likely then the Grail theory.

Historians who have studied the Cathars have pointed out that the area around Montsegur has many pagan connections. A few miles from the castle is the site of a Druidic altar dating from Celtic times and a Christian cross carved with pagan symbols. In nearby caves are evidence of the worship of Mithras and the site of Montsegur itself was reputed to have been a centre of pagan solar worship thousands of years before the arrival of the Cathars.

As we have seen, the Cathars had links with Middle East dualism, the Mystery cults and the Gnostics, and it is through these connections they can be linked with such secret societies as the Sufis and the Assassins who in turn influenced the Knights Templars. The Sufis are traditionally the followers of the secret tradition concealed within the orthodoxy of Islam. Today the religion founded by the prophet Mohammed is essentially patriarchal but the original religion of Arabia was centred on the worship of the feminine principle. The Caaba or mosque in Mecca, which is the holy centre of Islamic belief, was originally the site of a pagan temple. It is believed that the mysterious black stone worshipped inside the Caaba, given to the prophet Abraham by the Archangel Gabriel in Islamic lore, was in fact the cult object of a pre-Islamic centre of Goddess worship.

In Islamic belief Friday is a sacred day and in the classical world this day was dedicated to the goddess of love, Venus. The traditional colour of Mohammed is green which is associated with the Great Mother Goddess in her Egyptian aspect as Isis, the Lady of Nature. The Islamic symbols of the scimitar and the crescent have been identified variously as the Moon or the morning star Venus. It is possible that Mohammed had contacts with the Gnostic belief system. He was certainly taught by Christian monks and acknowledged their contribution in the founding of his new religion. Although Islam and Christianity were political rivals in the Middle Ages there were several connections between the two religions. Both were monotheistic, patriarchal and derived their spiritual inspiration from a common Semitic source. The followers of Islam recognized Jesus as a great spiritual teacher, although they did not accept his divinity, and revered many of the Old Testament patriarchs.

While the Sufi tradition allegedly originated in Islam there is the suggestion that its beliefs were far older. In his posthumous book *The Masters of Wisdom*, J.G. Bennett describes how he was taken by the Russian mystic, Gregori Gurdjieff, to see the prehistoric cave paintings at Lascaux. Gurdjieff showed Bennett the wall drawings of herds of reindeer crossing a river and explained this was a symbolic depiction of an ancient initiation ritual. According to Gurdjieff the number of antlers on the deer represented the level of spirituality reached by the initiates whose totemic emblem they were.

Gurdjieff confided in Bennett that these ancient Mystery schools dated back 30,000 to 40,000 years and that he had learnt about them while studying cave drawings in the Caucasian mountains and Turkestan. The Russian mystic had received initiation from Sufi masters so when, in the same passage of the book, Bennett reveals that there is a tradition in Sufism that it originated in Central Asia 40,000 years ago we do not need to guess the source for this startling information.

In common with early Christianity, the introduction of Islam was resisted by those Arabs who still followed the worship of pagan gods. Following the death of Mohammed several heretical sects arose promoting alternative forms of Islam and secret societies were founded based on these philosophies. They included the Ismailis, the Batimis, the Karmathites, the Fatimites and the Druses. Several of these heretical sects were inspired by Gnostic and Manichean ideas and some claimed to be preserving the Arabian occult tradition.

The most powerful and well documented Islamic secret society which operated in the Middle East was the sect known popularly as the Assassins. Their origins are shrouded in mystery but they seem to have been loosely connected with Gnosticism. In the eleventh century CE a mystic called Abdullah appeared in Persia with the mission to establish a pantheistic religion to replace Islam. He founded a secret society to propagate his beliefs which were derived from a mixture of Hinduism and the teachings of the Persian heretic Mani. Initiates into this society were offered nine degrees of illumination which were similar to the Eleusian Mysteries practised in ancient Greece.

The initiates were taught the mystical significance of the number seven which in the occult tradition was the number of planes of existence from the material to the spiritual. They were also taught that God had sent seven great teachers into the world to lead humanity to spiritual perfection. These teachers were Adam, the first man; Noah, survivor of the Flood; Abraham, the Chaldean founder of the religion of Yahweh; Moses, the Egyptian initiate and founder of the Cabbala; Jesus; Mohammed and Ishmael. Members of the society were also taught the Greek philosophies of Plato and Aristotle and were indoctrinated with the esoteric teachings of the Sufis.

Abdullah's secret society spread throughout the Middle East gathering in small groups to conspire against Islam until it was suppressed in 1123. One of its initiates was Hasam-i-Sabbah who organized an offshoot branch, called the Order of the Devoted, in 1093. The new Order renounced the mystical pantheism of the original society in favour of the positive virtues of the Koran. It was this Order of the Devoted which developed into the sect known as the Assassins.

It is alleged that the Assassins derived their title from the Arabic *hashishmar* or 'eater of hashish' which was the hemp plant they used for ritual purposes. Other authorities claim that it is derived from the Arabic *hass* meaning 'to destroy' or *asana* which means 'to lay snares'. Hasam took the traditional title of Sheikh al Jebal or Mountain Chief, hence his popular title of the Old Man of the Mountains. He and his followers established a castle at Alamut or the Eagle's Nest in Persia. Perched 600 feet above a valley gorge and surrounded by hostile mountains it was virtually impregnable. From this lofty fortress the Assassins waged an international war of terrorism against anyone who opposed them.

Hasam died in 1124 but the Assassins lived on as hired mercenaries willing to kill at a price. Several well-known European crusaders used the Assassins, including the English king Richard Coeur de Lion and Frederick II of Sicily who was excommunicated by the Pope for using them to murder the Duke of Bavaria.

The Assassin stronghold was finally overrun by the Mongols in 1256 and the Order was scattered. However, as late as 1754 the British consul at Aleppo claimed that the Order of Assassins still survived in Persia, Syria and India. It is alleged that they had taught their murderous skills to the Hindu cult of the Thuggee who worshipped the goddess of destruction Kali and practised human sacrifice during the days of the British Raj. In 1866 the Assassins were mentioned in a court case in Bombay featuring a Persian prince who claimed to be a direct descendant of the original Grand Master of the Order.

Some authorities have attempted to provide concrete links between the Assassins and the Sufis, who have been identified as Goddess worshippers because of their use of the double axe symbol (associated with ancient Goddess worship) and the shamanic nature of their rituals involving dancing and chanting. Pottery painted with the pentagram or five pointed star and the *vesica piscis* – an abstract symbol of the female vulva – have been unearthed from the ruins of the Assassins' mountain stronghold. They also wore white tunics and a red sash, symbolizing innocence and blood, which is similar to the costume adopted by the Zoroastrians, the Sufis, the Cathars and the Templars.

In the period when the Assassins were operating, the Catholic Church was launching its first crusades to extend its political power into the

Middle East to reclaim the Holy Land from Islam. The beginning of the Crusades can be dated from the 1060s when Pope Alexander II granted indulgences to the knights who had fought the Moorish invaders in Spain. In 1096 an eccentric monk, Peter the Hermit, led a Peasants' Crusade consisting of several thousand men, women and children across Europe to liberate Jerusalem from the Arabs. The majority of these unfortunates were massacred en route by bands of outlaws and the armies of the Byzantine Empire, which included the modern countries of Bulgaria, Yugoslavia, Greece and Turkey. This early disastrous crusade was followed by others which were well organized and led by trained knights who achieved considerable military successes and finally established a Christian kingdom in Jerusalem in the early twelfth century.

Despite the establishment of a Christian army of occupation in the Holy Land, European pilgrims travelling to the sacred sites still faced many dangers. At Easter 1119 a group of 300 pilgrims travelling from Jerusalem to Jordan were attacked and killed by the Saracens. King Baldwin II of Jerusalem was so shocked by this atrocity that he took steps to prevent it ever happening again. Baldwin had in his employment a Frankish knight called Sir Hugh de Payens who had spent three years fighting in the Holy Land. The king suggested to de Payens that he organize a chivalric order of knights to defend the pilgrim routes and he granted part of his palace as the headquarters for the new organization. The palace was inside the enclosure of a mosque which stood on the site of Solomon's original temple and for this reason Sir Hugh called his new order the Templi Militia or Soldiers of the Temple, but later changed this to the grander Knights of the Temple of Solomon in Jerusalem.

Baldwin initially funded the Knights Templars but de Payens decided to travel to Europe seeking patronage for he knew that if the Order was to succeed it needed support from the Church. He had already decided that the Templars would be warrior monks and he accepted the patronage of St Bernard of Clairvaux, founder of the Cistercian monks, who wrote the monastic rules for the Order and interceded on their behalf with the Pope, who granted his approval.

With the religious patronage of St Bernard the Templars took oaths of poverty, chastity and obedience to Christian principles and declared their intention to protect the routes to the Holy Land for the pilgrims. They dedicated themselves to the *Mère de Dieu* or Mother of God (Virgin Mary) swearing to 'consecrate their swords and their lives to the defence of the mysteries of the Christian faith'. Considering the history and later

Seal of the Order of the Temple

downfall of the Order this vow is very significant.

Although the above account is the generally accepted version of the foundation of the Templars, controversy still surrounds its origins. In their best-selling book *Holy Blood, Holy Grail* its authors claim that the Templars were an offshoot of an even older secret society called the Priory of Sion. This organization was dedicated to the reestablishment of the Old Merovingian dynasty to France, allegedly descended from Jesus and Mary Magdalene, and was the *eminence gris* behind the Order of the Rosy Cross.

The foundation of the Priory can be traced back allegedly to the Gnostic adept Ormus who lived in the first century CE. He was converted to the heretical version of the Christian message by Mark, a disciple of Jesus of Nazareth, and he formed a secret society which united

Esoteric Christianity with the teachings of the pagan Mystery schools. Ormus adopted as his symbol a cross surmounted by a rose to signify the synthesis of the new and old religions. The red cross was later to be adopted by the Templars while the rose cross was the sigil used by the medieval Rosicrucians.

A Knight Templar

Whatever the origins of the Order, with the support of St Bernard the Templars seem to have gone from strength to strength. Pope Honorius gave them his papal blessing and the Order adopted a white mantle with a red equal-armed cross as their uniform. At first the Templars adhered to their vows of chastity and poverty but shortly after its foundation the Order began to acquire political aspirations. The Templar tradition was firmly based on the revival of the chivalric ideal of knighthood which had been severely weakened by the Crusades. Knights who had left Europe with a strict moral code of warfare had been brutalized by their battles with the Saracens and had indulged in an orgy of bloody slaughter, raping and looting. The Templars wanted to restore the principles of knighthood and establish a new golden age of chivalry. Their ultimate aim on a political level was a united Europe, ruled by Christian principles, although their version of Christianity differed greatly from that of the Vatican.

Inspired by the Grand Masters of the Order who followed Sir Hugh de Payens, the Templars acquired both political and material power. Even while de Payens was alive the Order had become internationally established. In 1129 de Payens had visited both England and Scotland and contacted wealthy patrons who had donated land and money to his cause. The Order had also established itself in France and Spain and in the Holy Land had built a network of castles to defend the pilgrim routes and the sacred places of Christendom.

By the beginning of the thirteenth century the Templars had become the international bankers of Europe and were appointed treasurers to the French Royal family and the Vatican. The Grand Masters of the military orders of warrior monks, which included the Templars, the Knights of St John and the Teutonic Knights, had gained considerable political power. By the thirteenth century their Orders controlled 40 per cent of the frontiers of Europe. Ships owned by the Templars and other military orders carried not only fighting men to the Middle East but also ferried wealthy pilgrims as paying passengers. On their return trips the ships brought back cargoes which included spices, perfumes, and silk which were sold to merchants at high prices.

In January 1162 Pope Alexander III issued a special papal bull granting the Templars extraordinary powers. They were released from all spiritual obedience except to the Pope himself, were allowed to have their own chaplains and burial grounds and were freed from paying tithes but could receive them instead. Once a knight became a Templar he was forbidden to leave unless he transferred to another military order. This papal bull strengthened the political power of the Order even more and the Grand Master is reputed to have told Henry II of England, 'You shall be king as long as you are just', suggesting that he had the power to topple him from his throne.

The money-making schemes of the Templars were legendary. It is said that a group of knights were sent to a convent near Damascus where a miracle had taken place. A statue of the Virgin Mary had become clothed in flesh and from her nipples spurted a rich liquid which had the power to heal the sick and wash away sin. The Templars returned from the convent with a large supply of the liquid from the Virgin's breasts which they bottled and sold to gullible pilgrims.

Rumours of misconduct by the members of the Order were, however, beginning to circulate. As early as 1208 the Pope had censured the Grand Master because he claimed that while the knights wore the Christian cross few followed the teachings of Jesus. He alleged that many of the men admitted to the Order were guilty of adultery and other unspecified sexual offences. The activities of the Templars in the Crusades were also receiving adverse criticism from those who considered them disloyal to the Christian cause.

In 1219 the Templars professed their obedience to a papal legate when he headed an expeditionary force against Damascus. However, the knights disobeyed his orders and acted on their own. When King Frederick II of Sicily undertook his first crusade to Egypt the Templars conspired with the Sultan so that his campaign was a failure. The king retaliated by seizing the Templars' estates in Italy and Sicily and they duly responded by dispossessing the Teutonic Knights, founded by Frederick, of their estates in Syria.

It became generally believed that the Templars were engaged in forming secret pacts with the Saracens. This rumour seems to have been confirmed when the Order entered into an alliance with the Emir of Damascus against the Hospitallers of Knights of St John. In 1259 relations between the two Orders had degenerated to such an extent that open warfare broke out and a battle was fought between the Templars and the Hospitallers. There were frequent examples of the Templars forging alliances with the Saracens and they even had contacts with the Order of Assassins in a plot to give them the rulership of Tyre, the ancient centre of Goddess worship and birthplace of Hiram Abiff.

Because the Templars were so powerful few would openly challenge them but events were taking place which would lead to a weakening of their political power with fateful consequences for the future of the Order. These events coincided with the loss of their headquarters on the site of Solomon's Temple in Jerusalem and expulsion of the Templars from the Holy Land in 1291 when it was recaptured by the Saracens.

In 1307 King Phillip of France was facing bankruptcy and owed the Templars a considerable amount of money. Phillip heard that accusations were being made against the Order by two renegade members, Roffo Dei and the Prior of Montfaucan, who had been imprisoned by the Templars for unknown crimes. The two men had escaped and sought the protection of the French king which he freely offered in exchange for incriminating evidence of the secret activities of the Knights Templars.

Phillip IV passed the information on to Pope Clement V and the king and the pontiff conspired to lure the Grand Master of the Order, Jacques de Molay, into a trap on French soil. The Pope requested the Grand Master to visit Paris from his headquarters in Cyprus to discuss a new crusade in the Holy Land to recover Jerusalem from the Arabs. De Molay left Cyprus accompanied by his personal bodyguard of knights, 150,000 gold florins and six pack horses loaded with silver. This treasure he deposited in the Templar chapter house in Paris.

In order to provide de Molay with a false sense of security, Phillip made the Grand Master the godfather of his son and invited him to

Jacques de Molay, last Grand Master of the Order of the Temple

attend the coming funeral of his sister-in-law and act as a pallbearer. In reality the wily king was plotting the downfall of the Templars and the death of de Molay. The knights were staying at the Templar citadel in Paris and on the 13 October 1307 the king executed his plan. Troops surrounded the building and everyone inside was placed under arrest. Within forty-eight hours warrants had been issued ordering the detaining of every Templar in France, even though this was technically illegal as the Order was answerable only to the Pope and not to civil laws. On the 22 November however, the Pope issued a bull to all the Christian rulers in Western Europe ordering them to arrest any member of the Order residing in their countries. The fate of the Templars was sealed.

The list of charges made against the Order was a familiar one as they had been used against the Cathars in Southern France but there were some interesting new elements. Specifically the Templars were accused of denying the tenets of the Christian faith, spitting or urinating on the crucifix during secret rites of initiation, worshipping a skull or head called Baphomet in a dark cave, anointing it with blood or the fat of unbaptized babies, worshipping the Devil in the shape of a black cat and commiting acts of sodomy and bestiality.

Other lesser charges alleged that the Templars swore allegiance only to the Order, made secret pacts with the Saracens and carried out Islamic practices, murdered anyone who opposed their aims and buried them secretly in unconsecrated ground, broke their vows of chastity and procured abortions for their female lovers, and finally, that the Grand Master of the Order heard the knights' confessions and absolved them of all sins they performed in the name of the Templars.

What basis, if any, do these charges have in fact? It is easy to see the sensational allegations, which were supported by confessions extracted under torture, as pretence concocted by a bankrupt king to allow him legally to take the Order's wealth. The Pope supported the plan because he had become fearful of the Templars' political power which was creating a church within the Church, which threatened his own position as the anointed head of Christendom. However, the Templars had spent many years in the Middle East and the Order had been founded on the site of King Solomon's temple. Two important Templar citadels were located at the ports of Tyre and Sidon which were ancient centres of Goddess worship associated with the pagan origins of Freemasonry. The Templar uniform of red and white was also worn by the Assassins, with whom the knights had allegedly made pacts. One of the charges made against the Templars was that they wore a magical girdle or cord given to them at their initiation ceremony. This suggests connections with the Zoroastrians, the Cathars and the Sufis.

In their confessions the knights said that Templar initiation ceremonies took place at night in candlelit chapels. Initiates were forced to renounce their Christian faith as a sign of their loyalty to the Order and to spit, urinate or trample on a crucifix. Blasphemous as this may seem, it is possible the initiate was told to perform this act because, in common with the Cathars, the Templars rejected the crucifix as an evil symbol of suffering and death. Some initiates confessed that they had been told by their superiors in the Order that Jesus was a false prophet and that they should not respect the crucifix because it was 'too young'. This suggests elements of both Gnostic dualism and paganism.

Candidates entering the Order also had to kiss their initiator on the mouth, the navel, the penis and at 'the base of the spine'. These kisses were regarded by critics of the Order as proof of their perverted sexual activities but in the occult tradition the naval, sexual organs and the perineum are the physical locations of the psychic centres of the human body, known in the East as the *chakras*. The perineum marks the *Kundalini chakra* which is the psychic source of sexual energy in the body. Various occult techniques can be practised which liberate this energy so that it travels up the spinal cord to illuminate the brain. It is possible that during their sojourn in the Middle East the Templar Order contacted adepts from the Arab Mystery schools who taught them the secrets of sex magic. This theory is supported by confessions of Templars who said that at the climax of the ceremony the initiate indulged in an act of sodomy with the chaplain.

Speculation has always been rife as to the exact nature of the cult object venerated by the Templars. This was an image in the shape of a skull or head, called by the knights Baphomet, which is a word of unknown derivation. Baphomet has been variously described as an androgynous deity with two faces and a long white beard, or a human skull, which uttered oracular prophecies and guided the destiny of the Order. Some writers on the Templars have even speculated that this image was the Turin shroud, allegedly the garment used to wrap the body of Jesus after his death.

The nineteenth century occultist Alphonse Constant, a former Roman Catholic priest who took the Jewish pseudonym Eliphas Levi when he took up the magical path, wrote extensively about the deity of the Templars. Levi regarded Baphomet as a magical and pantheistic figure representing the Absolute in a symbolic form. He reproduced an illustration of Baphomet which seems to be based on an effigy of the deity found on the Commnaderie of Saint Bris le Vineux, which was a building owned by the Order. The gargoyle is in the form of a bearded horned figure with pendulous female breasts, wings and cloven feet. It sits in a cross-legged position which resembles statues of the Celtic stag god, Cernnunnos or the Horned One, worshipped in Gaul (France) before the Roman occupation.

In Levi's illustration Baphomet is a goat-headed figure with androgynous features who sits on a cube. A torch blazes between the goat's horns which represents cosmic intelligence and spiritual illumination. In occult tradition Lucifer – who is regarded by the Church as the Devil – is called the lightbringer because he grants his disciples spiritual illumination through incarnation on the physical plane. According to Levi the head of Baphomet combines the characteristics of a dog, a bull and a goat which represent the three sources of the pagan Mystery tradition. These are Egypt – the jackal god Anubis who was the guide of the dead to the Underworld and is identified with the Greek Hermes; India – the sacred bull who may be the origin of Mithras; and Judea – the scapegoat sacrificed in the wilderness to cleanse the sins of the tribe.

On the forehead of the Baphomet figure, marking the physical site of the pineal gland or third eye, is the magical sign of the pentagram or five pointed star which represents humankind in its unperfected state. It is also a symbol of the morning star, Venus, which was associated with Ishtar and Astarte. The morning star was also a title given to Lucifer describing his fall from heaven in the Bible.

The androgynous figure of Baphomet has female breasts and the lower part of its body is veiled portraying the mysteries of generation. However the phallic nature of the goat god is symbolized by the caduceus symbol of a wand entwined with two serpents which was carried by Hermes. This symbol hides the erect penis of the Baphomet figure. Its belly is covered with scales representing the reptilian origin of the human race in the evolutionary process.

Baphomet's androgynous nature is emphasized by the fact that one arm is masculine while the other is rounded and feminine. One hand points upward and the other downward representing the Hermetic axiom 'As above... so below'. The hands point to one black and one white crescent moon signifying the waxing and waning lunar phases. These symbolize the duality of human nature and the male and female principles whose union brought the universe into manifestation and the powers of light and darkness.

What does the word Baphomet represent? The late Montague Summers, who wrote several books on witchcraft and demonology from an extreme Catholic viewpoint, derived the word from the Greek *Baph metis* meaning 'the baptism of wisdom' which referred to a secret ritual only known to the Grand Master of the Templars. The late Madeline Montalban, a well known occultist and founder of the Order of the Morning Star, told us that she had translated, Baphomet to read *Bfmaat* which is a word derived from the Enochian language. According to Montalban, Enochian was the language spoken on the lost continent of Atlantis and although known to occult initiates since the earliest times it was only revealed to the outside world by the researches of the Elizabethan astrologer and magician Dr John Dee. In Enochian the word Baphomet or *Bfmaat* can be translated, according to Montalban, as 'the Opener of the Door'. Madeline Montalban further interpreted the Baphomet figure as a glyph of the Zodiac sign Capricorn. This astrological sign symbolized the material ambitions and political aspirations of the Templars. On an esoteric level the goatish emblem of Capricorn is regarded as a symbol for the occult initiate who climbs the celestial mountain to achieve oneness with the Divine.

Idries Shah, the writer on Sufi themes, claims that Baphomet comes from the Arabic word *Abufihamat* which can be translated as 'the Father of Understanding' or 'the source of wisdom and knowledge' and is a title used to describe a Sufi master. It is quite possible that the Templars were exposed to the beliefs of Sufism during their period in the Holy Land and the Gnostic dualist philosophy. Many of the Templars were Middle Eastern by birth including the Grand Master Philip of Nablus, elected in 1167, who was a Syrian by birth.

Levi alleged in his writings that if the letters of Baphomet were reversed they would read TEM OHP ABI. When this anagram is extended and translated into Latin it reads *Templi omnivm hominum pacis abbas* or 'The Father of the Temple of Peace of all men'. Levi regarded this as a reference to the temple built by Solomon whose esoteric purpose was to bring peace to the world.

It has been alleged that the Templars were secret Goddess worshippers. One of the objects found in the Templar chapter house in Paris was the silver image of a female figure. Inside this figurine were some human bones wrapped in red and white linen. Dr Hugh Schonfield, an expert on the Dead Sea Scrolls, has claimed there is a link between the Templars and the Essenes. He states that the name

Baphomet can be translated, by reference to a secret Essenic code, to read Sophia. This is the Greek word for wisdom and the name of the goddess worshipped in the Gnostic religion. In addition, the mysterious black cat worshipped by the Templars has been identified by some occultists as an image of the Egyptian cat goddess, Bast, or the lion headed goddess, Sekhmet.

The accounts of the worship of Baphomet were largely derived from confessions extracted under torture during which several members of the Order died. Many members however confessed without recourse to torture and confirmed stories which the agents of King Phillip infiltrated into the Order had obtained. On the 22 October Jacques de Molay confessed before an assembly of academics at the University of Paris that the charges made against the Order were true. He wrote to his fellow members in an open letter instructing them freely to confess the evil practices they had indulged in while members of the Order. As a result of this letter one of the leading members of the Order who confessed was the Grand Treasurer, Hugh de Pairuad. He said that he had been responsible for initiating many knights into the Order and had seen the Templars' god which granted them their wordly wealth, made the land fertile and caused the death of their enemies.

The investigation of the Templars' crimes was thorough and lasted several years. It was not until 1312 that the Pope officially disbanded the Order. Templars who had been found innocent of the charges or if guilty had submitted to the Church were freed and granted pensions. Those who refused to recant were ordered to be burnt at the stake. King Phillip obtained sizeable parts of the Templars' estates and revenue while the balance was shared by the Knights of St John.

In March 1314, after several delays caused by the inability of the Pope fully to accept the guilt of the Templars, De Molay was offered the chance to submit to the Church and when he refused he was burnt to death at the stake. The pyre was lit on a small island in the Seine between the gardens of the Royal palace and the church of the Hermit Brethren. Just before he died de Molay announced that he was innocent and cursed the French king and the Pope. He said that Phillip would be summoned to his maker within twelve months and the Pope before forty days. Clement died on the 20 April and Phillip died on 29 November.

Although the Templar Order was decimated in France it did not suffer so badly in other European countries. In England King Edward II reacted slowly to the papal bull condemning the Templars. He did place its members under arrest but the English Master of the Temple was allowed to draw a pension. Within a month of the arrests however Edward confiscated all the Templars' property in the country and used their financial resources to swell his own coffers. Although one Templar priest confessed to denying Jesus at his initiation no action was taken against him. Members of the Order freely submitted to the Church to avoid any further punishment and were pardoned.

In Germany, Portugal, Switzerland and Aragon the Templars were declared innocent and in Cyprus, where the Order had its headquarters, all the knights were acquitted of the charges brought by King Phillip. Before his execution de Molay had nominated a trusted knight called Larmenuis as his successor and told him to secretly reorganize the Order and gather together its scattered knights. It is from this point in history that the Templars disappear effectively from public view. They emerged in the following centuries as a clandestine organization working underground promoting the occult tradition and subversive politics.

3

THE ROSICRUCIAN CONNECTION

After the suppression of the Templars rumours were circulating in Europe that the secret tradition which they had followed was still being practised. In the late Middle Ages the influence of the masonic guilds was still considerable and the rumours connected them with the Templar Order. It was said that during the Crusades a small group of Syriac Christians, who claimed descent from the Essene sect, were rescued from the Saracens by the Knights Templars and placed under their military protection. These Christians were initiated into the innermost circle of the Order and were taught all its occult mysteries. When the Syriac Christians left the Holy Land they travelled across Europe and eventually settled in Scotland. In their new homeland they founded a new chapter of the Templar Order which later merged with a lodge of speculative Freemasonry.

Following the destruction of the Templar Order the masonic guilds had attracted many men of learning into their fold who were non-masons, in the sense that they were not members of the building trade. It is through the influence of these newcomers, who included occult initiates, that the esoteric symbolism of the masonic lodges was revived and speculative Freemasonry was established as a metaphysical system teaching the perfection of the human spirit through the symbols of the operative mason's working tools. Many crusaders had made contact with the Sons of the Widow and Sufi Masonry while living in the Middle East, and on their return to Europe were instrumental in reviving the spiritual aspects of the masonic craft.

The Templar tradition seems to have gone underground at the beginning of the fifteenth century due to the Church's holy crusade directed at the practitioners of witchcraft. The medieval witch hunt, which lasted from the end of the fifteenth century to the beginning of the eighteenth century, claimed nearly a million innocent lives and was instigated by the publication in 1484 of the *Malleus Malefiracum*. This evil book was written by two Dominican monks, Heinrich Kramer and James Sprenger, who were members of the Inquisition set up in 1215 to root out and kill heretics.

Before the publication of the infamous *Malleus Malefiracum*, or *Hammer of Witches*, the medieval Church had dismissed witches as ignorant peasants suffering from delusions that they worshipped pagan gods, but the Dominican monks changed this view. In their opinion witchcraft was a diabolical heresy which conspired to overthrow the Church and establish the kingdom of Satan on Earth. Pope Innocent VIII agreed with their diagnosis and in 1486 issued a papal bull condemning witches, which plunged Christian Europe into an orgy of bloody persecution which lasted nearly 250 years.

In this dark atmosphere of bigotry anyone who professed magical powers or claimed to follow occult beliefs did not dare proclaim them in public. The occult tradition went underground and only surfaced briefly in the next few decades, usually among the Establishment whose members were exempt from the persecution that decimated the lower classes who dabbled in the magical arts and witchcraft.

Vague references to the Templars were made in the available occult literature although, in the context of the paranoia which surrounded the witch hunt, they were largely misrepresented as black magicians and Satanists. In his book *De Occulta Philosophia* written in 1530 the German occultist and magician, Henry Cornelius Agrippa, mentioned the Templars in connection with the Gnostics and the worship of the pagan fertility god Priapus, whose symbol was a huge erect penis, and the Greek goat-footed god Pan. He identified the Order with the survival of paganism, suggesting that as a practising occultist he had some special insight into the sensational allegations which led to its downfall. It is claimed that Agrippa was a member of a secret society which claimed descent from the Templars and wrote his description of their occult practices from inside information.

The fifteenth and early sixteenth centuries were very important in respect of the growth of the underground occult tradition. The Moors, who had invaded Spain from North Africa in the tenth and eleventh centuries and had even penetrated areas of southern France until they were driven back by the Christian kings, had introduced both the secret teachings of the Arab Mystery schools and the Jewish mystical system, known as the Cabbala, into Europe. By the beginning of the 1500s there had been a revival of interest in the Gnostics and the Hermetic philosophy was also well known to the educated student of the occult sciences.

In 1460 a Greek manuscript consisting of an almost complete copy of the *Corpus Hermeticum*, the standard text book on Hermiticism, had come into the hands of a monk hired by the de Medici family in Italy to locate rare manuscripts. The monk's patron, Cosmos de Medici, arranged for the manuscript to be translated and it was published in 1463. Its publication marked the great occult revival of the period which was to culminate in the flowering of the Renaissance when artists, writers and poets inspired by classical paganism produced the great works of art and literature which are so highly valued today as the spiritual and material treasures of European culture.

It was also during this important cultural period in Western history that the existence of one of the most influential secret societies in the esoteric tradition was revealed to the outside world. This society had as its ultimate aim the re-establishment of the ancient Mysteries in a form which, unlike the Manichean heresy and the Templar Order, would be publicly acceptable. The earliest writings about this society, which was known as the Brotherhood or the Order of the Rosy Cross, began to circulate in Europe around the year 1605. They were contained in a manuscript called *The Restoration of the Decayed Temple of Pallas* and provide the earliest known constitution of the Order. A history of the Rosicrucians was written by an unknown author in 1610 but did not appear in print until four years later. It was entitled the *Fama Frateritatis* and provided a legendary history stating that the Order had been founded as early as the 1300s by a German mystic who was born into an aristocratic family.

This mystic, known only by the pseudonym Christian Rosenkreuz, had been placed in a monastery by his parents while he was still a young boy. He rebelled against the stifling authority of the clerical life and took the chance offered to him by an older monk to travel to the Middle East. His companion died en route in Cyprus but the young man travelled on to Damascus. There he became the student of a group of Cabbalistic adepts who lived in the city. Rosenkreuz eventually returned to Europe, stopping in North Africa where he studied with Arabian occultists in Fez, and Moorish Spain. During his studies in Fez the young monk was taught the magical art of conjuring up elemental spirits and was tutored in the secrets of alchemy or the transformation of lead into gold.

The fact that Rosenkreutz travelled extensively in the Middle East,

Fama Fraternitas, 1614

studying with Arabian occult adepts, suggests strongly that the Rosicrucians were familiar with the teachings of Sufism. Idries Shah has compared them with a Sufi secret society founded in Baghdad in the twelfth century called the Path of the Rose. It was founded by a Sufi master, Abdelkadir Gilani, whose personal symbol was a red rose. This Sufi group, in common with the Rosicrucians, practised alchemy as a metaphor for spiritual transformation from matter to spirit.

When Rosenkreutz returned to Germany he continued his occult studies, locking himself away for five years conducting magical rituals and alchemical operations. At the end of this period of isolation he decided to inform the world of his new found knowledge. Rosenkreutz possessed political ambitions and believed that the arts and sciences in Europe were in a state of decay. He believed that only by an injection of spiritual inspiration could European culture be saved from total moral degradation. To this end Rosenkreutz attempted to spread his message to his fellow Europeans but met only hostility, ridicule or indifference. Realizing that an open approach was doomed to failure, Rosenkreutz decided to conceal his political and cultural reforms behind the mask of a secret society. This group would work clandestinely behind the sences influencing in a subtle way important people who could bring about the social changes Rosenkreutz dreamed about.

Rosenkreutz revisited the monastery where he had been a novice monk before leaving for the Middle East. He persuaded three of its senior members, known in Rosicrucian literature as the Three Wise Men, to leave their monastic orders and join his venture. He asked them to swear an oath not to violate the secrets he was to give them and then revealed, over a period of several months, the occult knowledge he had received from his Arab masters. Rosenkreutz provided each of his students with a secret cipher to use to pass coded messages to each other. He also helped them build a house which became the repository for the thousands of volumes of esoteric wisdom he had collected over the years.

Four other monks were introduced to the group and these eight scholars were the nucleus of the Fraternity of the Rosy Cross. As soon as the Order had been safely established, seven of its members set out across Europe secretly spreading its occult doctrines, leaving Rosenkreutz in Germany to continue his arcane researches. They decided not to reveal their true identities to outsiders and agreed on six rules of conduct which all of them would follow without question. These were that they would heal the sick without charge, wear no special garment which revealed their occult beliefs, that every year on an allocated day they would meet at the headquarters of the Order to report their progress, that each member would nominate a worthy candidate to replace him when he died, that they would use the initials RC as their identifying mark, and that the existence of the Order would remain secret for at least a hundred years.

It was agreed by the early brethren of the Rosy Cross that when they died their bodies would be buried secretly and without ceremony. Therefore when Rosenkreutz himself died none of the other members knew where he was buried until by accident his secret tomb was discovered some 120 years after his death. His tomb was in the form of a seven-sided vault illuminated by a perpetual light whose source none of the brethren could discern. Rosenkreutz's body was perfectly preserved inside the tomb despite the length of time which had passed since his death.

Although this is the generally accepted legend of the foundation of the Rosicrucians some authorities claim that the Order's true origins date back several thousand years. It has been alleged that the original Order of the Rosy Cross was founded by the Pharoah Thothmes III in the fifteenth century BCE. He gathered together all the learned scholars, priests and philosophers of his time and formed them into a secret brotherhood of initiates who met to practise their rites at a temple on the banks of the Nile. In modern Rosicrucianism the cartouche or personal seal of Thothmes is used as one of the symbols of the Order in both private and public documents. The purpose behind the foundation of the Order in Ancient Egypt was to exert a civilizing influence on the ancient world and preserve the wisdom teachings of the Mysteries.

Thothmes III was one of the most significant Egyptian rulers during the XVIII Dynasty (1587–1375 BCE). As a young man he was co-regent to Queen Hatshepsut, his sister, and when she died in 1480 BCE Thothmes, whose name means 'born of Thoth' – the ibis-headed god of wisdom who was the Egyptian equivalent of Hermes – , ruled on his own as supreme Pharoah. There were rumours that the young man had murdered his sister to gain the crown but there is no proof to support this allegation.

Following Hatshepsut's death, Thothmes began a campaign of military expansion which transformed Egypt into a world power. He invaded Palestine, Syria and Nubia and extended Egyptian influence as far north as the Euphrates. The fear of Egypt's military might during his reign prevented attacks from outsiders and allowed the Nile civilization to develop in peace. The Pharoah's court received tribute from Egypt's conquered enemies including gifts of precious stones, perfumes, spices and gold which swelled the Royal coffers. With the guidance of the new Pharoah, Egypt became the wealthiest and most politically powerful nation in the Mediterranean area.

Thothmes was renowned for his hot temper and impetuous personality but he was also widely respected as a general and a statesman. He was feared by his enemies but deeply loved by his people. He never killed the rulers of the countries he conquered but deposed them and replaced their rule with Egyptian governors. At home the Pharoah was responsible for establishing a legal system which insisted on the impartiality of the judges and treated all men and women as equals, showing no favours to members of the Establishment. Thothmes was a cultivated man who was interested in the arts and sciences. He arranged for many rare plants, trees and animals to be brought back to Egypt from the countries occupied by the army and is credited with being the first founder of a zoo and a botanical garden in the ancient world.

When Thothmes died he was described by poets as 'a circling comet which shoots out flames and gives forth its substance in fire'. It was written about him that, 'there was nothing he did not know, he was Thoth in everything. There was no affair he did not complete.' Special references were made to the great temple the warrior mystic built at Karnak in co-operation with his son who ruled Egypt after his death as Amenhotep II.

Rosicrucianism, according to the mythical history of the order, survived the demise of the old pagan religions and the rise of Christianity. It is even claimed that the three Magi who travelled from the east to pay their respects to the infant Jesus at Bethlehem were initiates of the Order. The Emperor Charlemagne of the Holy Roman Empire, who was an early patron of the masons who built the Gothic cathedrals, is said to have founded a Rosicrucian lodge at Toulouse in the ninth century CE. In 898 CE a second lodge was established in France and in the year 1000 a group of heretical Roman Catholic monks founded the first Rosicrucian college which flourished in secret from the eleventh to the sixteenth centuries.

Some of the notable Grand Masters of the Rosicrucian Order have allegedly included such famous historical personalities as Raymond VI, the Count of Toulouse; the Italian writer, poet, and philosopher, Dante; the German magician, Cornelius Agrippa, who wrote about the Templars; the mystic and healer, Paracelsus; the Elizabethan astrologer, Dr John Dee; the Hermetic philosopher, Giordana Bruno, who was burnt at the stake as a heretic by the Inquisition; Sir Francis Bacon, chancellor of England in the reign of King James; the philosopher, Spinoza; the English scientist, Robert Boyle; Sir Christopher Wren, who designed St Paul's cathedral in London; Benjamin Franklin, who was actively involved in the American Revolution of 1776; the occultist and founder of Egyptian Masonry, Comte Cagliostro, and Thomas Jefferson, President of the USA. In more recent years the alleged Grand Masters of the Order have included the English writer and statesman, Lord Bulwer Lytton, the composer Claude Debussy.

Some modern Rosicrucians regard the legend of Christian Rosenkreutz as a symbolic fable published to reveal the existence and teachings of the Order to the general public. The Order itself had been operating in secret for at least 1500 years since its foundation in Ancient Egypt. In common with the Templars, the source of the esoteric knowledge possessed by the Rosy Cross initiates was the Middle East, specifically Egypt and the Mystery schools of Arabia. The Rosicrucians' political manifesto included the establishment of a social system which treated all people equally within a democratic framework. The three political aims of the Order were, initially, the abolishing of the monarchy and its replacement by a government composed of wise rulers, the radical reformation of the sciences and philosophy in accordance with spiritual principles and the discovery of a universal medicine or elixir of life which would cure all illnesses and diseases. When this manifesto was published in the seventeenth century the medieval system of feudalism was only slowly being replaced by more democratic forms of government. It would be nearly two hundred years before any major attempt was made to democratize the European systems of government (in the French Revolution) and in the colonies of North America. The English Civil War in 1640 laid the foundation for both these revolutions when the divine right of the monarch to rule without consulting the people was challenged in a bloody conflict which ended in the death of the king.

Many writers on the Order of the Rosy Cross have alleged that the fraternity was founded by ex-members of the Templar Order after their suppression by Pope Clement. It is claimed that before the Crusades, members of the Rosicrucian Order were secretly working in the Holy Land for the common good of humanity. Certainly both the Templars and the Rosicrucians used the symbol of the rosy or red cross and were dedicated to political and religious reform. Both groups, while nominally Christian, seem to have been secretly engaged in occult and pagan practices under the cover of orthodoxy.

The medieval Rosicrucians were popularly credited with possessing a wide range of magical powers, including the ability to prolong youth by occult techniques, the knowledge of summoning spirits, making themselves invisible, creating precious stones from thin air and transforming lead into gold. The term Rosy Cross was said to derive from the Latin ros meaning 'dew', and crux or 'cross' which refers to the chemical sign for light. According to this translation the Rosy Cross is an occult symbol of the alchemical operation of transforming matter into spirit, represented by lead and gold.

In common with Freemasonry the occult symbolism of the Order of the Rosy Cross represented the evolution of humanity from materialism to spiritual perfection. This symbolism coloured the Order's political

The Rosy Cross symbol

aims which involved, as we have seen, the restoration of the sciences of
the ancient world destroyed by Christianity, the promotion of medical
care for the poor, social reform and the universal establishment of
democracy. The Rosicrucians were linked with Freemasonry at an early
date. As far as is known the earliest written reference to speculative
Masonry is a poem written in 1638. This refers to both the Masons and
the Rosicrucians in the following words, 'For what we pressage is not in
grosse, for we be brethen of the Rosie Crosse, we have the Mason's Word
and second sight, things to come we can foretell aright....' This informs
the reader that the Rosicrucians knew the inner secrets of Freemasonry
and possessed the psychic power to predict the future.

Because it used the symbol of the Rosy Cross in its symbolism the Order of the Garter has been linked with the Rosicrucians. The Order was founded in 1348 by King Edward III of England and dedicated to the Virgin Mary, the Christianized version of the pagan Great Mother Goddess. Edward was a student of the Arthurian legends and meetings of the Order took place in a special chamber in Windsor Castle around a table modelled on the one used by King Arthur's Fellowship of the Round Table.

The insignia of a knight of the Order of the Garter consists of a jewelled collar composed of gold and red roses with five petals contained within tiny garters. These roses alternate with twenty-six gold knots, each representing a member of the Order. Hanging from the collar is a representation of St George, the patron saint of England, killing the dragon. This is enamelled with gold and set with diamonds. In addition to this magnificent collar the knights wore a velvet garter with enamelled red and white letters spelling out the Order's motto, *Honi soit qui mal y pense* or 'Evil be to he who evil thinks'. This motto was apparently the comment made by Edward when he picked up the garter dropped by the Countess of Salisbury while they were dancing and it was this event which, according to legend, persuaded the king to found the premier chivalric order in English history.

The association of the Order of the Garter with the Rosicrucians may not be as fanciful as it seems at first glance. It is recorded that the son of Edward III had connections with a group of knights who had fought in the Holy Land and had been inducted into the Templar tradition. On their return to England these knights founded an esoteric lodge which practised the occult arts. It is also true that many famous men who were either Rosicrucians or Masons have over the centuries been knighted as members of the Order of the Garter, a privilege which can only be granted as the personal gift of the reigning monarch.

Connections between royalty and the Rosicrucians, despite the Order's aim to abolish the monarchy, were even closer in Elizabethan England. One of the alleged Grand Masters of the Order, Dr John Dee (1527–1608) became the confidant of Elizabeth I and was involved in many of the political intrigues of the sixteenth century. As well as practising as an astrologer, Dee was also renowned as a mathematician, navigator, cartographer, magician, Hermeticist and natural scientist. He studied at Cambridge University and tavelled extensively all over Europe, studying occult doctrines from leading Cabbalists, mystics and philosophers. He spent some time in Bohemia with Emperor Rudolf II of the Habsburg dynasty who was a practising occultist and he was a well-known figure at many European Royal courts.

On his return to England Dee was invited to cast the horoscope of Mary Tudor and the young Princess Elizabeth. Unfortunately, in May 1555, a warrant for his arrest was issued following an accusation that he had bewitched the Queen. Dee spent several months incarcerated in prison before the charge was declared false and he was released.

It is popularly believed that Dee was a charlatan and a sorcerer but his library at Mortlake indicates he was well versed in ancient religious ideas, especially the pre-Christian teachings of Hermes Trismegistus, Zoroaster and the Gnostics. He owned a copy of the *Corpus Hermeticum* and had made a deep study of the pagan Mysteries and the mythology of ancient Egypt. It is therefore not surprising that the Rosicrucians should claim this learned occultist as one of the leading members of their secret society.

Despite his brief spell of imprisonment during the reign of Queen Mary, Dee seems to have received the Royal patronage of Elizabeth when she ascended the throne. It is recorded that the Queen often rode out to Dee's house in Mortlake, by the side of the River Thames, to discuss affairs of state with her favourite astrologer. Dee's advice was highly regarded by the Queen and in 1592, when he requested a living in rural Hampshire to pursue his occult studies, Elizabeth refused the request as she wanted to keep him close at hand.

Politically Dee was an imperialist who wanted to see England take her rightful place in world history as a maritime power. In 1577 he wrote his *Treatise on Naval Defence* which provided the blueprint for an imperial fleet which would rule the waves and form the bodyguard of a future British Empire. It seems that Dee's imperialistic vision was also shared by others in Elizabeth's court whose influence on the Queen was even greater then that of the Mortlake astrologer.

When he was not writing about politics, Dee took an active role in diplomatic and intelligence matters which helped further the imperialist aims of Elizabethan England. Dee was closely associated with one of the Queen's most trusted advisors, Sir Francis Walsingham, who is credited with founding the British Secret Service. Walsingham was a wily character who had risen from obscurity to become one of the Queen's favourites and he served her loyally until his death.

Walsingham was first employed at court as a personal bodyguard to the Queen, with the task of searching her apartments for signs of poisons. Elizabeth was the proposed victim of several assassination plots during her reign, including one conspiracy organized by the Jesuits. Walsingham soon developed a natural ability to acquire information by clandestine means and swiftly established an intelligence network which extended beyond the shores of England to the Continent. It was rumoured that, like Dee, Walsingham was a student of occultism and that he used the underground organization of witch covens in Tudor England to gather material for his intelligence service. The risk he took at a time when the practice of witchcraft was a capital offence cannot be overestimated but, in common with intelligence officers ever since, Walsingham took the risk of indulging in illegal activities because he regarded the defence of the realm as more important then his personal safety.

Walsingham's embryonic Secret Service was initially involved in counter-espionage and the threat to national security presented by the assassination plots directed towards Elizabeth. Although she was a popular Queen, she could boast a cult of personality which bordered on her being worshipped as the personification of the virgin goddess Diana, so Elizabeth was always in danger from her enemies. The Spanish were the leading contenders in the assassination stakes and Walsingham and his agents played an important role in exposing the activities of foreign spies sent to England to infiltrate the court and high society.

In 1570 Walsingham was appointed the ambassador to France and it was while he was in this position that he extended his spy network across Europe. Dee was useful to the spymaster because during his European travels the astrologer had made many important contacts in aristocratic and Royal circles, including high-placed occultists who were members of secret societies. He passed information on to Walsingham about these people and the head of the Secret Service was able to contact them and seek recruits for his network of agents on the Continent.

While Walsingham was in Paris he became involved in the negotiations for the proposed marriage between Queen Elizabeth and the Duke of Anjou. He worked to undermine it at every stage, believing it would be disastrous for the future of England. Frustrated by the lack of progress in the negotiations, Elizabeth instructed John Dee to visit Walsingham in Paris and find out what was going on. Dee was asked to cast a horoscope based on the suitability of the proposed marriage between the English Queen and the French prince. He reported to Elizabeth that the stars did not predict a happy union and he advised against it.

In common with most intelligence agents, Walsingham was fascinated by secret codes and ciphers. In consultation with Dee, the spymaster formulated a series of codes which were used by his agents to spread messages. He also employed skilled code-breakers who were used to translate the codes used by England's enemies. In 1562 Dee had discovered a book on cryptography written by the Abbot of Spanheim. He utilized the ideas in this book to write his occult volume called *The Monad*. This book has always been regarded purely as a study of esoteric symbolism but Sir William Cecil, a leading member of Elizabeth's government, stated quite clearly that it was work which had been of great value to the security of the realm. This suggests that Dee wrote it so that it could be of use to both occultists and secret agents. It has even been claimed that the records of the conservations in the Enochian language received by Dr Dee from the angels through the mediumship of Edward Kelly were also used to conceal secret messages relating to the magician's work for the Intelligence Service

Dee was not the only Rosicrucian openly involved in political work. Following the publication of the *Fama Fraternitatis* several lodges of the Order were founded and the members of these groups claimed that the Rosicrucians had been active in the events which surrounded the Reformation and the rise of the Lutheran movement in Germany and Switzerland. The Order had good political reasons for initially supporting the Protestant cause. On the surface, as heirs to the pre-Christian Ancient Wisdom, the secret societies would have gained little from religious reform. However, by supporting the Protestant dissidents they helped to weaken the political power of the Roman Catholic Church, the traditional enemy of the Cathars, the Templars and the Freemasons. At first the Rosicrucians believed that the religious reformers behind the Protestant movement would be the creators of spiritual tolerance so they gave them their support. In practice Protestantism was to become as spiritually bankrupt as the Roman version of Christianity and in fact exorcized from the faith those elements of paganism which gave it some substance of esoteric credibility.

In Austria the Rosicrucian influence on the Reformation was centred around Johann Valentin Andrea, a Lutheran clergyman born in 1586 who had visited Switzerland and been impressed by the social reforms carried out in that country. When he returned to Austria the cleric set up a mutual protective association on Swiss lines among the workmen of his local cloth factory. In 1620 Andrea also made contact with several liberal Austrian noblemen and with their help founded several Rosicrucian lodges in the country. At one stage he was credited with the authorship of

SVFFICIT.

N.
MDLX
XXVI
AVG
XVII

O
MDC

IOH VALENTINVS
ANDREÆ

Johan Valentin Andrea

the *Fama Fraternitatis*, although he always denied writing it. He certainly propagated Rosicrucian tenets, including the foundation of a college of wise men and women who would act as social reformers, and he was a close friend and supporter of Martin Luther. It was noted that Luther used as his personal seal the symbol of a rose and a cross but whether he was a Rosicrucian initiate is debatable.

The new Protestant version of Christianity proved to be no more tolerant of alternative spiritual beliefs than the Catholics. Religious intolerance is a pernicious evil which has permeated exoteric Christianity since the days of the early Church. The Protestants reacted savagely to what they regarded as the 'paganism' inherent in the Roman belief system and promoted a puritanical form of religious worship. During the English Reformation instigated by Henry VIII, the destruction of churches and cathedrals can hardly be justified, even by the corruption of the clerical establishment at that time. The Protestants also devalued the role of the Feminine Principle in the Christian faith by rejecting the Virgin Mary leaving a spiritual vacuum which was only partly filled in the eighteenth and nineteenth centuries by the rise of Anglo-Catholicism within the Church of England, which restored some of the old mysteries to the Protestant religion.

Many people in high places who had positions of power and influence were attracted by the utopian ideals of the Rosicrucians. One of these was the antiquarian Elias Ashmole (1617–1692) who was a close friend of Charles II, a knight of the Order of the Garter, founder of the famous Ashmolean museum and library at Oxford, and a speculative Freemason. Ashmole was also a friend of the astrologer William Lilly and was involved in the formation of the Royal Society which was based on Rosicrucian concepts. In 1652 Ashmole revealed his connection with the Rose Cross by stating that one of the first members of the Order was an Englishman who cured the Duke of Norfolk, Grand Marshal of England, of leprosy. Ashmole could only have known this as a member.

In 1650 Ashmole published a book called *Fasciculus Chemicus*, written by Arthur Dee who was the son of the Elizabethan astrologer. Dee was the personal physician to Czar Ivan the Terrible from 1621 to 1644. On the death of Ivan the *boyars* plotted to replace him by a non-Russian ruler but with the help of Dee, the Romanov dynasty was established on the throne. Dee, like his father and Ashmole, may have been a Rosicrucian initiate but he was certainly an agent for the English Secret Service.

Ashmole and William Lilly founded a Rosicrucian lodge in London in 1646 based on the utopian ideal of the creation of a new Atlantis, which symbolized the golden age before the Fall when humanity was spiritually perfect, and the rebuilding of Solomon's temple as revered in the Templar tradition. Ashmole and Lilly may have been influenced by the beliefs of Sir Francis Bacon, who was the Viscount of St Albans, and had written *The New Atlantis* which promoted the Rosicrucian manifesto. The position of the Freemasons and the Rosicrucians during the English Civil War and the Commonwealth is confused. The social reforms and attacks on the religious establishment which characterized the activities of Oliver Cromwell during the 1640s would suggest that the secret societies supported his cause. Many Rosicrucians and Masons, however, were aristocrats whose natural inclinations, despite their liberal beliefs, would have been to support the Royalist cause. Although the original Rosicrucian manifesto advocated the abolition of the monarchy this aspect of the Order's beliefs seems to have been diluted considerably.

It is claimed that after the Restoration the more progressive Puritans, including possibly some members of groups such as the Levellers and the Diggers who had been persecuted by Cromwell, infiltrated the Masonic lodges. It is possible that some of these elements were associated with the foundation of the Royal Society in 1660. The Society was formed to reform science, religion and the arts and was based on the Rosicrucian concept of the Invisible College. Several of the leading members of the Royal Society were either Masons or Rosicrucians.

By the late 1640s the neo-Rosicrucian Order had become firmly established throughout Europe. Although threatened by clerical persecution, the Order had formed lodges in Nuremburg, Hamburg, Paris and Amsterdam. At the beginning of the eighteenth century the lodges of speculative Masonry were also coming out into the open. One of the most important Masonic personalities of this period was the Chevalier Andrew Ramsay, a supporter of the Jacobite cause to bring the Stuart dynasty back onto the British throne. Ramsey lived for a long time in France and, in 1736, he addressed a gathering of French Masons and referred to the Templar tradition. He revealed that Masonry was the heir to the secrets of the Templars who in turn had inherited the ancient wisdom of the pagan Mysteries.

Freemasonry had been introduced into France by English aristocrats who supported the Stuarts. They were members of the Society of Legitimists who campaigned on behalf of the Scottish princes claiming the British crown. Lord Derwentwater founded the first lodge in France, at Dunkirk in 1721, with a charter granted by the Grand Lodge of England. Many Frenchmen joined the new Masonic lodges even though the government issued orders prohibiting membership. The king decreed that no member of the court should join a lodge and if they did they faced imprisonment in the Bastille. Innkeepers were threatened with fines of 3,000 francs if they used their premises for Masonic meetings. Despite this official disapproval Masonry flourished and by the 1750s numerous lodges practising the Scottish Rite, which had higher degrees than the English version of Freemasonry and seems to have been Rosicrucian-inspired, were established all over France.

In 1738 the Roman Catholic Church officially condemned Masonry. This event was precipitated by the public declarations of the Grand Master of the French lodges, the Duc d'Anton who preached the revolutionary ideals of liberty, universal brotherhood, love and equality. He was succeeded by the Comte de Clement under whose Grand Mastership French Freemasonry split into several rival groups. On the Comte's death in 1771 the Duc de Chartres was elected as his replacement and was installed as the leader of the Grand Orient, the independent ruling body of French Freemasonry which separated it from the Grand Lodge of England.

The Grand Orient had links with several other occult secret societies, including the Martinists or followers of Martinez de Pasqually who was a Rosicrucian adept. He handed on his mantle to Louis Claude Saint-Martin who had given up a promising career in the French army to follow the mystical path. Saint-Martin taught that humanity could achieve union with the Godhead through direct contact with the divine, as taught by the Gnostics. He also believed that all men were kings and supported the political aims of equality and democracy for all.

One of the most political Masonic lodges of the eighteenth century was founded by Savalette de Lage who formed a secret society called the Friends of Truth. The political philosophy of this group mapped out the ground-plan of the social reformation which was later to become the inspiration for the French Revolution. Another politically-orientated Masonic lodge called *Neuf Soeurs* was founded in Paris which had links with de Lage. This lodge had the task of creating an alternative education system as the established one was firmly in the hands of the clerical authorities who used it to promote their own version of Christian education.

Public lectures were given by members of the *Neuf Soeurs* lodge on history, literature, chemistry and medicine at an establishment called the College of Apollo, the Greek Sun god. During the Revolution this college changed its name to the *Lycée Republican* and its tutors addressed the students wearing the Phrygian cap of the revolutionary militia. Among the leading members of this radical lodge were the Duc de la Rochafoucard, who translated the American Constitution into French; Captain Forster, who sailed with the explorer Cook to the Pacific; the philosopher Voltaire; the American politician and scientist Benjamim Franklin and the revolutionary Paul Jones.

It was in the eighteenth century that the Templar tradition, forced underground for nearly 400 years, began to emerge as an influential factor in Masonic and Rosicrucian beliefs. Ramsay had hinted at the Templar influence but it was Karl Gotthelf, the Baron von Hund, who established it firmly within the Masonic tradition with his foundation of the Strict Observance Rite. Von Hund had been initiated into a Masonic lodge in Paris which was led by Lord Kilmarnock, the Grand Master of Scottish Freemasonry, and which claimed to be the guardians of the Templar tradition. This group may have been the inheritors of the Templar beliefs imported into Scotland by the Syriac Christians or descendants of the lodge founded by the son of Edward III in the fourteenth century. Alternatively, supporters of the Jacobite cause alleged that a Masonic lodge had been founded in Scotland in the early 1700s which drew its charter from a surviving Templar chapter in Bristol that had been operational for several hundred years.

At his initiation into Masonry, von Hund claims he was introduced to a mysterious figure called the Knight of the Red Feather who he later identified as Prince Charles Stuart. This person gave von Hund permission to found a German branch of the neo-Templars in Germany. According to von Hund's version the original Scottish chapter of the Knights Templars had been founded by two English members of the Order who had discovered the elixir of life and practised alchemy.

The popular myth circulating in occult circles in the eighteenth century was that the Templars had been initiates of a Gnostic teaching passed down by the Essenes who had also initiated Jesus into its mysteries. Neo-Templarism was therefore an attempt to combine pagan wisdom with Christian ideals. In Freemasonry the influence of the Templars was felt in the myth current in the eighteenth century which compared the three renegade knights who betrayed the Order to King Phillip of France with the fellow masons who murdered Hiram Abiff in Solomon's temple. Masonic references were also made to the assassination of a prominent Templar, Charles de Monte Carmel, who was ritually murdered shortly before the Order was suppressed. His murderers concealed his body by burying it under a thorn bush where it was discovered by other Templars. This murder was regarded by eighteenth-century Masons as a turning point in the Templars' history and instrumental in its eventual downfall.

The survival of the Templar tradition was, according to Masonic historians, masterminded by the last Grand Master, Jacques de Molay, while he was in prison. On the night before his execution de Molay sent a trusted confidant to the secret crypt in Paris where the bodies of the Order's past Grand Masters were always entombed. This messenger took from the tomb various symbolic objects which were sacred to the Order, including the crown of the king of Jerusalem, a seven-branched candlestick from Solomon's temple and statues from the church which marked the site of the alleged burial place of Jesus.

De Molay told his trusted aide that the two pillars which stood at the entrance of the Templar tomb were hollow and contained large sums of money. He was told to use this wealth and the symbolic objects to recreate the Order so that its secrets would not be lost. The two pillars of the crypt's entrance were probably copies of the obelisks at the gateway of Solomon's temple. In addition to gold coin, the hollow pillars also possibly contained manuscripts detailing the occult teachings of the Templar Order.

As well as von Hund there was another claimant to the Templar revival in Germany. This was Johann Augustus Starck who had encountered Masonic Templarism while teaching languages in St Petersburg. He also made a separate contact with a surviving Templar tradition in southern France which practised in the Cathar style. Starck believed that the original Templars had inherited their occult lore from Persia, Syria and Egypt and this had been passed to them by an Essenic secret society operating in the Middle East during the Crusades. His version of neo-Templarism received the patronage of European aristocrats and membership of the new Masonic Templar lodges included dukes, counts and princes. In Sweden Gustav III became the patron of neo-Templarism because he believed it had been founded by Charles Stuart and he was a supporter of the Scottish pretenders and the Jacobites.

In 1771 there was a grand convention of all the Masonic lodges which claimed mythical descent from the Templar Order. Starck's group was amalgamated with the lodges founded by Baron von Hund who, because he could offer no documentary evidence of the origins of his version of Templarism, was forced to retire and took only an honorary position in the new organization. At the time of the grand convention, which established neo-Templarism's place in the Masonic tradition, Prussia was ruled by the mystical Frederick the Great, who was both a Freemason and a student of the occult. In 1767 Frederick founded two neo-Masonic lodges called the Order of the Architects of Africa, which was devoted to the Manichean heresy, and the Knights of Light, which practised the magical arts. Frederick was a financial supporter of orthodox Freemasonry and in 1768 he commissioned the building of a Grand Lodge for use by the Prussian brethren. One of the many titles used by the Masonic secret societies founded by Frederick was the Illuminati. A few years later this name was to be adopted by a group of occultists who, despite their short public exposure, are regarded as the key figures in the secret political history of the next 200 years.

More sensational nonsense has been written about the Illuminati than any other secret society, yet the real facts about this mysterious organization and its role in the revolutionary movements of eighteenth-century Europe are extraordinary. The Illuminati were founded in 1776, the year of the American Revolution, by a young professor at the Bavarian University of Ingoldstat, Adam Weishaupt. He was of Jewish descent but as a young boy had been educated by the Jesuits in the Catholic faith. However, when Weishaupt began to teach law at the University he became an active supporter of the Protestant cause and was involved in a series of bitter arguments with prominent Catholic clergymen.

While an undergraduate Weishaupt studied the ancient pagan religions and was familiar with the Eleusinian mysteries and the theories of the Greek mystic Pythagoras. As a student he had drafted the constitution for a secret society modelled on the pagan Mystery schools but it was not until he was initiated into Freemasonry that Weishaupt's plan for the ultimate secret society was spawned.

Weishaupt first made contact with a Masonic lodge in either Hanover or Munich in 1774 but was sadly disappointed by what he discovered. In his opinion the other members of the lodge were ignorant of the occult significance of Masonry and knew nothing about its pagan symbolism. His contact with the Masonic tradition had, however, given Weishaupt an insight into the structure and organization of a secret society and he used his experience in Masonry to found his own clandestine fraternity.

On 1 May 1776 Weishaupt announced the foundation of the Order of Perfectibilists which later became more widely known as the Illuminati. The first meeting of the Order was only attended by five people but it soon attracted the notice of influential members of Bavarian society who shared Weishaupt's egalitarian and socialist political ideas. Within a

Adam Weishaupt

short period of time the Illuminists had lodges all over Germany and
Austria, and branches of the Order were founded in Italy, Hungary,
France, and Switzerland. Weishaupt conducted a secret operation to in-
filtrate Masonic lodges and established a power base within Continental
Freemasonry as part of his long-term plan to use his secret society for
political change in Europe.

Weishaupt's political vision was of a utopian superstate with the
abolition of private property, social authority and nationality. In this
anarchistic state human beings would live in harmony within a universal
brotherhood, based on free love, peace, spiritual wisdomC and equality.
Speaking before the French Revolution Weishaupt said 'Salvation does
not lie where strong thrones are defended by swords, where the smoke of
censers ascends to heaven or where thousands of strong men pace the rich

fields of harvest. The revolution which is about to break will be sterile if it is not complete.' This suggests that Weishaupt's principal targets for reform were the monarchy, the Church and the rich landowners who kept the European peasants in servitude.

The anti-Royalist and anti-clerical nature of the Illuminati was graphically illustrated by the mystical symbolism of the initiation ceremony into the highest grade of the Order. The candidate was led into a room where in front of an empty throne stood a table on which were placed the traditional symbols of kingship – a sceptre, a sword and a crown. The initiate was invited to take up these objects but was told that if he or she did they would be refused entry to the Order. They were then taken into a second room draped in black. A curtain was pulled back to reveal an altar covered in a black cloth on which stood a plain cross and a red Phyrigian cap as used in the Mithraic Mysteries. This ritual cap was handed to the initiate with the words 'Wear this – it means more than the crown of kings.' This ritual is very similar to the initiation into the Mithraic Mysteries when the neophyte is handed a sword and a crown and rejects them saying, 'Mithras alone is my crown'.

Weishaupt established a network of Illuminist agents throughout Europe who had access to cardinals, princes and kings. These agents reported back to their Grand Master the gossip and intrigues of the courts which Weishaupt used for his own political purposes. Both men and women were initiated into the Order and Weishaupt taught sexual equality. He came into conflict with the Church because he also taught his disciples that religious freedom was the right of everyone. He believed that once the masses had been de-Christianized they would demand political freedom and the right to enjoy life without the moral straitjacket imposed by the puritanical teachings of the Church on sexual matters. Some writers on the Illuminati, especially those who present Weishaupt as a proto-Communist, have described the Order as ultra-materialistic. It is true that Weishaupt had an almost pathological hatred of established religion but it cannot be denied that he was a spiritual person, although his spirituality would have horrified the clerics who opposed him.

He firmly believed in the redemption of humanity and restoring human beings to the state of perfection which had existed in the halycon days before the Fall. In common with the Rosicrucians and the Freemasons, Weishaupt believed this redemption was possible by the application of the occult traditions preserved by the pagan Mystery schools who were the guardians of the Ancient Wisdom. He also believed that the Church was a corrupt organization which had lost the original teachings of Jesus and was only concerned with holding on to power for materialistic reasons. The secret doctrine of Christianity, he believed, was still preserved by the Rosicrucian and Masonic traditions. Where he differed from those two secret societies was in his determination to overthrow the existing political system, even if that could only be achieved by violent methods. It was the Illuminist attempt to overthrow the Hapsburgs in 1784, exposed by police spies who had infiltrated the Order, which led to the Bavarian government banning all secret societies and driving the followers of Weishaupt underground.

The Illuminist participation in the events leading up to the French Revolution of 1789 has been the subject of considerable speculation and sensationalism. One of the founders of the Revolution, the Comte de Mirabeau, is said to have been a prominent Illuminist. It is also reputed that the groundplan for the uprising was discussed at the Grand Masonic Convention in 1782 at Wilhelmsbad which Mirabeau attended as an observer. Mirabeau allegedly confessed to other delegates at the Convention that he was a disciple of the Albigensi heresy whose aim was to bring down the French monarchy and destroy the Catholic Church so that the 'religion of love' could be established in France.

When he returned to France, Mirabeau introduced the philosophy of Illuminism into his Masonic lodge whose members included several political activists who became leading revolutionaries and later served under Napoleon. By 1788 nearly every lodge in the Grand Orient had been infiltrated by supporters of Weishaupt who were active in spreading the political policies of terrorism against the state, the abolition of the monarchy, religious freedom, sexual permissiveness and social equality.

One of the most colourful figures who played an important role in the political intrigues which culminated in the French Revolution was the Comte Cagliostro. His real name was Joseph Balsamo and he had been born in Parlemo, Sicily in 1743. As a young man Cagliostro travelled around Europe and Asia as the disciple of an Armenian mystic called Althotas who claimed to possess the Philosopher's Stone which could transform base metal into gold. In Rome Cagliostro married a young noblewoman, Lorenza Felicioni who, it is alleged, the Comte controlled by using hypnotism which had been taught to him by his fellow Mason, Dr Mesmer. It was Lorenza, freed from her hypnotic spell, who was later to denounce her husband to the Inquisition for practising heresy.

Cagliostro had been inducted into Freemasonry in Germany and was also an initiate of the Illuminati. On an esoteric level Cagliostro's contribution to the occult tradition was the creation of Egyptian Freemasonry. This he claimed returned Masonic symbolism to its rightful position as the centrepoint of the Ancient Egyptian Mysteries. Lodges were established in Germany, France and England practising a combination of Egyptian Masonry, Cabbalism and ceremonial magic. Men and women were initiated into these new lodges and this fact, coupled with stories of strange magical practices where the initiate was breathed upon in a mysterious manner by the Grand Master or Mistress, led to rumours of sex orgies and perversions.

Politically, Cagliostro was involved with the Society of Jacobins who supported the French Revolution. He had also attended the Grand Masonic Congress of 1785 when further plans were made by the Illuminati to create the atmosphere for mass uprisings in France against the monarchy. Cagliostro received funds from the Illuminati and travelled all over Europe as their agent, spreading the gospel of revolutionary politics. He lived in Paris for several years and set up an apartment in the Rue St Claude decorated with effigies of the gods and goddesses of ancient Egypt and an altar on which stood a stuffed monkey and a human skull. Cagliostro sold medallions of his own likeness as talismans and was mobbed by admirers in the street. He initiated members of Parisian high society into his Egyptian lodge and was patronized by the Royal family. Few knew of his real mission hidden behind this facade of occult mumbo jumbo.

In 1785, Cagliostro was the focal point of the Diamond Necklace Affair which was an illuminist plot to discredit the monarchy in the eyes of the French people. Cagliostro was asked by Cardinal de Rohan, a French priest who dabbled in the occult and had fallen in love with Queen Marie Antoinette, to purchase a diamond necklace on the cardinal's behalf for the queen. Rohan was under the impression that he had been corresponding with his Royal love but in fact his letters had been intercepted by the Comtesse de la Molte who had pretended to be the Queen. Cagliostro purchased the jewels and handed them over to the cardinal who duly delivered them to the palace where they were received by the Comtesse. She and her secretary broke up the necklace and sold the individual stones in Paris and London. Unfortunately the fraud was discovered by the Queen, and King Louis XVI arrested the conspirators, including Cagliostro, throwing them into the Bastille.

Foolishly, the king decided to have the ringleaders of the plot tried by the Parliament, which at that time was strongly anti-Royalist and had been infiltrated by Illuminist and Masonic agents. Cagliostro was acquitted, although the Comtesse de la Molta and her accomplice were found guilty. The resulting scandal inflicted severe damage on the reputation of the French Royal family and the Church which created the seeds of the public's simmering suspicions about the degenerate court life of the monarchy.

Following the court case, Cagliostro was forced into exile and fled to England. There he set up his headquarters at 50 Berkeley Square, which is today reputed to be the most haunted house in London. In 1787, while he was living in London, Cagliostro wrote to his friends in Paris predicting the coming Revolution, the fall of the Bastille, the overthrow of the monarchy, the destruction of the Church and the founding of a new religion based on love and reason. These accurate predictions were probably more based on his inside knowledge of the plans of the Illuminists then any psychic faculty he might have possessed.

Cagliostro's mentor was the legendary Comte de Saint-Germain. This mysterious occultist claimed Russian, Polish and Italian blood, and was an alchemist, spy, industrialist, diplomat and Rosicrucian. Saint-Germain was active in Europe from 1710 to 1789, during which time he always had the appearance of a man in his early forties. It is said that while studying occultism in the East the Comte was introduced to the secret rites of Tantric sex magic which provided him with a technique to prolong his youth. In 1743 he lived for several years in London writing music, and he became a close friend of the Prince of Wales. He was forced to flee from London after becoming entangled in a Jacobite plot to restore the Stuarts, and was exposed as an agent of the French Secret Service. In 1755 he travelled to the Far East to become the pupil of occult adepts in Tibet but he also found time to engage in spying operations against the British India Company.

As the secret agent of the French Royal Family, the Comte de Saint-Germain became involved in several political intrigues. He negotiated on behalf of the French king with Frederick the Great during the Seven Years War and was responsible for the alliance between France and Prussia. He was also involved in the plot to overthrow Peter the Great in 1762 and replace the Russian Czar with Catherine II. She allegedly placed the Masonic lodges in Russia under her personal protection in gratitude for the Comte's help in her rise to power. In 1770 Saint-Germain, this time acting as an agent for the French king, was involved in the partition of Poland and the Treaty of St Petersburg by which the Austro-Hungarian Empire, Russia and Prussia shared the spoils.

The Comte founded two secret societies of his own called the Asiatic

Brethren and the Knights of the Light, and was allegedly a leading member of the Illuminati, although he does not seem to have shared all their radical political ideals. He was heavily engaged in Masonic, Rosicrucian, and Templar activities with his patron Prince Kar l von Hesse-Kassel. As early as 1780 Saint-Germain warned Marie Antoinette that the French throne was in danger from an international conspiracy. The Comte was supposed to have died in 1784 but he was seen by several witnesses with Cagliostro and Mesmer at the 1785 Masonic Congress. In 1788, he appeared in Paris warning aristocrats of the impending holocaust, and in 1789 he was in Sweden preventing an Illuminist plot against King Gustav III. Rumours continued to circulate for many years after his alleged death that Saint-Germain was still alive working behind the scenes in European politics or studying obscure occult doctrines in some Himalayan lamasery with Tibetan monks.

From 1785 to 1789 several of the Masonic lodges in France were working full-time to undermine the monarchy and the established government. However, many of the French Masons remained loyal to the Royalist cause during the Revolution and it was only a select few who took an active part in the radicalism of the period. Even within the ranks of the revolutionaries there were indications that liberal elements were in opposition to the role played by the secret societies. In 1789, the Marquis de Luchet who supported the Revolution claimed, 'There exists a conspiracy in favour of depotism, against liberty, of incapacity against talent, of vice against virtue, of ignorance against enlightenment. This (secret) society aims to govern the world'.

Whether prompted by Saint-Germain's warning or not, in June 1789 the French king tried to forestall the revolutionary elements by introducing a programme of social reforms. Unfortunately, he also demanded that the monarchy should be preserved with the nobility having the power of veto on any modifications of policy. Within weeks of this announcement the absolute power of the monarchy was challenged by popular revolts in towns all over France which climaxed in the storming of the Bastille. This event led to the major political reforms of the Revolution including the founding of a republic, the secularization of the Church and eventually the mass executions of the aristocracy and the Royal family.

The overt influence of the Masonic-Illuminist tradition in the Revolution was marked. In Revolutionary literature of the period the Illuminist symbol of the eye in the triangle appears on book covers and the red Phrygian cap, borrowed from the Mithraic Mysteries and the initiation rites of the Illuminati, was adopted as the headgear of the citizens' militia. Mirabeau allegedly said when the Bastille was stormed, 'The idolatry of the monarchy has received a death blow from the sons and daughters of the Order of Templars.' The Masonic tenets of equality, liberty and fraternity became the rallying cry of the mob while the red banner, a Masonic symbol of universal love, was openly carried in the streets by the revolutionaries. It is said that when the French king was executed a voice cried out from the crowd 'De Molay is avenged.'

In the early days of the Revolution the anti-clericism of the Illuminati was consciously adopted by the mob with attacks on the Church and the destruction of clerical property. A lithograph was published showing a naked man staring upward at heaven. He holds a mattock in one hand and stands on a tree which has been chopped down. In the branches of the tree are emblems of the state and the Church. In the background a lightning flash illuminates the stormy sky and sets a crown ablaze. In this cartoon the archetypal man, symbolizing the common people, is addressing himself to the Supreme Being which suggests that despite their anti-clerical stance the revolutionaries still believed in a form of spirituality.

At the height of the political reforms even the fanatical Robespierre attacked unenlightened people who supported the Revolution but preached materialism. He also condemned those intellectuals who could find no place in their theories of life for the concept of God and another leading political activist, Cemot, said 'To deny the Supreme Being is to deny Nature itself.'

Within a year of the beginning of the Revolution the land had been divided up between the peasants, slavery had been eradicated from the French colonies, price controls were introduced to protect the living standards of the poor and a democratic constitution was created. The Committee of Public Safety passed laws introducing free education, free medical services, and the guidelines for a welfare state. The price for these reforms was high. The threat of foreign invasion and counter-revolution led to a centralized dictatorship of a new ruling class and to the Terror which destroyed all opposition to the alleged betrayal of the original aims of the Revolution. As with all radical political movements, those who advocated the replacement of the *status quo* were soon seduced by the power they had gained and became oppressors worse than the tyrants they replaced.

The role of the Illuminati and the Masons in the French Revolution was confused by the abandonment of the high ideals of the political movement which instigated the original social reforms. The radicalism of the Masonic lodges before the Revolution had alienated their traditional following among the aristocratic classes in France. Even before 1789 the aristocrats had begun to resign from the lodges which were promoting socialism and, as a result, their organization was seriously weakened. By 1792 very few Masonic lodges were practising and the movement was in a state of apathy. Those lodges which had survived faced hostility from the revolutionary government. At Versailles in 1792 the former Grand Master of a Templar lodge was lynched by an angry mob. Elsewhere Masonry came under suspicion as its role as a secret society was seen by those in power as a cover for counter-revolution. Having been instrumental in the Revolution it is ironic that within the space of a few years it became the victim of the monster it had helped to create.

As early as 1791 allegations concerning the role of the Masons and the Illuminati were already beginning to circulate. They were largely based on the confessions of Cagliostro who had been arrested by the Inquisition in 1789. In an attempt to save his life, Cagliostro told his accuser about the international conspiracy by the Illuminati, the neo-Templars and the Freemasons to start revolutions all over Europe. He revealed that their ultimate objective was to complete the work of the original Knights Templars by overthrowing the Papacy or infiltrating agents into the college of cardinals so that eventually an Illuminist would be elected as Pope.

In his confession, Cagliostro admitted that large sums of money had been placed by representatives of the Illuminati in banks in Holland, Italy, France and England to finance future revolutions in those countries. He even claimed that the House of Rothschild, the international banking family founded in 1730, had supplied the funds to finance the French Revolution and that they were acting as agents for the Illuminists. No evidence to support this wild allegation has ever been uncovered and one can only presume it was a figment of Cagliostro's imagination or a deliberate libel for personal reasons which are unknown.

By 1796 the allegations of Masonic and Templar involvement in the French Revolution were becoming a cottage industry. It was pointed out that de Molay had been imprisoned in the Bastille which was the first target of the mob. Connections were made between the Templars and the Jesuits on the flimsy evidence that both groups were dedicated to the setting up of a 'church within the Church'. It was alleged that the Duc d' Orleans, the Grand Master of French Freemasonry and a close friend of Mirabeau, was involved in the Illuminist plot against the French Royal family. It was also said that he had practised a secret occult ritual using relics belonging to de Molay. Whether these were the sacred objects smuggled out of the Templar crypt in Paris on the eve of the Grand Master's death is unknown.

In France in 1796 *The Tomb of Jacques de Molay* was published which claimed that the Revolution was the work of anarchists who could trace their lineage back to the Templars and the Assassins. In 1797 a Jesuit priest, Father Bamuel, published his *Memoires pour serir de l'histoire du Jacobinisme* in which he traced the survival of the Manichean heresy through Catharism, the Assassins, the Templars, the Freemasons and the French Revolution. He even claimed that the English Civil War was a Templar conspiracy.

The exposure of the Illuminist plot for universal revolution was greeted with shock by the other Royal families in Europe. They had seen what had happened in France and thought they were next in line. Before the French uprising the police in Prussia and Austria had been placed on alert to counteract threats of subversion by secret societies. In 1790 the Bavarian government decreed membership of the Illuminati to be a capital offence. The fear of the secret societies even extended to England when Parliament debated the Unlawful Societies Act which would have prohibited Freemasonry. It failed because the English Craft had never dabbled in politics and was supported by both the aristocracy and the Royal family.

With the rise of Napoleon in France in the post-revolutionary era the Masons faced a bleak future. Bonaparte was aware of the Illuminist role in the Revolution but decided to use Freemasonry for his own political ends. He infiltrated the surviving lodges in Paris with his agents and installed his brothers Joseph and Lucien as successive Grand Masters of the Grand Orient. Their sponsorship attracted many leading members of the Napoleonic administration and by the end of his reign the Grand Orient could boast over 1,200 lodges in France. By the early 1800s Masonry had spread to the French colonies overseas and was also well established in the Civil Service at home.

The tolerance of secret societies during the Napoleonic dynasty led to a revival of Templarism. In March 1808 a neo-Templar Order held a public requiem for Jacques de Molay. This requiem was held in the Church of St Paul in Paris and was presided over by the Abbé Pierre Romains, the Canon of Notre Dame, who was the primate for the revived Order. The Templars were dressed in the medieval uniform of the knights and were escorted by a detachment of soldiers from the French

Army. The alleged bones and personal sidearms of de Molay were exhibited in the church and the piebald banner of the Templars was carried in procession through the streets to cheers from a crowd of onlookers.

In 1809 a secret Masonic lodge was founded in France which modelled itself on the Illuminati called the *Sublimes Maitres Parfait* (Sublime Perfect Masters), a title which also has overtones of Catharism. This new society professed extreme republican views and actively worked for socialist reforms including the abolishing of the concept of private property. The Perfect Masters were opposed to Napoleon who they regarded as a traitor who had betrayed the ideals of the Revolution. They sought to establish links with other European secret societies dedicated to political subversion and revolution. Exactly what the Perfect Masters achieved is unclear as little is known of their activities after the 1820s when the group's existence was revealed to the public, thus destroying its credibility as a secret society.

Meanwhile the pro-Royalist Masonic lodges in France were secretly working behind the political scenes to restore the monarchy. They claimed success in 1814 when Napoleon abdicated in favour of King Louis XVII and were allegedly behind the Paris revolt of 1830 which placed Louis Philippe on the throne. He placed the Freemasons under his protection and appointed his son, the Duc d'Orleans, as the new Grand Master. On his death in 1842 he was succeeded by his brother but, at the Masonic convention that year in Strasbourg, the seeds of the 1848 Revolution were sown by the radical elements in European Masonry. The convention was attended by both German and Italian republicans representing secret societies who preached anarchism and socialism. With the establishment of a provincial government in 1848 the French Masons began openly to demand liberty and political freedom but this attempt at radicalizing political opinion in France ended with the restoration of the Empire.

Napoleon III was hostile to Freemasonry and its dabbling in political matters. In 1850 he decreed that the Grand Orient and its lodges should not interfere with the politics of the country. However, Masonry still received the private support of politicians and in 1852 the French President's cousin was elected Grand Master. He remained in office until 1861 when he was forced to resign for supporting the Pope in a debate in the Senate.

The Illuminati had apparently failed in its attempt to create an ideal social order in France but their philosophy had influenced another revolution many thousands of miles away. In 1776 the American colonists had finally challenged the British in the War of Independence and the blueprint for a unique society based on democracy, religious freedom and social equality had been drawn up in the New World. It was a blueprint which had originated in the founding of the first European colonies in North America in the seventeenth century by spiritual dissidents who included members of the Rosicrucian Order. The American Revolution provides an example of the most successful social experiment ever attempted by the secret societies in human history. Its political ramifications are still being experienced today in our modern world as the young nation seeks to justify its early spiritually-inspired beginnings.

4

THE AMERICAN DREAM

Following the suppression of the Templars in the fourteenth century the Order in Portugal was exonerated of all guilt in an inquiry ordered by the king. Instead of disbanding, as the Order was forced to do in most other European countries, the Knights Templars in Portugal were reformed. This new Order took the name of the Knights of Christ and survived until at least the late-sixteenth century. Its members included several famous navigators and explorers and it is said that the father-in-law of Christopher Columbus belonged to the Order. The discoverer of America had inherited from his relative the charts and maps which made his voyage to the New World a success.

This historical curiosity is interesting because it offers an indication of the occult influences which surrounded the foundation of America and its development into a world superpower. It has been suggested that Columbus' association with the Templar tradition may have been closer than just marrying the daughter of a Knight of Christ. He may in fact have been a member of a secret society which had connections with the Templars and the Albigensi heresy.

Some historians claim that Columbus was an illiterate sailor who was educated by a guild of weavers based in the Italian city of Genoa. At this period the craftsmen's guilds were often used as a cover by members of esoteric groups seeking to conceal their identities and true motives. Opposing this view, other historians see Columbus as a well-educated scholar and the volumes of writings he composed during his lifetime tend to support this image of the explorer.

Columbus was associated with a political group that supported the ideas of Dante, one of the alleged Grand Masters of the Order of the Rosy Cross, who is known to have used codes and ciphers in his writings, a practice associated with membership of a secret society. Columbus' voyages of discovery were sponsored by Leonardo da Vinci and Lorenzo de Medici, both initiates of secret societies, who found the explorer wealthy patrons among European Royalty and aristocracy. Whether Columbus was actually initiated into the Order of the Rosy Cross or any other secret society cannot be proved. He was certainly religious and believed he had a special mission in life, wearing a brown robe and girdle similar to the habits worn by Franciscan monks. He also heard spirit voices while in trance, and believed when he landed in America that God had led him to the New Jerusalem. The idea of America as the fulfilment of a Biblical prophecy concerning the foundation of a spiritual Utopia on Earth was a central belief in the Rosicrucian philosophy of the seventeenth century. In contrast to this religious piety, Columbus had an appalling attitude to the Native Americans whom he regarded as potential fodder for the slave market. These illiberal views would instantly disqualify him from membership of any Rosicrucian-inspired fraternity.

Columbus was the human instrument by which the New World was discovered, or perhaps 'rediscovered' is the best word, but the next stage in the political development of America devised by the secret societies was to be the task of a true initiate of the occult tradition – Sir Francis Bacon (1561–1626), who was rumoured to have been the son of Queen Elizabeth I and the Earl of Leicester. In his early career as a lawyer Bacon became a member of a secret society called the Order of the Helmet. This group worshipped the Greek goddess of wisdom, Pallas Athene, who is depicted wearing a helmet and carrying a spear. As a young man he was also a student of Hermetic, Gnostic and neo-Platonist philosophy and had studied the Cabbala.

Bacon, like many of his contemporaries, was a Utopian who received his inspiration from some ancient, half-forgotten Golden Age when humanity lived in harmony without war or violence. He projected this vision forward into the future when he hoped enlightened religion, increased education and the benefits of science would create the new Jerusalem. Unfortunately, many of the Utopians were hopeless romantics whose visions of the future seldom extended beyond the limits of their overworked imaginations. Bacon, on the other hand, had formulated a blueprint for the new Golden Age which, although not published until after his death, provided the *raison d'être* for his life and political career.

His *magnum opus* was a novel called *The New Atlantis*, which was published in 1627 after the foundation of the English colonies in the

Americas. It is the story of a family who are shipwrecked on a mysterious island ruled by philosopher-scientists who have flying machines and ships which travel under the sea. In this fantasy novel Bacon refers to America as the New Atlantis and describes the creation of a scientific institute on the lines of the Invisible College advocated in Rosicrucian writings. This was later to provide the impetus for the Royal Society founded by the Order of the Rosy Cross in the reign of Charles II.

Bacon's books often featured title pages with Masonic symbols, including the compass and the square, the two pillars of Solomon's temple and the blazing triangle, and the eye of God, indicating his association with the secret societies who supported his Utopian concepts.

Bacon's reason for supporting the English colonization of the New World was the threat from the Spanish who had already established a foothold in both North and South America. The Spanish were fiercely resisting the religious reforms which had swept Europe in the sixteenth century. Bacon was aware that the ships of the Spanish Armada had carried not only troops but agents of the Inquisition who had planned to restore the Catholic faith in England by sword and fire. If Bacon's plans for the New World were to be realized he knew that the Spanish had to be prevented from founding American colonies on a large scale.

Early attempts to colonize America spanned a period of nearly seventy years, although it is the epic voyage of *The Mayflower* in 1620 which is clearly remembered today. In fact as early as 1550 the Spanish had colonized most of the Caribbean, Mexico, California, and South America. The French were busy colonizing Canada and in the 1580s English colonies were settled in Newfoundland. However the rapid colonization of the New World by English settlers did not really begin until the reign of James I.

In 1606 James set up the Virginia Company which was granted Royal authority to begin settlements in the province of Virginia, named after Elizabeth I, who had been popularly called the Virgin Queen. The Union Jack first flew on American soil at Jamestown in Virginia as a permanent fixture in the spring of 1607, and in 1609 the first governor of the new colony was appointed. In this same year James granted a charter to found the Bermuda colony, and three years later settlers from the original Virginia landing took up residence on the islands.

The early members of the Virginia Company were aristocrats who supported the Church of England and the Royalist cause. They included Lord Southampton, the Earl of Pembroke, the Earl of Montgomery, the Earl of Salisbury, the Earl of Northampton, and Sir Francis Bacon who became a member in 1609. As Chancellor of England, Bacon was able to persuade the king to issue the charters which enabled the new colonies to proliferate in the New World.

As early as the 1600s the seeds of the American Revolution in the following century were being sown. The English colonists were already divided into those who supported the monarch's right to rule from London and others who wanted the new colonies to be independent. Although Bacon's insistence on the founding of the English colonies was prompted by the Spanish menace, his long-term political objectives were centred on the creation of a democratic society based on spiritual principles.

Bacon expressed his views on this subject several times claiming 'This kingdom now first in His Majesty's (James I) time hath gotten a lot or portion in the New World by the plantation of Virginia and the Summerlands (Bermuda). And certainly it is with the Kingdom of Earth as it is with the Kingdom of Heaven. Sometimes a grain of mustard seed provides a tree.' He was more explicit in a speech to Parliament when he made a reference to the establishment of 'Solomon's House' in the American colonies and mentioned his unpublished novel, *The New Atlantis*, as the blueprint for the country. In his clear reference to King Solomon's temple in Jerusalem, Bacon was stating that the founding of the colonies in Virginia was a spiritual, as well as a political, act.

The Virginia Company members who actually settled in America included several members of the Bacon family, and friends of his who were initiates of the Rosy Cross. They were to be followed later by the Puritan faction, which embraced the Pilgrim Fathers who sailed on *The Mayflower* escaping religious persecution in Europe and founding the colonies in New England and Massachusetts. In addition to these religious separatists it is claimed that as early as the 1620s Masonic lodges had been formed in the American colonies, although officially speculative Freemasonry did not emerge in Europe until the start of the eighteenth century.

As well as the Puritans and Rosicrucians there were other spiritual dissidents escaping persecution of a different type. One of these was Thomas Morton, an English lawyer who founded his own colony which he called Merrymount in Massachusetts in 1624. Morton was a rebel who forged alliances with the local Indians, sold them muskets and warned them of the genocidal tendencies of the Puritan colonists. In May 1628 Morton ordered a maypole to be erected in the centre of his colony. Around this phallic symbol danced the members of his colony, local

Indians and refugees from the Puritan settlement who had rebelled against the strict code of the Pilgrim Fathers. The participants in this pagan revel wore stag antlers, bells and clothes of many colours and elected a Lord and Lady to rule over their orgiastic celebrations. On the evening of Mayday, news of these erotic antics reached the ears of the Puritans and an armed group raided the Merrymount colony to arrest Morton. The Indians were scattered into the woods by gunfire and the refugees from the Puritan faction were rounded up and marched back to the colony where they were put in the stocks for defying their elders. The Maypole was cut down and charges of practising witchcraft were prepared against Morton. Due to insufficient evidence the charges were dropped and Morton returned to the colony in 1629 and promptly erected another Maypole. Following a year of threats and harassment the Puritans arrested Morton again, burnt down his house and sentenced him to deportation.

On his return to England Morton organized a political attack against the Puritans, using his knowledge of the law to challenge the legal validity of the charter granted to found the Massachusett Company and accusing the colonists of religious hypocrisy and corruption. In England Morton played down his pagan beliefs and presented himself as a dedicated Anglican who was resisting the Puritan excesses of the other colonists. His plan to dislodge the Puritans was nearly successful but was prevented by the outbreak of the Civil War. In 1643 Morton returned to America but was rearrested and spent two years in prison. He was finally released in 1645 but his health had been affected and he died two years later.

In the 1650s the Masonic influence was spreading in the colonies. A group of Dutch settlers who were third degree Masons arrived in Newport, Massachusetts in 1658. They introduced Masonry to the colony and members of the family operated a Masonic lodge in the area until 1742. In 1694 a mystic called Johannes Kelpius chartered an English ship to take himself and a group of followers to a colony in Pennsylvania. Kelpius was a German student of the Cabbala, a practising magician, astrologer and alchemist who had founded the mystical Order of Pietists. This group based their beliefs on spiritual revelations received from spirit sources by psychic methods which predicted the imminent Second Coming.

The modern American occultist and writer, Manly Palmer Hall, has refuted claims made by nineteenth-century writers that the Pietists were a bona fide Rosicrucian group. However he does concede that the Order introduced Cabbalism, astrology, alchemy and the Hermetic tradition to the new colonies. It is possible that contact was made between the Pietists, the Freemasons and the Rosicrucians in the New World which led to a mutual exchange of esoteric knowledge.

It is difficult to imagine how the high ideals of the original colonists were broken by colonial rule but it happened in a series of political mistakes by the British crown and government. A set of circumstances arose in which the American colonists were forced to take a radical stand against British misrule and from this defiance was born the political and spiritual impulse that led to independence and the creation of the United States of America.

Arguments about the taxes levied on the American colonies by the British had been simmering for years but they finally came to a head in 1773 with the passing of the Tea Act. The British government, attempting to save the East India Company from bankruptcy, arranged for them to deliver their tea direct to the colonies. In revolt against the new tax they had to pay on tea, a group of Boston citizens disguised as Indians raided the East India Company's ships in the city harbour and threw their cargo overboard. The members of the Boston Tea Party were all Freemasons who belonged to the St Andrews lodge in the city.

The British seem to have totally underestimated the strength of feeling in the American colonies over the Tea Act, hence perhaps the popular saying, 'It's just a storm in a tea cup'. In March 1774 they introduced a bill closing the Boston port until compensation was paid to the East India Company for the loss of their goods. Events quickly escalated and when a small force of colony militia tried to seize an ammunition store at Concord and fired on the British Redcoats, the American Revolution had effectively begun.

One of the most influential figures in the American Revolution was the writer, philosopher and scientist Benjamin Franklin. He was a Quaker but had become a Freemason in 1731 when he joined the Lodge of St John in Philadelphia, which was the first recognized Masonic lodge in America. At the time he was inducted Franklin was working as a journalist and he wrote several pro-Masonic articles which were published in *The Pennsylvania Gazette*. In 1732 he helped draft the byelaws of his lodge and in 1734 he printed the *Constitutions* which was the first Masonic book ever issued in America. He eventually rose to Grand Master of the St John's lodge and in 1749 was elected Grand Master of the Province. While in France in the 1770s, as a diplomat for the American colonies, Franklin was made Grand Master of the Nine Sisters Lodge in Paris. Members of the Lodge included Danton, who was to play a crucial role in the French Revolution, the Marquis de Lafayette and Paul Jones, both of whom fought in the American War of Independence. While he was in Paris Franklin used his Masonic contacts to raise funds to buy arms for the American rebels.

Franklin's diplomatic activities in the years before the American Revolution brought him into contact with those in positions of power who shared his Masonic and occult interests. One of these was Sir Francis Dashwood, the English Chancellor of the Exchequer who was also the founder of a secret society called the Friars of St Francis of Wycombe, more popularly known in the coffee houses of London as the Hell Fire Club.

Dashwood, the eldest son of a businessman, had married into the aristocracy. He sat in the House of Commons for over twenty years and the House of Lords for nearly another twenty, served as Chancellor from 1762 to 1763 and was a close friend of and political advisor to George III. While on the Grand Tour of Europe as a young man, Dashwood was initiated into a Masonic lodge in Florence. When he returned to England he founded the Society of Dilettanti which catered to the hard-drinking habits and debauched sexual activities of wealthy rakes. Dashwood also began to rebuild his ancestral home at West Wycombe using ideas he had picked up in Italy. The ceilings were painted with murals depicting the Greek and Roman gods and statues of these deities were scattered in the gardens. Dashwood also had a special lake created in the grounds on which were staged mock battles using large-scale models of sailing ships.

In 1739 Dashwood returned to Italy and made contact with several Continental Masons. He also visited Rome to witness the election of a new Pope, even though he was anti-Catholic. The previous pontiff had prohibited the practice of Freemasonry in 1738 and excommunicated all Catholics known to be members of the Masonic lodges. The Grand Master of the Florence lodge, Lord Reynard, who was the son of the Lord Chief Justice of England, had been forced to close down the lodge and destroy all its papers to avoid arrest by the Inquisition.

On his return to England, Dashwood founded the Friars of St Francis and meetings were held in the mansion in a special room decorated as a Masonic temple. At this time Dashwood was also a member of a neo-Druidic Order called *An Ulieach Druidh Braithreachas* or the Druid Universal Bond. This organization had been founded in 1717 to revive the old Celtic religion and included as its Chief Druid, from 1799 to 1827, the visionary poet William Blake, who is also listed as a Grand Master of the Rosicrucian Order. Following the rumours about sex orgies performed by the so-called Hell Fire Club at West Wycombe, the Druid Order withdrew Dashwood's charter to practise Druidism in 1743.

In 1751 Dashwood purchased Medmenham Abbey at Marlow on the River Thames and he converted the thirteenth-century house, once owned by the Cistercian monks, into a Gothic style folly. In the gardens he erected statues of the classical gods and goddesses, including Venus who bends over to extract a thorn from her foot. Unsuspecting walkers, rounding a corner, are faced with her exposed buttocks, and Priapus displaying a huge erect penis.

Exaggerated rumours and gossip about the activities at Medmenham Abbey carried out by Dashwood and his friends began to circulate in London high society. It was whispered that prostitutes dressed as nuns attended orgies at the house. Satanic rites were practised, such as the Black Mass which involved prayers recited over the naked body of a woman as the altar. In fact, the Medmenhamites were actually practising a revival of the pagan old religion. According to one member of the Hell Fire Club it was dedicated to the worship of the *Bonea Dea*, or the Great Mother Goddess, and the practice of the Eleusian Mysteries. Some of its members may have indulged in pseudo-Satanic rites although only as a prelude to their sexual antics which were an important aspect of the parties held after the meetings were finished.

In 1760, when George III was crowned, several Hell Fire Club members were given high office. They included John Stuart, the Earl of Bute, who was made Secretary of State for the Northern Department, and Dashwood himself who became Chancellor of the Exchequer. Among other important people who later joined the Hell Fire Club were the Lord Mayor of London, the son of the Archbishop of Canterbury, the Prince of Wales and Benjamin Franklin.

In 1758 Franklin visited England seeking support for the American colonists in their efforts to obtain more independence from the British crown. He stayed with Dashwood at West Wycombe and the two Masons discussed ways in which the worsening relations between the colonies and the government in London could be improved. Franklin was worried that the situation was becoming dangerous and would eventually result in bloodshed. Dashwood seems to have worked for the American colonists as their representative in this country and in 1770 put forward a plan to the British government for reconciliation between them and the Americans, but it was turned down.

Franklin again visited Britain in 1773 and met Dashwood. He informed him that time was short and unless some compromise was found the Americans would revolt against British rule. Franklin and Dashwood visited Oxford University and Sir Francis introduced his American friend to Lord North, the First Lord of the Treasury. The three men discussed the deteriorating relationship between Britain and the colonies and possible solutions to the problem. Unfortunately nothing came of this meeting and Franklin's attempt to negotiate a settlement failed.

Dashwood's influence in the matter was considerably weakened by the stories of sexual excesses at Medmenham. This gossip developed into a full-blown scandal with the revelations of a radical politician, John Wilkes MP, who had been a member of the Hell Fire Club. Wilkes was a self-styled defender of democracy and liberty who supported the American colonists in their attempt to rid themselves of British imperialist rule. He claimed that the inner circle of the Hell Fire Club were political conspirators plotting to deprive the Americans of their democratic rights. Considering Dashwood's involvement with Franklin and the fact that the two men were Freemasons, this seems very unlikely. It is obvious from the role played by Freemasonry in the creation of the new American nation that the Masonic fraternity supported freedom and independence for the colonies but they wanted to see the new country born without the spilling of blood, while Wilkes obviously had his own reasons for demeaning the efforts of Dashwood and Franklin to avoid conflict.

With the outbreak of war between the British and the Americans it was only to be expected that a man of destiny would arise capable of guiding the immediate future of the nation that arose from the ashes of the old order. The man who took this role in history was General George Washington, the descendant of a twelfth-century knight from the north of England who had served English Royalty. The Washingtons were staunchly Royalist and one of Washington's ancestors, a relative of the Duke of Buckingham, had fought on the side of the Cavaliers in the English Civil War. With the triumph of Cromwell two members of the family had emigrated to Virginia to escape Puritan persecution. They quickly established themselves as landowners, merchants and local politicians creating the Washington dynasty of New Americans which eventually gave birth to the first president of the United States on 11 February 1732.

Washington seemed set for a modest career as a farmer and landowner but, with the death of his brother in 1752, he inherited property, a seat in the House of Burgesses and, most importantly as future events would show, a post as major in the colonial militia. Within two years Washington was fighting the French and with the encouragement of John Adams who was a Freemason and a member of the secret Order of the Dragon, had begun a military career which led him to become commander-in-chief of the rebel forces in the American Revolution.

George Washington was himself a high-ranking Mason. He had taken his first degree initiation at a lodge in Fredericksburg, Virginia in 1734. Among the fifty-six American rebels who signed the Declaration of Independence only six were not members of the Masonic Order. The majority of the military commanders of the American revolutionary army which fought the British during the War of Independence were practising Freemasons.

The secret influence of the esoteric societies in the American Revolution, both Masonic and Rosicrucian, is illustrated by the occult symbolism of the American flag and the Great Seal which is the national symbol of the country. The design for the Stars and Stripes was a joint effort by a committee whose members included Benjamin Franklin and Washington, but it seems they were helped by the strange intervention of a mysterious person whose real name and identity is unknown.

Preparations for designing the flag took place in the house of a rebel leader in Cambridge, Massachusetts in December 1775. At a dinner party attended by the flag committee a stranger staying with the family of the house was introduced. He was referred to merely as the Professor and was described by those who met him as an elderly man who was very well read and extremely knowledgeable about the historical events of the previous century as if he had witnessed them. He was a vegetarian, was accompanied by a large oak chest containing rare books and ancient manuscripts and seemed to know Franklin. The stranger put forward several proposals about the design of the flag which were eagerly accepted by the committee without argument.

When the dinner party broke up and the other committee members left for home, the Professor remained in conversation with Franklin and Washington for several hours. He predicted to the two statesmen that America would soon take its rightful place as a new nation recognized by all the governments of the world and was destined to be a future leader of civilization.

The designing of the Great Seal of America, which is the country's symbolic coat-of-arms, was also an act surrounded by occult significance and mystery. A committee was formed on the afternoon of 4 July, 1776 after Congress had formally signed the Declaration of Independence creating the new American nation, and a resolution was passed requesting Franklin, John Adams and Thomas Jefferson to design a device to be used as the official seal for the new country. Several of the colonies already had their own seals but Congress wanted one which would be universally recognized as representing the inspiration for the American Revolution and the destiny of the American people.

A French artist, Eugene du Simtière, was commissioned by the committee to draw designs based on their ideas and, if necessary, add his own. Each committee member proposed a different design for the Seal. Franklin suggested Moses leading the Israelites across the Red Sea to escape Pharoah's army. Jefferson selected a similar scene from the Bible depicting the Children of Israel marching through the wilderness towards the Promised Land. The exodus from Egypt to Canaan was symbolic both of the route taken by the Ancient Wisdom in the days of Moses and the emigration of the Masonic-Rosicrucian tradition from Europe to the New World in the seventeenth century.

John Adams in contrast took a theme from Greek mythology for his illustration for the Great Seal. He depicted the god Herakles, or Hercules, resting on his club and facing a choice between Virtue and Sloth. This can be interpreted as the twin choices facing the new nation. However it should also be noted that in Plato's description of the mythical utopia of Atlantis he describes it as situated beyond the Pillars of Hercules in the Atlantic Ocean. Bacon's Utopian romance *The New Atlantis* was widely accepted as a blueprint for the new America and it would have been well known to people like Adams and Franklin.

Du Simtiere's design for the seal was more mundane but no less significant. Following tradition, he proposed a shield divided into six quarters on each of which were represented the heraldic devices of the six European countries who had provided settlers for the seventeenth-century colonies - the Tudor rose of England, the thistle of Scotland, the Celtic harp of Ireland, the fleur de Lys of France, the eagle of Germany and the lion of Holland. The shield was supported by twin goddesses personifying liberty and justice. The shield was surrounded by thirteen smaller ones representing the number of original colonies. It was surmounted by the Illuminist symbol of the eye of God in a triangle with the Latin motto *E pluribus unum* or 'One out of many'.

Congress was not happy with any of the proposed designs and in 1780 another committee was formed and additional work was carried out. In May 1782 a third group was appointed which submitted several designs including a shield with thirteen pentagrams or five pointed stars - the occult symbol of humanity representing the old colonies and thirteen red, white, and blue stripes. On the reverse of the seal was a truncated pyramid with thirteen steps surmounted by the eye of God surrounded by rays of light.

While Congress accepted the design on the reverse they were still not satisfied with the obverse side of the seal. They commissioned the Secretary of Congress, Charles Thomson, to modify the design. Thomson had formerly been a teacher at a school in Philadelphia run by Benjamin Franklin and was a member of the American Philosophical Society. This organization had been founded by Franklin and other leading Masons to promote the arts and sciences in the colonies. It operated in the same tradition as the Royal Society in England which was based on the Rosicrucian concept of the Invisible College.

The design of the Great Seal as it exists today is owed to Thomson and his colleague William Barton. On the obverse side is the bald-headed American Eagle which in astrological symbolism represents the Zodiac sign of Scorpio. This sign is associated with death, rebirth, sexuality and regeneration. The eagle is holding in its talons a bundle of arrows and an olive branch. This represents the conflicting forces of war and peace which have characterized the American nation over the years. In occult terms it symbolizes the dualistic concept of good and evil, light and darkness, the male and the female which the Masonic-Templar tradition inherited from the Gnostics and the Manicheans.

On the chest of the eagle is a heraldic device in the form of a shield and above its head is a cloud containing thirteen pentagrams. In its mouth the eagle holds a scroll with the words *E pluribus unum* written on it. The general interpretation of this phrase is that it refers to the creation of the new American nation from the original colonies, the many becoming one. This phrase however also has an occult meaning and is used by initiates to refer to the ancient belief that all gods are one God. Even the most polytheistic pagan religions recognized the existence of a Supreme Creator who ruled over all the other gods and goddesses in the pantheon. This concept is to be found in the Rosicrucian teachings, and in Freemasonry the phrase is used to refer to the one (God) in relation to the many (humanity).

The reverse side of the Great Seal designed by Thomson also reveals a wealth of occult symbolism. It shows the truncated pyramid with its steps representing the thirteen colonies. On the bottom step are the Roman numerals MDCCLXXVI or 1776, the year of the Revolution. This was also the date of the foundation of the Illuminati. Above the

1894 poster by Albinet advertising the Salon Rose-Croix. It shows Hugh de Payens, First Master of the Templars, represented as Dante and Joseph of Arimathea, 'first Grand Master of the Grail', as Leonardo da Vinci. (Michael Holford)

Membership certificate of the Bristol Lodge of the Rosicrucians, issued by W G Westcott, Supreme Magus, 19 May 1984. (Collection – Gerald Yorke. Picture – Michael Holford)

'Saviour of the World': a figure common on gnostic gems. French Revolutionary period. (Collection – Gerald Yorke. Picture – Michael Holford)

Washington as a Freemason. (Library of Congress, Washington DC)

Sir Francis Dashwood (1708-81), Chancellor of the Exchequer, Founder of the Hellfire Club. (Hulton Picture Library)

Gregory Efimovitch Rasputin.
(Hulton Picture Library)

Aleister Crowley.
(Hulton Picture Library)

Crowley dressed as a black magician.
(Hulton Picture Library)

Franz Ferdinand of Austria with his family. (Hulton Picture Library)

Comte de Saint Germain.
(Bibliothèque Nationale)

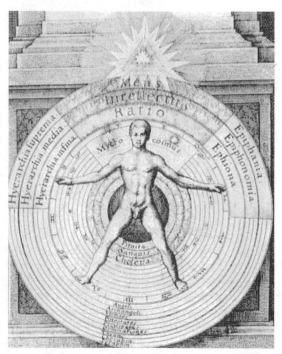

Man as microsm, the Universe in miniature. From 'Utriusque Cosmi Historia' by Robert Fludd, 17th century mystical philosopher.
(Ann Ronan Picture Library/ E P Goldschmidt & Co Ltd)

Certificate of membership of the Ordis Tempis Orientalis, issued by Theodore Reuss, 18 August 1912.
(Collection – Gerald Yorke. Picture – Michael Holford)

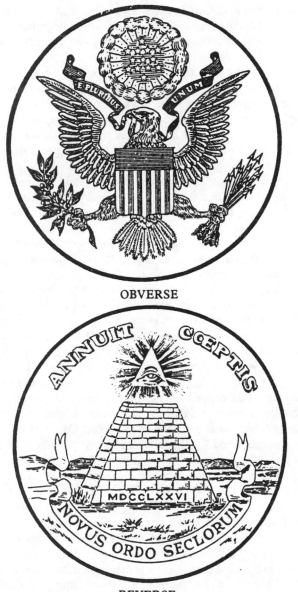

OBVERSE

REVERSE

The Great Seal of the United States

pyramid is the eye of God in a triangle surrounded by rays of light. This was the identifying symbol of Illuminism which appeared on the covers of radical political texts published during the French Revolution by supporters of the Masonic tradition.

In occultism the truncated pyramid represents the loss of the Ancient Wisdom which occurred when the Christian Church achieved political power and began to repress the old pagan religions which were driven underground into secret societies. In Ancient Egypt, when the pyramids were used as initiation chambers, each pyramid had a special capstone made either from natural crystal or an alloy of precious metals. This capstone attracted cosmic rays and occult forces which created the right conditions for the initiate inside the pyramid's inner chamber to experience spiritual illumination. Symbolically on the Great Seal the eye in the triangle represents the missing capstone which now only exists on a metaphysical level.

Above the eye in the triangle symbol is the motto *Annuit Coeptis* which is translated as 'He favours our undertaking'. This is a reference to the belief that the American Revolution was a divine event fulfilling an historic destiny for the future of the world. Washington is said to have been approached by an angel at Valley Forge who granted him a vision of the Utopian role America was to play in the centuries to come. Washington was a God-fearing man and believed that he had been chosen as the divine instrument who would bring this prophetic vision into reality. He was certainly an instrument for the Freemasons and Rosicrucians who planned the American Revolution and recognized in him the attributes needed for the first leader of the embryonic nation.

Below the pyramid, on the reverse side of the seal, is a scroll bearing the words *Novus Ordo Seclorum* or the 'New Order of the Ages'. This motto was borrowed by the colonists from the works of the Roman philosopher Virgil. In its original form it is rendered *Magnus ab integro seclorum mascilir* and was inspired by a passage from the mysterious Sibyline books. These documents were said to contain details of the destiny of the Roman Empire. On an exoteric level this plagarism of a phrase from Imperial Rome could easily be seen as an attempt to compare the new American republic with the glories of the ancient Roman Empire. On another level from the Masons and Rosicrucians, who were behind the creation of the new nation, the words 'New Order' would either refer to the replacing of monarchistic rule with republicanism or to the New Age of Aquarius. This New Age, which is about to dawn, replaces the old Piscean Age that began around the period when Jesus was preaching in Galilee. The occult conspirators believed that America would play an important role in the transition from the Piscean to the Aquarian Age, this transition spanning a period of 250 years, from the American Revolution of 1776 to the year 2025 CE.

The Masonic-Rosicrucian tradition had a profound influence on the formation of American democracy but there was another European secret society which had a place in the early history of the nation. This fraternity was centred round the Adams family who were, as we have seen, involved in the Revolution and provided the new republic with several Presidents. In 1823, the President John Adams ordered a tombstone to be erected to mark the grave of his ancestor Henry Adams who had emigrated to the colonies from the southwest of England in the early 1600s. This gravestone records that Adams fled from the Dragon persecution in Devonshire and founded a colony at Mount Walliston, which had been renamed Merrymount by the neo-pagan Thomas Morton.

It is claimed by the American writer Andrew E. Rothovius that Adams was not, as is generally assumed, a Puritan fleeing religious persecution but a leader of a secret society called the Dragons whose members attempted to revive the old pagan religion in the reign of Elizabeth I and James I. The Dragon title was a reference to the mysterious earth energy at sacred power centres and ley lines which form a network of ancient megalithic sites, such as standing stones and stone circles, across the British landscape.

The Dragons regarded King James' son Prince Henry as the only hope for the future of their country. James was a weak homosexual whose reign was overshadowed by attempts to remove him from the throne, including the infamous Gunpowder Plot of 1605. Henry had challenged his father's policies by seeking to instigate social reforms. He had even tried to persuade the king to abdicate once he was old enough to take over the reigns of power. This event was anticipated by the Dragons who seemed to have regarded Henry as a reincarnation of King Arthur destined to bring about their Utopian dream of a perfect society ruled by spiritual principles and laws. Disaster struck, however, on Henry's eighteenth birthday when he fell ill and died within a few days. Rumours circulated that he had been poisoned, either by his father or by conspirators within the court who objected to his liberal ideas. It was this tragedy which prompted many Dragon members to leave England and set sail for the New World. The Adams family, who were some of the original Dragon colonists, concealed their pagan beliefs under a veneer of Puritanism when they reached America. A few did have some contact with the pantheist Thomas Morton but their long-term plan came to fruition with the American Revolution and the part John Adams took in its inception and aftermath.

In the early years after the Revolution, John Adams eagerly supported Washington's key political ideas which were based on geographical considerations. As an initiate of an occult tradition based on the sacred geometry of the prehistoric megalithic culture, Washington's theories made sense to Adams. The first president wanted to construct a national capital combining the government with a centre for national education. This capital would be at a central location in the country which was easily accessible to every citizen. A system of nationwide canals would be dug linking all the major cities of the new nation with the capital to form a communications network. In this way the government would not be isolated from the people and anyone could have easy access to its centre. For various reasons Washington did not pursue this ideal and became instead a disciple of the *laissez faire* school of capitalism, which today has become the byword for the New Right in both the United States and many European countries with conservative governments.

Adams was obviously disillusioned by Washington's abandonment of geo-politics but then, in 1799, ten years after Washington's death, the new Secretary of State revived the idea of the canal system and John Adams actively supported him. His purpose for doing this was prompted by his idealistic vision of an egalitarian society as proposed by the original Dragons who had colonized America. By transforming the new canals, roads, and eventually railroads, into a national transportation network Adams believed a nation could be created where all men and women were equal. Unfortunately this grand plan was blocked by Congress who voted against the supply of funds needed to finance it.

In 1824 his son John Quincy Adams became President and attempted to revive the national transportation system, but political events conspired against his success. Missouri had applied for statehood in 1820 and soon made it clear that it, and the other Southern states who practised slavery, would not support the idea, or any other policy which might assist the free passage of commercial goods or human beings across the South. In the North the industrialists were also suspicious of anything which promised greater freedom for their workers and, in a strange alliance, they joined forces with the slave-owning Southerners to create the new Democratic Party. They supported their own Presidential candidate, Andrew Jackson, who was an advocate of slavery. In the election of 1824, Adams narrowly missed defeat, becoming President by only a slim majority. Although established in the White House the new President spent much of his time in office fighting his political opponents and his attempts at social reform were frustrated.

During his period in office President Adams did try to pioneer the modern concepts of conservation and ecology. He attempted to force Congress to prevent the destruction of the virgin forests in Florida owned by Andrew Jackson and his associates, but failed. He also attempted to introduce laws forcing factory owners to treat their workers more humanely. In 1828 the election was fought again between Jackson and Adams with the former winning easily. The issue in the election was between the contrasting personalities of the two candidates, with Adams satired as an idealistic intellectual and Jackson projected as the no-nonsense war hero - a pattern which was to be repeated throughout American history. Adams left the White House embittered and disillusioned with the political process. He told friends that his spiritual vision of the new America had been destroyed by the alliance between the slave owners and the industrialists who had conspired to deprive him of re-election.

John Quincy Adams no longer held high political office but his family were still influential in shaping radical ideas which had germinated in the Dragon tradition. His two grandsons, Henry and Brook Adams, wrote books which offered an alternative vision of society based on spiritually derived values rather than materialism. Henry Adams visited the medieval cathedral of Chartres in France which had been one of the greatest achievements of the masonic guilds. Chartres had been built on the site of a Druidic temple and, in Christian times, the cathedral was dedicated to the Black Virgin, a version of the pagan Goddess. Following his visit to France, Adams wrote *Mont Saint Michel and Chartres* which was published in 1913. In the book he pointed out that in the three centuries since 1600, the beginning of American colonization by James I of England, influenced by the Rosicrucian Grand Master Bacon, humanity had developed more rapidly than ever before in history. Pessimistically he predicted that in the period between 1915 and 1920 the human race would reach the zenith of its spiritual development and then rapidly descend into materialism and barbarity.

His brother, Brooks Adams, also assumed the role of social prophet, publishing several important works on world affairs, the political role of America and its future destiny. A hundred years before the concept of the right and left hand sides of the brain (representing logical and intuitive thinking processes) received scientific approval, Adams explained human history in terms of cyclic alternations of the domination of the imaginative and calculative mind. He believed that we had entered a historical cycle dominated by the logical, rational mind with its emphasis on scientific progress, militarism and the centralization of political power in a ruling élite. He claimed that the seat of this centralized power structure when he was writing in the early 1890s was America, which would replace the British Empire as the leader of Western civilization. He predicted that the new century would see America taking an active role in a worldwide war which would establish the country as an imperial power ruled by a military-based government with a society devoid of spiritual or moral values and addicted to materialism. According to Adams' scenario, this situation would occur by 1920 and remain the dominant factor in American political and social life until the end of the century.

Although the spiritual vision of the Freemasons, Rosicrucians and Dragons was betrayed, there have been several attempts in American history to revive the original ideals of the seventeenth-century colonists and return the country to the spiritual path. The Presidency of Abraham Lincoln was a turning point in America's spiritual history. It marked the Civil War which, although thousands of lives were sacrificed, led to a new spirit of freedom, the emancipation of the slaves, the modern concept of human rights and the final union of the North and the South to create the United States of America.

Lincoln was known for his psychic interests and had become involved in the practice of Spiritualism after the death of his son. References were often made in newspapers hostile to Lincoln's reforming campaigns to his 'progressive friends'. This was a coded reference to the inner circle of Quakers, Spiritualists and occultists to whom the President turned for spiritual guidance. Lincoln himself possessed psychic powers, including clairvoyance, or precognition, and the ability to heal the sick.

The President was a close friend of a neo-Rosicrucian called Pascal Beverly Randolph. Born in 1825 Randolph had travelled in the East where he had been taught the secrets of Tantric sex magic. He was of mixed blood and fought during the Civil War when he led a Negro infantry company. After the war Lincoln appointed him as an educator of emancipated slaves in Louisiana. Randolph had begun his occult career in 1858 when he founded a Rosicrucian occult society called the Hermetic Brotherhood of the Light which taught sex magic. The early

Rosicrucians had been interested in the transformation of sexual energy into spiritual power and had used alchemical symbolism to conceal the process from outsiders. Randolph claimed to have been initiated into 'the white magic of love' by a 'dusky maiden of Arabic blood' in Jerusalem. This may refer to an actual sexual encounter in the East or might be a coded reference to the Goddess worshipped in King Solomon's temple in Jerusalem.

Attempts have been made to dismiss Randolph as a charlatan who used occult practices for his own personal sexual gratification but he was aware of the history of the Rosicrucian Order. He regarded Christian Rosenkreutz as the one who revived rather than founded the Order, and alleged that he too had been initiated into Tantrism while studying in the Middle East. The aim of these practices was the creation of the Elixir of Life which prolonged youth. Randolph claimed that this elixir was the mixed secretions of men and women produced at the height of sexual excitement. His belief that the sex act was a sacred ritual, which could be used to achieve spiritual enlightenment, led to his arrest in Boston for advocating free love. The prosecuting counsel described Randolph as 'the most dangerous man in the world' but he was acquitted.

Randolph was not the only Rosicrucian to publicly announce his existence in the nineteenth century. The formation of neo-Rosicrucian groups in England, which ultimately resulted in the Hermetic Order of the Golden Dawn, inspired a group of Freemasons in Pennsylvania to form a Masonic Rosicrucian Order in 1879. This group, today known as the Societas Rosicruciana Civitatibus Foederatis, is only open to Master Masons and, in 1980, it had a total of 773 members. There is no evidence that Randolph was connected with these Masonic Rosicrucians but links can be traced between his organization and the Ordo Templi Orientis, or OTO, which claimed to be following the Templar tradition. When R. Swinburne Clymer became the head of Randolph's group he rejected the Tantric sex magic of its founder for more orthodox Rosicrucianism. Randolph however had already passed on his knowledge of Tantrism to a group of French occultists who in turn passed them to the German founder of the OTO.

The Ancient and Mystical Order Rosae Crucis (AMORC) was formally established in the United States by H. Spencer Lewis (1883–1939). Lewis claimed that AMORC was directly descended from an early American Rosicrucian group which had formed a lodge in Philadelphia in 1624, but he also said he had received instruction in the occult mysteries from a Rosicrucian Order in Toulouse, France in 1909. According to Lewis the authority to found AMORC was given to him by a member of the English branch of the Order who was descended from Oliver Cromwell and had received her authority from the Grand Master of the Order who lived in India.

AMORC symbol

The circumstances of Lincoln's assassination had some mysterious elements which have prompted some conspiracy theorists to represent it as an example of the workings of the secret societies in American history. The President's killer, John Wilkes Booth, was trapped in a burning barn after the murder and shot dead by a soldier named Boston Corbett. Apparently Corbett was a religious fanatic who had castrated himself for spiritual purposes. He was later committed to a mental hospital but escaped and was never seen again. It has been suggested that he was a secret member of the infamous Skoptsi sect which flourished in eighteenth- and nineteenth-century Russia. This weird cult traced its origins back to the pagan Mysteries of the goddess Cybele whose priests wore women's clothing and castrated themselves as a sacrificial offering at her altars. This sect may have been introduced into nineteenth-century America by Russian immigrants. Rumours persist that Booth escaped from the fire in the barn and lived until 1903 under an assumed name, financially supported by Lincoln's replacement in the White House.

Another intervention by the Masonic-Rosicrucian-Illuminati tradition in American history took place in the 1930s and coincided with the Presidency of Franklin Delano Roosevelt whose New Deal introduced socialism into the American political system and led to allegations by his extreme right-wing enemies that he was a crypto-Communist. Roosevelt was allegedly a member of a secret society called the Ancient Arabic Order of Nobles and Mystics and held the grade of a Knight of Pythias. This Order claimed to be an offshoot of the Illuminati and included among its past members Mirabeau, Frederick the Great, Goethe, Spinoza, Kant, Sir Francis Bacon and Garibaldi. This list of notables suggests there was some confusion between it and the Order of the Rosy Cross.

Two nineteenth-century Freemasons, Walter Flemming and William Florence, were the co-founders of the American branch of the Order. Florence had been initiated into a French Lodge of the Order in 1870 while staying in Marseilles. He was later inducted into another lodge in Algeria and returned to found the first American lodge in New York in 1871. Membership of the Order was open only to Freemasons who had reached the thirty-second degree of the Ancient and Accepted Scottish Rite or were members of Masonic Templar lodges.

The Order's mythical origins date back to the seventh century CE, or earlier, and it was allegedly founded by a descendant of Mohammed. He in turn had derived the idea for the Order from a politico-religious secret society in medieval Europe whose members included Arabs, Christians and Jews. The symbol of the Order is a crescent moon, made from the claws of a Bengal tiger, engraved with a pyramid, an urn and a pentagram. The crescent is suspended from a scimitar and in the Order is a representation of the Universal Mother worshipped in ancient times as Isis. The horns of the crescent point downwards because it represents the setting moon of the old faith at the rising of the Sun of the new religion of the brotherhood of humanity.

In 1945 Roosevelt arranged for the obverse design of the Great Seal to be printed on the back of the dollar bill. He had been given the idea by Henry Wallace, the Secretary of Agriculture who was a practising occultist. Wallace had suggested to the President that a new dollar coin should be minted showing the Great Seal design of the Egyptian pyramid and the eye of God. Roosevelt agreed with the idea but suggested that it would be more practical to include the design on the existing currency rather than create a new coin.

Wallace's idea originated with the Russian mystic and artist Nicholas Roerich who acted as a guru to the Secretary for Agriculture. Roerich had worked with Stravinsky on his ballet *The Rite of Spring* and had designed scenery for Diaghilev's famous Russian ballets. He had spent

Part of US Dollar bill

many years travelling through Nepal and Tibet studying with the lamas in the Buddhist monasteries of those countries and searching for the lost city of Shambala – the legendary home of a fraternity of occult adepts or masters who had secretly influenced world affairs throughout history. These adepts were known in occult circles variously as the Secret Chiefs, the Hidden Masters or the Great White Brotherhood, and were believed to be the *éminence grise* behind the formation of all-important esoteric groups including the Freemasons, the Sufis, the Knights Templars, the Rosicrucians, the Hermetic Order of the Golden Dawn and the Theosophical Society.

Roerich was a supporter of world peace and was associated with the League of Nations founded after the First World War to prepare for the establishment of a world government. In 1935, the same year as the Illuminist symbol appeared on the dollar bill, Roerich was active in the drawing up of a pact signed by twenty-two countries pledging themselves not to destroy cultural treasures. The symbol used to illustrate this pact was composed of three spheres symbolizing the trinity of love, power, and wisdom. These spheres were enclosed within a larger circle representing the world.

The Secretary of Agriculture was well versed in occult knowledge. In a letter to his Russian guru he stated, 'The search – whether it be for the lost word of Masonry, or the Holy Chalice, or the potentialities of the age to come – is the one supremely worthwhile objective. All else is karmic duty. But surely everyone is a potential Galahad? So may we strive for the Chalice and the flame above it'. The chalice he refers to is the Holy Grail, regarded by the Rosicrucians as a feminine symbol for perfection, and 'the age to come' is the dawning of the Aquarian Age.

His relationship with the Russian mystic was to have serious political consequences for Wallace. Critics of the Secretary for Agriculture managed to obtain copies of the correspondence he had with Roerich. They used it to expose his occult beliefs and to discredit his bid for the Presidency. They also alleged, without any evidence apart from the fact that he was Russian, that Roerich was a Communist sympathizer. Roerich was an internationalist and, whilst he may have supported the original democratic aims of the 1917 Revolution, he was an ardent critic of the excesses of Communism as practised under Stalin in the 1930's. In fact, as a student of the esoteric tradition and an agent of the Great White Brotherhood, Roerich was an internationalist and would have found the ultra-materialism of Communism less then attractive as a political ideology.

Wallace's reasons for wanting to introduce the reverse side of the Great Seal onto the American currency were based on his belief that America was reaching a turning point in her history and that great spiritual changes were imminent. He believed that the 1930s represented a time when a great spiritual awakening was going to take place which would precede the creation of the one-world state. According to Wallace's own account written in the 1950s, when he presented the idea to President Roosevelt he was excited by the idea. Roosevelt was eager to have on the American currency the Masonic symbol of the all-seeing eye, which he said was a sigil of the Grand Architect of the Universe. Before passing on the idea to the Treasury, Roosevelt asked his Cabinet colleague James Farley if the Catholics would object to the introduction of a Masonic symbol on the dollar bill. When he was told there would be no objections, Roosevelt instructed the Treasury to start printing the new dollars.

Although Wallace failed in his attempt to become US President he continued his occult researches and studies. In later years, the ex-Secretary of Agriculture became involved in psychic research. He was responsible for supporting the pioneering work of Dr Andrija Puharich, a scientist who was responsible for fostering the psychic talents of a young Israeli called Uri Geller and promoting him to the outside world through the media.

The strange incident of the one dollar bill may represent one of the last attempts by the Masonic-Rosicrucian-Illuminati tradition openly to influence American politics. They are however rumoured to have worked secretly behind several political organizations in the United States since the days of Roosevelt. The American Dream was finally to come to a tragic end on a November day in Dallas in 1963. This event was followed by a period of national suffering which was characterized by the Vietnam war, the civil rights struggle, Watergate and the recent Iran-Contra scandal. It is very difficult to see the United States today taking its predicted role as the civilizing leader of the New Age although the new era of detente with the Soviet Union offers hope for the future. In all difficult times history produces men and women of destiny and there is still time for the real American dream to be realized.

GERMAN NATIONALISM AND THE
BOLSHEVIK REVOLUTION

In the years following the French and American Revolutions there were events happening in Europe which generations later had a profound effect on the lives of millions of people. Political alliances were forced, creating the conditions that allowed the rise of the three major European superpowers of the nineteenth century. These powers were personified by the dynamic families who were their hereditary rulers – the Romanovs of Russia, the Habsburgs of the Austro-Hungarian Empire and the Hohenzollerns of Prussia who became the Kaisers of Germany.

The bloody conflict which ensued between these great European dynasties was to include the British and French Empires and involve America in a European commitment which has lasted to modern times. Specifically, Russia and Germany were destined to dominate nineteenth-century politics in Europe and gave birth to conflicting political ideologies which were instrumental in bringing about the holocausts of two world wars in our own century. It would be too easy to dismiss these wars as isolated events, but the fact is that their causes date back to events in the nineteenth century and to the political doctrines which had been germinating for several decades before the outbreak of the Great War of 1914–18.

On the surface, the motivation of the Romanovs, the Habsburgs, and the Hohenzollerns was purely territorial and political. Each family had imperial aspirations, especially the Habsburgs who had been Holy Roman Emperors by papal decree since medieval times. The tensions these aspirations created eventually led to the First World War but at the beginning the leaders of each nation were more interested in self preservation than conquering neighbouring countries. The extra element in the historical tragedy which unfolded was the influence of mysticism, the occult and secret societies on the lives of the leading characters in this drama. Orthodox historians have chosen to ignore this aspect because they believe it has no real significance in politics. In fact it is only through the revealing of the occult conspiracy that the events under discussion can be fully understood and placed in their true historical perspective.

In Russia the Romanov family had come to power and were to rule the country for 300 years from the seventeenth century until they were deposed in the Bolshevik Revolution of 1917. The Romanovs emerged as the ruling dynasty during a period of anarchy and chaos and the crowning of Mikhail Romanov, who allegedly ascended the throne with the help of the Rosicrucian Dr Arthur Dee and the British Secret Service, established a dynasty under whose influence Russia would grow into a mighty empire and whose influence was exerted from Eastern Europe to Asia.

Before their rise to power the Romanovs were credited by their enemies with practising witchcraft and possessing occult powers. In 1598 when Feodor Romanov plotted to seize the throne he placed his trust in Boris Godunov who also wanted to wear the Russian crown. Godunov bribed the servants in the Romanov household and placed false evidence in the house to prove that the family dabbled in the occult. The Romanovs were found guilty of practising sorcery and spent many years in exile before Feodor's son, Mikhail, achieved the goal of the family and was crowned Czar.

It was during the reign of Czar Alexander I (1801–25) that the secret societies exerted their greatest influence on the Russian court and the country's political objectives. The first Masonic lodge was officially founded in Poland in 1750 and within a few years Masonry had spread rapidly from there to Mother Russia. By the end of the eighteenth century Freemasonry, Rosicrucianism and Martinism were flourishing in the spiritual hothouse climate of Russian society, where bizarre mystical cults and wandering holy men were accepted as a natural product of the orthodox religious experience.

In both Poland and Russia the secret societies dabbled in radicalism and their membership included activists engaged in socialist, revolutionary and nationalist politics. One of the most active advocates of mixing radical politics with the occult was Count Thadeus Grabianka who was under the mistaken impression that he had been divinely chosen as the king of Poland. He set up a court-in-exile at Avignon in France, one of the medieval haunts of the Cathars, and built a replica of Solomon's temple which was the site of quasi-magical rites. In 1803 the Count was forced to flee from France to avoid criminal charges for fraud. He found asylum in Russia and at St Petersburg founded a secret society which combined

Rosicrucianism, Martinism and radical politics.

The Empress Catherine the Great, wife of Peter III, had been ruling since 1762. She was an autocrat who was suspicious of anything resembling political reform which might weaken the power of the Czars. She had been horrified by the outbreak of the French Revolution in 1789. When she was told of the execution of the French king she became physically ill and was ordered to bed by her physicians. When she recovered Catherine reacted by recalling all her subjects from Paris, breaking off diplomatic relations with France, ordering all French citizens to leave Russia or take an oath of loyalty to her, closing all Russian ports to French shipping, granting asylum to aristocrats fleeing the Terror and providing funds to the counter-revolutionaries. Her disquiet at the events in France was not helped by the revelation in 1794 of an Illuminist plot to overthrow the Habsburgs.

The young Alexander, who had been born in 1777, does not seem to have shared his grandmother's fears. In fact he was later to express sympathy for the aims of those who started the French Revolution. Alexander stated several times that he believed all men and women should be equal and had the right to liberty. He also expressed sadness at the destruction of Polish nationalism which had been ruthlessly crushed by his grandmother's armies.

Alexander had been named after St Alexander Nevsky, a Russian national hero who had defeated the Swedish army and the Teutonic Knights. His religious education was in the hands of a Russian orthodox priest André Samborsky, who had been derided as a heretic by his clerical opponents. Samborsky had served as the official chaplain to the Russian legation in London and had married an English-woman. His enemies claimed that Samborsky had become tainted with degenerate Western values while living in England. When he returned to Russia he had abandoned his clerical garb and worn an ordinary frock coat, shaved off his beard and spoken with an English accent. The Empress had deliberately selected this heretic priest to teach her grandson because she thought his open-minded attitude to religion would help Alexander come to terms with spiritual matters in a more progressive way than his predecessors.

Alexander's father, Paul, was also a religious rebel who had circulated among Freemasons and Martinists as a young man. He had opposed his mother's suppression of the Martinist Order which had acquired several important converts in the aristocracy who supported their belief in a democratic society based on equality and liberty. Catherine had outlawed

the Martinists in the wake of the French Revolution because she resented
their radicalism.

Even before he ascended to the Russian throne, Paul had expressed
enlightened views. He had built new churches and schools, supported the
rise of Lutherism, financed new industrial enterprises and promoted
advanced agricultural techniques. Paul had even erected a hospital where
peasants working on his country estate could get free medical treatment
and his image was that of a social reformer who wanted to improve the
living conditions of the Russian people.

In November 1796 the Empress Catherine died of a heart attack. Paul
became Czar and the liberals thought that he would begin a programme of
social reform and democracy. In fact Paul's character had been changing
for several years, indicating that he was suffering from a progressive
mental illness. His mother had been so concerned by his mental state that
she had contemplated naming Alexander as her heir to prevent Paul from
taking the throne after her death.

Paul had formed his own private army to rule his country estates which
he had modelled on the Prussian Army corps. He had also surrounded
himself with a group of brutish ex-Russian Army officers who obeyed his
every command without question. This obsession with military matters
and a series of extra-marital affairs led to tensions in his marriage which
were later to affect his rulership. Soon after he became Czar, Paul started
to exhibit paranoid tendencies imagining that cabals of conspirators were
plotting to overthrow him. He withdrew his patronage from the
Martinists and the Freemasons and ostracized the aristocrats in his court
who still supported the secret societies and their political ideals.

The relationship between Paul and his son Alexander was virtually
destroyed by Paul's rigid attitudes, bordering on dictatorship, and the
Grand Duke's desire to see social reform. As early as the autumn of 1797,
Alexander wrote to liberal friends criticizing his father's regime and
promoting his own destiny as an imperial reformer who would bring
enlightenment to the Russian people. There was a mutual distrust
between the two men which bordered on hatred because Paul was aware
that his mother had favoured the Grand Duke and he suspected his son of
a plot to replace him. Alexander had already drafted secret plans for
reform but decided not to present these to the new Czar because of his
worsening mental condition which caused him to act in an unpredictable
manner.

By 1801 large sections of the Russian army were in open revolt against
Paul's dictatorial style. The Czar had hinted that he was planning to adopt

a young German prince and name him as his heir and threatened Alexander with death if he opposed the adoption. At this stage a group of court officials conspired with Alexander to force the Czar to abdicate in his favour. They believed if this did not happen soon the people would rise up and the monarchy might be destroyed in a popular revolution.

On the night of 11 March 1801 the conspirators, assisted by rebel Army officers who had pledged their troops to the coup, faced Czar Paul and demanded that he sign the document of abdication. When he refused, Paul was knocked to the floor and strangled. The Grand Duke Alexander was informed of his father's death and was so horrified that he refused to accept the crown which he said was stained with blood. However he was quickly persuaded by the Army officers who told him that unless he did the country would be plunged into revolution. Alexander reluctantly accepted and an announcement was made that the old Czar had died of apoplexy during the night.

Early in his reign Alexander lifted the prohibition on the Martinists and he actively supported the role of the secret societies in political life. The new regime was characterized by the formation of a group of advisors to the Czar who called themselves the Secret Committee. This group modelled itself on the Committees of Public Safety which operated during the French Revolution. It consisted of radicals who admired the Cromwellian principle in English politics and the revolutionary government of France. Their aim was the creation of a democratic society in Russia but they believed social reformation could only be reached if the monarch were still in absolute control of the political process so they rejected the republicanism of their French counterparts.

The new social reforms Alexander planned were postponed by the war with Napoleon in 1805. Alexander seems to have regarded this war as a divine mission and it is during the period of the military campaign that he first seems to have had difficulties discerning fact from fantasy. The idea of the divine mission was the result of predictions given to the new Czar by Madame von Kruderer, a famous psychic who was a student of the Swedish mystic Emmanuel Swedenborg. She acted as Alexander's spiritual guide and persuaded him that it was his duty to defeat the French Emperor and restore the House of Bourbon to the throne in France.

In 1815, while in Russian-occupied Paris, Alexander installed Madame von Kruderer in a hotel near the Elysée Palace and consulted her daily. She went into trance and on one occasion informed the startled Czar that he was the reincarnation of Jesus! Even Alexander could not accept this statement and the psychic's influence on his life began to wane after this.

Alexander's campaign against Napoleon had kindled in him new spiritual insights. Increasingly he began to believe that his life destiny was to be the creator of an international brotherhood based on love and peace. He came under the spell of one of his courtiers, Koshelav, who had contacts with the Martinists, the Rosicrucians, the Piestists, the disciples of Swedenborg and the Quakers. He had been involved in the foundation of the Russian Bible Society which, despite its dull name, was a group of religious zealots who practised a heretical form of mystical Christianity.

Koshelav offered the Czar initiation into Freemasonry but Alexander refused. He regarded himself as the chosen instrument of divine power and as such he could not be initiated into a secret society. The Czar did however accept tutelage from Koshelav in the secret teachings preserved in the Masonic lodges which the occultists freely offered him. Koshelav was associated with the Skotpsi who practised castration as a religious rite. The cult had first appeared in Russia in the 1750s among the Society of Flagellants, who were later known as the People of God. This extreme religious sect was described by one critic as practitioners of a mixture of Christianity and pagan rites.

The leader of the castration cult in the reign of Alexander was Kandvah Selivanov who attracted many disciples among Russian high society and in the Czar's court, although few made the final sacrifice required to enter the inner circle of the sect. Selivanov had delusions that he was the new messiah and called his home the House of God or the New Jerusalem. One of his female devotees, Catherine Tatarinova, founded a secret occult society based on the practices of the whirling dervishes who belonged to the Sufi brotherhood. She was a close friend and leader of the castrators' cult and through him was introduced to the Czar. Alexander paid her an annual salary of 6,000 roubles and consulted her about the esoteric meaning of the Bible.

Koshelav was the occult teacher who inspired Alexander's political dream which dominated the rest of his life. This was the creation of a united Europe where politics and religion would work hand in hand for the good of humanity. By 1815, however, Alexander had begun to question the legitimacy of the secret societies and had become a convert to a mystical form of fundamental Christianity which rejected the paganism inherent in the Masonic and Rosicrucian teachings as heathen superstition.

Alexander pursued his idea of a politically united Europe and proposed a Holy Alliance between Russia, Prussia and the Austro-Hungarian Empire. These allied powers would rule the new European federation in accordance with Christian values and morality. By this time Alexander had identified the political forces working in Europe for radical change as the agents of the satanic powers of darkness which had to be exterminated. The Grand Duke Alexander, the liberal reformer, had been transformed into Czar Alexander, the reactionary enemy of social progress. The shock of his father's violent death which had brought him to power and the mental conflict between his autocratic power and championing reform had finally caused him to lose touch with reality.

A pact forming the Holy Alliance was signed in September 1815 by Alexander, the Emperor Francis von Habsburg and the king of Prussia. Spain, France, Sweden and the independent kingdoms of Naples and Sardinia were invited to join but the Vatican and Britain refused to have anything to do with the new alliance. English aristocrats such as Lord Castlereagh and the Duke of Wellington dismissed it as 'mystical nonsense' and expressed amusement at a political pact which united three kings dedicated to the Russian Orthodox, Catholic and Protestant religions.

In 1820 Czar Alexander and the Habsburg Emperor acted together as members of the Holy Alliance to prevent revolution in Italy. They believed that the new revolutionary fever in the country had been encouraged by a secret society known as the Carbonari or Charcoal Burners. This sect had originated in Scotland at the time of Robert the Bruce and had spread to France, Germany, Poland and Italy. In common with Masonry, the Carbonari were a medieval guild organized by charcoal burners who travelled the country selling their wares. Although nominally Christian the charcoal burners practised rites which had pagan features and, in defiance of the Pope, preached religious freedom and the ending of oppression and tyranny. Allegedly the Carbonari had connections with both the Freemasons and the Illuminati.

With over 60,000 members in Italy it was easy for the Carbonari to seize power in Naples and Piedmont. King Ferdinand was forced to take an oath of allegiance to the society and wear their symbol of the red, white and blue tricolour. The Czar reacted to these developments in Italy with his usual melodrama stating 'Our purpose (in invading Italy) is to counteract the empire of evil which is spreading by all the occult means at their disposal the Satanic spirit which directs it.' Despite his fighting words Alexander was facing mutiny among his army officers who did not support his divine mission to rid Europe of the secret societies. Although the Russian army stood in readiness it was the Austrians who actually crossed into Italy, put down the revolts in Naples and Piedmont and drove the Carbonari underground.

Increasingly Alexander became more and more under the malefic influence of extreme elements in the Russian Orthodox Church. They recognized in his sudden conversion to Christianity the chance to undermine the power of the secret societies in Russian society. In 1822 Alexander issued an Imperial edict outlawing Freemasonry and closing the lodges. It had been alleged by the Church that Russian Masons were conspirators in an international plot with their English and Polish brethren to overthrow the Czarist regime. Alexander's attack on the Freemasons was a disastrous move for instead of reducing opposition to his rule it increased resistance and many converts to the liberal political movement were recruited from the armed forces.

Alexander himself seems to have suffered from guilt for in November 1824 when St Petersburg was flooded and 500 people died he interpreted this disaster as a sign from God that he had failed Him in the divine mission to unite Europe. At the same time there was unrest in the army and reports reached Alexander of plans to stage a military *coup d'état*. His health was suffering and in the late autumn of 1825, having exiled himself from St Petersburg on doctor's orders to recuperate in the Crimea, he died.

Russia was thrown into confusion by the Czar's death. Many people did not even believe it. Stories circulated that Alexander had faked his death and had become a wandering holy man or had entered a monastery. Alexander had no sons so his young brother Grand Duke Constantine was destined to be Czar. However, Constantine had married a Polish countess and relinquished his right to the throne in favour of another brother, Grand Duke Nicholas. Unfortunately Nicholas was unaware of this pact between Constantine and Alexander. When he heard of the Czar's death Nicholas swore allegiance to his brother in Poland. Constantine in the meantime had pledged his loyalty to Nicholas from his home in Warsaw and had no intention of returning home to claim the Romanov crown. For a period of two weeks Russia effectively had two Czars until, on 14 December 1825, Nicholas finally accepted his brother's rejection of the throne and agreed to be Alexander's heir.

In the chaos which followed Alexander's death, the liberal radicals decided to take advantage of the confused situation and revive the original aims of the old Czar's regime. The Decembrist movement, as it was later termed, was a group of intellectuals, writers and army officers who had continued the Masonic tradition in secret since it had been driven underground in 1822. It included among its members the famous writer Count Pushkin who had been the confidant of the wife of Czar Paul. The leadership of the Decembrist group consisted of army officers who had fought with Alexander in the campaign against the French. These officers had made contact with the surviving Illuminist elements in French Freemasonry and had attempted to revive radicalism within the aristocratic system. As the Czar became more and more reactionary they had decided that the only way political change would happen in Russia was by revolution. The confusion after the death of Alexander provided the Decembrists with the opportunity to stage a coup, seize control of the government and set up a new liberal regime.

On the morning of 14 December 1825, the date set for the coronation, Nicholas had become aware of an army plot but had decided to take no action. Stories were sweeping the barracks that Nicholas had usurped the throne and Constantine was the real Czar. Contingents of the Moscow Guard and the Grenadiers assembled in the centre of St Petersburg calling for Constantine to be crowned. Nicholas arrived in the square with the Horse Guards, who had remained loyal to him, and they charged the rebels. The ground was icy and several horses fell blocking the progress of the charge, which was repulsed by heavy fire from the rebel forces. Nicholas ordered the artillery to open fire on the rebel troops and a large crowd which had gathered to support them. The outcome was a massacre which led Nicholas to comment sadly, 'I am Emperor but at what price, the blood of my subjects.' The coup had failed and the leaders of the Decembrists were arrested. Five were executed for their part in the failed rebellion.

Nicholas I ruled Russia for thirty years and was succeeded in 1855 by his son Alexander II. Czar Nicholas had expressed a strong dislike for mystical matters during his reign. This allergy was probably caused by the circumstances which had surrounded his rise to power and the ending of the Decembrist plot. In contrast, Alexander II was a romantic who was not only very religious but soon became involved in the new religion of Spiritualism which was becoming popular in the salons of European high society. Alexander had married Wilhelma Maria of Hesse in 1841 and she shared his interest in occultism. In 1861 séances were held in the Winter Palace in St Petersburg, attended by the Czar and the Czarina, members of the Royal court and Russian aristocrats. The Royal family sat round a table while the Scottish medium D.D. Home, who was visiting Russia accompanied by the novelist Alexander Dumas, conducted séances to contact the spirits of the dead. Home later commented on the fact that the Czar had a private library crammed with thousands of books on the occult and spiritual matters.

Czar Alexander was a reformer as well as an occultist and knew that Russia had to be modernized. In 1856 he gave a speech vowing to abolish serfdom but he found his task more difficult then he had imagined. One of the reforms the Czar did achieve was to have the greatest political consequences for the future. This was the transition from an army based on aristocratic privilege to a citizens army. In common with his namesake, Alexander II tried to form a political and military alliance with other great Central European powers. In 1872 the Czar, Emperor Franz Josef von Habsburg, and Kaiser Wilhelm I forged an alliance which was ratified in 1873 as the League of the Three Emperors. Political changes were taking place however which were to seal the doom of these three imperial powers and would lead to the First World War which marked the end of German imperialism, the Romanovs and the Habsburgs.

In January 1871, through the political conspiring of Otto von Bismarck, King Wilhelm of Prussia was crowned as Kaiser or Emperor of the Second German Reich. This not only marked the birth of modern Germany but also inspired the rise of a pan-German nationalist movement which drew its spiritual strength from occultism and its ideology from the esoteric philosophies of the secret societies. Within this new political movement lay not only the imperialism which formed the political background to the 1914–18 war but also the extreme racialist doctrines which, in the 1920s, spawned National Socialism.

As early as the 1850s political movements had arisen whose aim was the union of all the German speaking peoples of Europe. These movements could be identified by extreme nationalism and their anti-semitic, anti-capitalist and anti-liberal views. By the 1870s this political movement had established a mystical framework for its racial views which seems to have been heavily influenced by the doctrines of the new Theosophical Society founded by a Russian medium, Helene Blavatsky, in 1875. Blavatsky's aim was to synthesize Eastern forms of religion and occultism, such as Hinduism and Tantric yoga, with the Western European occult tradition exemplified by Hermeticism, Freemasonry, Rosicrucianism and the Cabbala. Madame Blavatsky claimed to have been initiated into the occult mysteries while studying in India and Tibet. During her visits to these remote locations she had contacted the Great White Brotherhood, including the Comte de Saint Germain and the Master Koot Hoomi, who is believed by some occultists to be the reincarnation of Thothmes III.

Blavatsky was influenced by the romantic novels written by the English statesman and occultist Lord Edward Bulwer Lytton (1803-73). These occult novels had themes involving secret societies, mysterious initiations and the existence of a clandestine tradition behind the orthodox religion. Bulwer Lytton was a prolific writer whose novels were read not only in England but also in America and most European countries. It was widely rumoured that he was a practising member of the Rosicrucian Order and is claimed as one of their Grand Masters. He had been elected as a Liberal member for Parliament in 1831 and played an important role in the passing of the Reform Bill. Lord Lytton's real interest, however, was in occultism which dominated his private life. He had an extensive library of books on the subject, including many rare treatises on medieval magic. He also allegedly operated a small occult group which practised magical rituals such as the conjuration of elemental spirits and demons.

Bulwer Lytton's grandson claimed that his grandfather was a Rosicrucian and Grand Patron of the Order. Evidence exists which does prove that he was proposed as Honorary Grand Patron of the Societas Rosicruciana Anglia, a neo-Rosicrucian Order founded by Robert Wentworth Little in 1867. Wentworth was a clerk at Freemason's Hall in London who said he had access to secret documents in the archives showing a link between the masonic guilds and the Rosicrucians. These documents had been discovered by William White, the Grand Secretary of English Freemasonry until 1857. He had been initiated into a Rosicrucian Order by the Venetian ambassador in London. In collaboration with the occultist Kenneth McKenzie, who had been initiated into a German Rosicrucian Order and had been granted a charter to found an English lodge, Wentworth Little founded the SRIA. In 1888 this new Rosicrucian society gave birth to the famous magical fraternity known as the Hermetic Order of the Golden Dawn. This Order was founded by two SRIA members, Dr William Wynn Westcott and Samuel McGregor Mathers who said they had received their authorization from a German occult adept called Anna Sprengel who lived in Bavaria, the home of the Illuminati.

MacGregor Mathers was a supporter of the Jacobite cause and was rumoured to be a member of another secret society known as the Jacobite Legitimists. This group claimed that the true heir to the Scottish throne was Princess Maria Theresa, wife of Prince Ludwig of Bavaria. They demanded home rule for Scotland and supported Irish nationalism. In

February 1893 the House of Commons was in uproar when the banning of the society's official newspaper *The Jacobite* was debated. A Belfast MP said that unless the journal was banned, loyalists in Ulster would rise against the British government. The Jacobite cause also had supporters in the Theosophical Society including Bishop C.W. Leadbeater who was to be disgraced in a homosexual scandal involving young boys.

Bulwer Lytton may have been a member of the SRIA but there is no evidence that he attended any of its meetings. His honorary membership was granted because of his knowledge of Rosicrucian beliefs expressed in his best-selling novel *Zanoni*. In 1870 Bulwer Lytton was approached by the occultist Hargraves Jennings who had written a lengthy treatise on the sexual meaning of Rosicrucian and pagan symbols. Jennings sought the help of the politician to secure employment as a librarian as he was finding it hard to make a living writing on obscure occult subjects. Lytton replied that he could not help him find suitable employment but congratulated him on tracing the Order's connection with earlier (pagan) religions.

One of Bulwer Lytton's closest friends was Benjamin Disraeli, who shared his interest in secret societies and the occult. In common with his aristocratic friend, Disraeli wrote several novels involving secret societies and political conspiracies. In 1856, in the House of Commons, Disraeli spoke out against the threat posed by the secret societies in Europe. He warned of the danger of supporting the revolutionary movements in Italy because of the influence the secret societies had in them. He said, 'The government of this country has not only to deal with governments, kings and ministers but also with secret societies, elements which must be taken into account which at the last moment can bring all our plans to nought, which have agents everywhere, who incite assassinations and can if necessary lead a massacre.'

Blavatsky had read Bulwer Lytton's novels and was very impressed by their occult content, especially *Zanoni* and *The Last Days of Pompei*. The latter was published in 1834 and dealt with the time between early Christianity and the Mysteries of Isis in Italy in the first century CE. Blavatsky's esotericism was virulently anti-Christian but this tendency was modified by her successor as leader of the Theosophical Society, Annie Besant.

Besant was a socialist, trade union organizer and strike leader until she joined the Theosophical Society in 1889. Previously she had been a member of the National Secular Society, the Fabian Society, the Social Democratic Federation and the Free Thought and Radical Movement.

From 1874 to 1889, when she became a Theosophist, Annie Besant had campaigned on a wide range of reforms including women's suffrage and sexual equality, anti-vivisection, penal reform, the organization of trade unions, the rights of ethnic peoples and the right to freedom of speech. Her political work was modified after she joined the Theosophist Society but in 1893 she attended the World Parliament of Religions in Chicago and was invited to visit India. As a result she became involved in Indian nationalism and founded the Home Rule League in 1916. As a result of her political work for the League she was interned for three months in 1917 by the British authorities.

Besant was responsible, in 1902, for founding the Co-Freemasonry movement whose lodges admitted men and women on equal terms. The Grand Lodge of England refused to accept Co-Masonry, which claims as its Grand Master the Comte de Saint-Germain on the spiritual plane, and the new Order affiliated itself to the Grand Orient of France. There is no suggestion that Co-Masonry shares with the French Freemasons their interest in radical politics. The lodges of Co-Masonry teach the inner wisdom of the Craft which has been lost to the orthodox Masonic Order in this country. Many Co-Masons are also members of the Liberal Catholic Church which promotes esoteric Christianity through the Theosophical Society. In 1912 Annie Besant also founded a neo-Rosicrucian offshoot of Co-Masonry which was called the Order of the Temple of the Rose Cross which was active until the end of the First World War.

Bulwer Lytton's novels not only had an impact on the Theosophists but they also affected the mystical aspects of German nationalism. His occult novel *The Coming Race*, published in 1871, presented the fictional idea of a subterranean matriarchal, socialist utopia ruled by superior beings who had mastered the so-called Viril, or Life Force. This was a mysterious energy which could be manipulated by the adepts who ruled this underground world to perform healing and telepathy. It also had destructive uses as a death ray which was similar to the modern laser. One of the German mystico-political groups called itself the Viril Society and took its philosophy from Bulwer Lytton's novel. The Viril Society was originally founded as the Luminous Lodge and combined the political ideals of the Order of Illuminati with Hindu mysticism, Theosophy and the Cabbala. It was one of the first German nationalist groups to use the symbol of the swastika as an emblem linking Eastern and Western occultism.

The racial ideas of Madame Blavatsky, concerning root races and the emergence of a spiritually-developed type of human being in the Aquarian Age, were avidly accepted by the nineteenth-century German nationalists who mixed Theosophical occultism with anti-Semitism and the doctrine of the racial supremacy of the Aryan or Indo-European peoples. One of the leading occult societies of this type was the Armanenschafft founded by an Austrian esotericist, Guido von List, who had spent a lifetime researching Teutonic mythology. List was a practitioner of the old pagan religion and was dedicated to re-establishing the ancient cult of Aryan Sun worship and reviving the priesthood of Wotan or Odin, the one-eyed shaman god of the runes.

List based his society on the Masonic degree system of Entered Apprentice, Fellow Craft and Master Mason. Initiates into the Order were not only expected to learn the mystical meanings of the runic system but were also taught the secret history of the priesthood of Wotan. List claimed that when the Church suppressed paganism its priesthood went underground and its traditions survived in the beliefs of the Templars, the alchemists, the Freemasons and the Order of the Rose Cross. He believed that the Templars and the Rosicrucians had inherited the spiritual and aristocratic aspects of the pagan priesthood while the Freemasons, who were political radicals, had inherited the democratic aspects of the occult tradition.

Guido von List had tenuous connections with two occult fraternities which shared his extreme right-wing views and adhered to his idea of a pan-German Empire based on spiritual principles derived from the pagan religion. The first of these groups was the Ordo Templi Orientis, or the Order of the Temple in the East, founded between 1895 and 1900 by two high-ranking German Freemasons, Karl Kellner and Theodor Reuss. The OTO had been born from the Masonic Rites of Memphis and Mizraim founded by an Englishman called John Yarker who was an associate of the SRIA. Yarker had authorized the foundation of a German lodge of this Masonic Rite by contact with Kellner, Reuss and Dr Franz Hartmann. The latter was a prominent occultist who had started the German Theosophical Society in 1896 and had links with various neo-Rosicrucian Orders.

The OTO's official history taught that its unique Tantric doctrine had been given to its founders by three Eastern adepts and that the Order possessed 'the key which opens up all Hermetic and Masonic secrets, namely the teachings of sexual magic and all the secrets of Freemasonry and all systems of religion'. When Kellner died in 1905 Reuss became the head of the OTO and within a short time branches of the Order were

Seal of the Ordo Templi Orientis

founded outside Germany, including France, England and Scandinavia.

Reuss was a complex character who as a young man had worked as a spy for the Prussian Secret Service. He had lived in London spying on socialist Germans in exile, including the family of Karl Marx. Reuss joined the Socialist League, whose members included Engels and the Utopian socialist William Morris, but he was exposed as an undercover agent and forced to resign from the organization.

There are some interesting connections between the OTO and the Hermetic Order of the Golden Dawn whose membership list included the poet W.B. Yeats and his close friend Maud Gonne, both active in Irish nationalism. Reuss had founded several Masonic-Rosicrucian lodges in Germany, with the authorization of William Westcott who was one of the founders of the Golden Dawn. Another member of the Golden

Dawn, Aleister Crowley, was to become the head of the OTO in England. Reuss had written to Crowley in 1912 accusing him of revealing the inner secrets of the OTO in his *Book of Lies* which contained coded descriptions of various magico-sexual rites veiled in Rosicrucian symbolism. These rituals included one involving mutual oral sex as a form of occult meditation. Crowley told Reuss that the rituals had originated in documents belonging to Adam Weishaupt, the founder of the Illuminati.

Reuss accepted this story because he believed that the OTO had links with the Illuminati. In fact, either Crowley or one of his disciples had written the rituals some years before. Crowley had broken away from the Golden Dawn in 1900 following a leadership fight with MacGregor Mathers, and because some of the other members had objected to his preoccupation with the use of sexual energy in magical workings. Crowley was delighted when Reuss appointed him as head of the English branch of the OTO and he took the magical name Baphomet from the idol worshipped by the Knights Templars.

Crowley may also have shared some of Reuss' political views as well as his interest in magical sex rites. When he was at Cambridge University the young Crowley had belonged to a Jacobite legitimate society and had dabbled in extreme right-wing politics. Crowley may have been responsible for the various theories which began to circulate concerning the OTO's origins. It was claimed that the Order had been founded in St Petersburg many years earlier than 1895 by a mysterious count, that it was a direct descendent of the Order of Illuminati, or it was founded by a medieval Sufi saint who had taught the Templars the secret of sex magic.

The second occult fraternity was the *Ordo Novi Templi* or the Order of New Templars, founded by Lanz von Liebenfels in 1907. Von Liebenfels was a romantic who had convinced himself he was descended from medieval German aristocracy, even though he was the son of a railway worker. He used his Order to further extreme right-wing, racist views based on the Templar tradition. Von Liebenfels was a fantasist who claimed that Lord Kitchener, who died in mysterious circumstances when his ship sank off Archangel during the Allied campaign to defeat the Bolsheviks after the First World War, was a secret supporter of the Order of New Templars. The ONT had established contact with several other radical right-wing groups with occult associations. It supported pro-Serbian nationalism, which was to play a crucial part in the events that led to the outbreak of hostilities in 1914, and assisted the Magyar nationalists in Hungary. During the 1920s, when Hitler was rising to power, the ONT acted as the international co-ordinator for European and American rightist groups. In the 1930s it acted as a front for the illegal National Socialist Party in Austria. This did not prevent the prohibition of the ONT by the Nazis in 1941 following the abortive peace mission by Rudolf Hess which led to the persecution of the occultists in the Third Reich.

A page from 'OStara', the official magazine of the Order of New Temples

An offshoot from the ONT and the Armanenschaft was the German Order founded just before the First World War. This anti-Semitic, racist, nationalist occult group used the swastika as its emblem and practised rituals based on Masonry. Its philosophy was centred on the purity and supremacy of the Aryan race, the revival of the pagan traditions of ancient Germany and the creation of a pan-German state. The German Order was the prototype of the Thule Society which later influenced the embryonic National Socialist movement. With the rise of the Nazis the mystical tradition of racial purity, neo-paganism and theosophical occultism was to be dramatically projected into the public arena and become the roots of a political creed of the most powerful nation in Europe.

Before the rise of National Socialism, the agents of the secret societies were engaged in activities which would result in the end of the old European Empires formed under the Holy Alliance of Czar Alexander I at the beginning of the nineteenth century. In Austria the Habsburgs ruled with an iron fist. Any faint hope that the wave of liberalism would affect the Austro-Hungarian Empire was destroyed in January 1889 at a hunting lodge in Mayerling. Crown Prince Rudolf von Habsburg allegedly shot dead his mistress Maria Vetsera and then committed suicide. Rumours circulated after the tragic deaths that the Crown Prince had been murdered by his political enemies who opposed his ultra-liberal ideas.

Rudolf may have been a notorious womanizer but he was also a philosopher who had studied the works of Descartes and Voltaire, the Masonic philosopher of the French Revolution. The Crown Prince was also a student of history, botany, physics and sociology and had travelled widely in the Far East. Rudolf wrote a massive twenty-four volume history of the Habsburg dynasty which is still regarded as the classic reference book on the subject.

The Crown Prince was an early supporter of the revolutionary concept of a world government saying, 'There will be wars until the people and the nations have completed their development, until they at last unite themselves and mankind has become one family'. He was in favour of a united Europe, secretly supported the Magyars and recommended that the Austro-Hungarian Empire should sever its ancient links with the Vatican. He spoke out against the corruption and excessive wealth of the church, called on the aristocrats to pay taxes and for the land to be divided up between the peasants. In other words he was the perfect target for assassination by those reactionary forces in European politics who were resisting social change.

Rudolf's fault, apart from his obsesssive sexual urges, was his idealistic naivety and faith in human nature. He truly believed that he could single-handedly stem the tide of anti-Semitism and extreme nationalism which was rising in the Empire. As an internationalist he believed that 'the principle of nationalism is based on common animal principles. It is essentially the victory of fleshly sympathies and instincts over spiritual and cultural ideas.' In 1882 he predicted, 'Dark and ugly times await us. One can almost believe that old Europe is outdated and beginning to disintegrate. A great and thorough reaction has to set in, a social upheaval from which, after a long time, a whole new Europe may blossom.'

In 1898, Rudolf's mother, the Empress Elizabeth, fell victim to an assassin while staying in Switzerland. The Empress was walking back to her hotel in Geneva with a lady-in-waiting when she was attacked by an Italian called Lucheni who stabbed her through the heart. When questioned by the police the assassin confessed he was an anarchist and said his original target had been the Prince of Orleans, the pretender to the French throne, or King Umberto of Italy. He told the police that 'other comrades' would accomplish these murders later. At his trial when he was sentenced to life imprisonment Lucheni shouted, 'Long live anarchy! Death to the aristocrats!'

Lucheni was a disciple of the Russian anarchist and Freemason Mikhail Bakunin (1814–73) who was the originator of the Nihilist movement. He believed that degenerate Western society could be saved only through atheism and anarchism. Bakunin's extreme anti-clericalism led him to be denounced as a Satanist and he is quoted as saying, 'Satan was the first freethinker and the saviour of the world. He freed Adam and impressed the seal of humanity and liberty on his forehead by making him disobedient.' Bakunin was Secretary General of the First International, a coalition of Nihilists, anarchists and communists, and was a political associate of Karl Marx and other revolutionary socialist leaders.

From 1900 to 1913 Europe was plunged into chaos as the revolutionary and nationalist movements attempted to force change on the old Imperial powers. In 1905 the Greeks revolted against Turkish rule in Crete; the Czar Nicholas II had been forced to use troops to put down riots in St Petersburg and a mutiny by sailors on the *Potemkin*. In 1908 both King Carlos I of Portugal and the Crown Prince were murdered. These assassinations were followed in 1910 by a revolution during which King Manuel II had to flee for his life. In 1912 Italy, Bulgaria, Turkey and Serbia were at war. By 1913 Russia had declared war on Bulgaria, and King George I of Greece had been murdered.

Against this backdrop of revolution, war and assassination, the old alliances which had held nineteenth-century Europe together, were crumbling. By the outbreak of the First World War, Russia and Germany were bitter enemies. The Czar wanted a new alliance with Britain and France to prevent Germany declaring war on Russia. He was confident that world peace could be achieved by the creation of a triple Entente of France, England and Russia to combat the growing threat of German expansionism.

The British, however, did not support this plan. While they believed the public would rally to the defence of France if she was attacked by the Germans they knew that they would not show the same eagerness if the Kaiser invaded Russian soil. The British government was still hoping for a reconciliation with the German Kaiser so that Russia's imperial ambitions in Persia and India could be resisted. Meanwhile, the Germans were negotiating with the ailing Emperor Franz Joseph of Austria to form an alliance to attack Russia. The Germans were also attempting to woo Rumania and Serbia to strengthen the new alliance. This involvement with Serbia was to cost Franz Joseph the life of his nephew, the Grand Duke Franz Ferdinand, and result in world war.

On 28 June 1914 Franz Ferdinand and his wife Sophia were in Sarajevo in Bostonia on an official visit. As their car travelled through streets lined by cheering crowds, a group of assassins, who for months had been planning the death of the ArchDuke and the Duchess, struck. One threw a bomb which hit the bonnet of the car, bounced off and exploded in the road, wounding twenty bystanders. The bomb thrower fled the scene and tried to commit suicide by drinking a bottle of cyanide but he was seized by the police before he could commit the act.

Panic spread through the streets in the wake of the bomb attack but the official convoy of cars continued on its route to the town hall. After making an official speech the ArchDuke decided to visit the local Governor's adjutant who had been injured in the bomb blast and taken to hospital. It was a decision which was to cost his life. Incredibly the assassination squad was still in the streets. The car containing the ArchDuke and his wife took a wrong turning and in the confusion which followed one of the assassins calmly walked up to the car and fired two shots from a Browning automatic pistol, killing the Royal couple.

The three principal assassins at Sarajevo were Gavrilo Princip and two of his friends who were all members of a nationalist group called the Order of the Black Hand. This secret society had been founded in 1911 as the Union of Death to fight for Serbian liberation. The seal of the Order was a clenched fist holding a skull and crossbones beside which was a knife, a bomb and a poison bottle. Members of the Black Hand included Army officers, civil servants, lawyers and university professors. Initiation ceremonies into the Order were performed in a darkened room and neophytes had to hold a revolver in one hand and a knife in the other. Then they repeated the following oath to defend the Serbian cause; 'By the Sun that warms, by the Earth that feeds me, by the blood of my forefathers, by God, by my honour and by my life.'

All of the Sarajevo assassins were selected because they suffered from tuberculosis and did not have long to live. In accordance with the Order's rules they had agreed that if they failed in their mission they would commit suicide by taking arsenic. The assassins were students with Bolshevik aspirations who previously had been involved in distributing socialist and anarchist pamphlets calling for world wide revolution and the overthrow of the European monarchy. As much as the Habsburgs they murdered, the assassins themselves – especially Princip who finally committed the act and was filled with remorse afterwards – were victims of international conspiracy.

Although the Order of the Black Hand was dedicated to Serbian nationalism, there were those within its ranks who had wider political ambitions and saw the deaths in Sarajevo as a means to an end. The Russians were soon implicated in the plot when it became known that a secret payment of 8,000 roubles had been given to the leaders of the Black Hand by the Russian military attaché in Belgrade. The Order was assured by Czar Nicholas that he would support Serbia if war broke out between his country and the Austro-Hungarian Empire.

It was also rumoured that representatives of the Black Hand had met with several members of the French and Grand Orient at the Hotel St Jerome in Toulouse in January 1914. One of the items discussed at this meeting was allegedly the murder of the Emperor Franz Joseph and the ArchDuke Ferdinand. This indicated that the assassination was a complex plot organized by the Order of the Black Hand with the support of the Czar and renegade elements of French Freemasonry. Their aim was to force Austria to invade Serbia and create the conditions for a major European war.

Following the assassinations the Kaiser invited the Austro-Hungarian ambassador to lunch and told him that military action had to be taken swiftly to neutralize Serbia and he offered him German support. The Kaiser was obviously not aware at this stage of the Russian involvement in the deed because he told the Austrian diplomat that German intelligence reports suggested that the Czar would not respond if the Habsburgs occupied Serbia. On 28 July 1914, four weeks after the assassinations, Austro-Hungary declared war on Serbia, even though the earliest its army could march into the country was mid-August. Russia responded by mobilizing her army in defence of Serbia and on 29 July the Kaiser informed the Czar that unless his troops stood down the German Army would also mobilize. On 31 July the Germans demanded that Russia halt its mobilization, and when this demand was ignored they declared war on 1 August.

The French were formally asked by the Germans to remain neutral in the war, but they refused. The Kaiser then falsely accused the French of violating his territory and declared war on France. Meanwhile the Kaiser was negotiating with the British to ensure their neutrality but on 2 August Britain warned the Germans not to attack French shipping in the English Channel. On 3 August the German High Command informed the British Foreign Office that their troops planned to march through neutral Belgium to attack the French. In a stern reply the Germans were informed that if one of their soldiers set foot on Belgian soil Britain and Germany would be at war. The First World War had effectively begun.

Sarajevo and its international repercussions were to cause not only the downfall of the Habsburgs and Hohenzollerns but also that of the Romanov dynasty which was swept away by the Bolshevik Revolution of 1917. In pre-war Russia, the Royal family were heavily involved in occult practices. Between 1900 and 1905 the French occultist Dr Gerard Encausse visited Russia and held magical séances for the Czar. Encausse was a member of the Cabbalistic Order of the Rosy Cross founded by two prominent French occultists, the Marquis Stanilas de Guaita and Josephin Paladin in 1888. Paladin came from an eccentric Catholic family who were religious fanatics and extreme supporters of the monarchic system. His brother Adrien was a homoeopathic doctor and Cabbalist who claimed to have been initiated into an ancient Rosicrucian Order in Toulouse in 1858. Encausse had also been initiated into the Golden Dawn lodge founded by Samuel McGregor Mathers in Paris which practised the Mysteries of isis.

At the magical séances held by Encausse, it is claimed, the French occultist conjured up the spirit of Czar Nicholas' father, Alexander III. In 1905 Russia was on the brink of revolution, there was rioting in the streets, strikes, and rumours of mutiny in the armed forces. Nicholas asked the spirit of his father for advice and was told to resist the revolutionary forces. If he did not deal severely with this outbreak of unrest the causes of the uprisings would return in a few years and his rule would be seriously threatened. Encausse seems to have stayed in contact with the Czar after he returned to France, with the occultist and the monarch exchanging letters at regular intervals. The French magician, however, confided to friends that he thought the Czar was relying too much on spiritual sources of advice in running the country and ignoring the advice of his ministers.

Encausse was particularly concerned when he heard that the Czar and

Symbol of the Cabalistic Order of the Rosy Cross

Czarina had come under the hypnotic influence of the mystic monk, Grigori Rasputin. He was a member of the Khlysty or People of God, a neo-Gnostic sect who practised flagellation and sexual indulgence as a method of making contact with Divinity. Rasputin was a product of the spiritual revival that had swept Russia in the early 1900s. Interest in the occult was widespread at all levels of society; weird religious sects proliferated and sexual permissiveness was encouraged. Wandering holy men, occultists and Spiritualists attracted thousands of followers, including members of the aristocracy and the Czarist court.

   The Czarina Alexandria seems to have been infatuated with Rasputin and was in awe of his healing powers which had allegedly saved the life of her son. Despite his dirty, unkept appearance Rasputin exerted a strange power over women. He was capable of withholding orgasm for long periods, and one titled lady who made love to him said that the experience was so sensual that she fainted from pleasure. Rasputin apparently believed that sexual domination could be used as a method of achieving spiritual enlightenment and told his many lovers that it was God's will that they surrender their bodies to him.

Rasputin's influence on the Royal family was regarded by many court insiders and those who opposed Czarist rule as sinister. Encausse warned the Czar that the monk was an evil influence claiming 'Cabbalistically-speaking Rasputin is a vessel like Pandora's box. He contains all the vices, crimes and filth of the Russian people. Should this vessel be broken its dreadful contents will spill across Russia.' His enemies claimed Rasputin was an agent of the secret societies working to weaken the Czar's rule. They alleged that at a secret Masonic conference held in Brussels in 1905 representatives of various European secret societies had plotted to use Rasputin to bring down the Romanovs.

Despite this, when war broke out in 1914, Rasputin advised the Czar not to involve Russia in the fighting. He predicted that the country would suffer a terrible defeat and the monarchy would be destroyed in the bloodbath to follow. It would seem there were several political factions in Russia who were attempting to prevent Rasputin exercising his influence on the Czar. In 1913 conspirators had plotted to castrate and murder Rasputin but the wily monk heard of the plan and took evasive action.

In June 1914, coincidentally on the same day as the Sarajevo assassinations, a prostitute called Gusyeva attempted to murder Rasputin while he was holidaying in the Black Sea resort of Yalta. She stabbed the monk in the stomach but although he lost a considerable amount of blood he survived. She told police she had attempted to kill Rasputin because he was a heretic and a fornicator who had seduced a nun. Gusyeva was diagnosed insane and committed to a mental hospital.

Following Sarajevo the Czarina sent a stream of telegrams to Rasputin asking his advice on the serious international situation. Rasputin replied by sending a telegram to the Czar telling him to prevent Russia being enticed into the war. If it were, he predicted, 'it will be the finish of all things.' Rasputin was obviously not aware of the Russian complicity in Sarajevo and Nicholas ignored the monk's advice. Rasputin was later to claim that if he had been well enough to have visited St Petersburg in person Russia would not have entered the war and the course of world history would have been changed.

As the war progressed, Rasputin's enemies used his anti-war sentiments to claim that the monk was pro-German, was in league with revolutionaries and was a secret agent in the Kaiser's Intelligence

Service. Meanwhile, hostility to the Romanovs was growing among the ordinary Russian people aided by the activities of socialist agitators who wanted to replace Czarism with a workers' republic. Rasputin seems to have had a premonition of his impending doom and the consequences it would have for Russia and the Romanovs. In 1916 he wrote to the Czar saying, 'If I am killed by common assassins, and especially if they are my brothers, the Russian peasants, you have nothing to fear. But if I am murdered by the Boyars (the nobles), if they shed my blood their hands will remain soiled with my blood. Brothers will kill brothers. They will kill each other. There will be no nobles in the country.'

In December 1916 right-wing factions within the aristocracy conspired to rid Russia of Rasputin. They believed that if he were allowed to live the Army would rise in revolt against the Romanovs. The conspirators, led by Prince Felix Yusupov, enticed the monk into a trap. He was fed chocolate cakes and wine laced with cyanide, which apparently had little effect on him. He was then shot in the chest at close range. The monk fell to the floor as if dead but a few moments later revived enough to attack his would-be assassins. Rasputin tried to escape but was shot twice more as he fled. His body was then bundled into a car, taken to the Petrovsky bridge and thrown into the river. Popular legend relates that he was still alive when he was thrown into the icy waters and actually died from drowning.

The Russian people reacted to Rasputin's death with indignation. He had been loved by the masses and after his death the mystic monk was treated as a martyr. The Czar's court was regarded as the source of the conspiracy which had killed a popular hero. In the months following Rasputin's death it was widely expected that a right-wing coup would oust the Romanovs from power. The Czarist secret police therefore concentrated their efforts on infiltrating extreme rightist groups and secret societies who, while supporting the monarchy, regarded Nicholas as a weak ruler. In fact the revolution, which finally toppled the unpopular Romanovs, was a product of the extreme left and began with the establishment of a liberal and democratic government.

In March 1917 food riots broke out in St Petersburg, renamed Petrograd, and the troops sent to quell the disturbances joined the protestors. With the breakdown of law and order, a right-wing Provisional government was formed to run the country. On 15 March, faced with mounting criticism of his policies, Nicholas abdicated in favour of his younger brother Mikhail. However the new Czar soon realized he did not have the confidence or support of the armed forces or the people and he abdicated handing over executive power to the provisional government. This move was widely welcomed by the leaders of the world's governments who believed that democracy was going to be established in Russia.

The provisional regime ruled for eight months until November (October by the Old Calendar still used in Russia at this time) and during that period it promoted democracy and promised freedom of religion, speech, assembly and the Press. However, in an attempt to disorganize the war effort, the Kaiser arranged for the revolutionary Lenin to return to Russia and he called upon the peasants to take control of the farms and factories. In July 1917, with the government still trying to fight an unpopular war and divided internally, radicalized soldiers, sailors and Bolsheviks attempted to seize control of Petrograd. The revolt failed due to the intervention of regular army units in the city which remained loyal to the provisional government.

On 7 November (October), 1917 the Bolsheviks finally came to power when soldiers of the Petrograd garrison, aided by sailors and workers militia from the Red Guard, stormed the Winter Palace and arrested the members of the Provisional government. The revolution was not bloodless for in 1918 fighting broke out between the Bolsheviks and the White Russians who supported the monarchy. The Allies intervened in the resulting civil war and detachments of American, French, British and Italian troops landed in Siberia to prevent the seizure by the Germans of war materials stored in the ports of Archangel and Mumansk. Allied forces blockaded the Russian coast from October 1919 to January 1920 and supplied the White Russians with military hardware including British-made tanks. They could not, however, prevent the defeat of the White army or the relentless progress of the Bolshevik revolution which created the modern USSR.

Rasputin's prophecy of the downfall of the Romanov dynasty had come true although he had not lived to see it. Even if he had survived the right-wing plots to kill him, it seems unlikely the mystic monk would have been tolerated for long in the new Soviet Union. One of the first acts by the Bolsheviks was to suppress the Russian Orthodox Church and outlaw the various religious sects which had flourished during the reign of the Czars.

NAZISM AND THE OCCULT TRADITION

During the First World War an Austrian artist called Adolf Hitler served in the 1st Company of the Bavarian Reserve Infantry Regiment and took part in the Battle of Ypres. He was one of 600 survivors from the regiment's total enlistment of 3,500 and was awarded the Iron Cross. This decoration was given to Hitler for capturing a French officer and fifteen men singlehanded and armed only with a Luger pistol. In 1916 Hitler was wounded in the leg but recovered to become a messenger carrying documents between regimental headquarters and the front line.

Hitler was regarded by his fellow soldiers as a rather peculiar character because of his habit of spending the long periods between engagements in silent meditation. After one of these contemplative sessions Hitler surprised his companions by leaping to his feet and shouting that Germany would soon lose the war. To the astonishment of his fellow soldiers he claimed that the German people faced invisible enemies who were a greater danger to the war effort than the Allied troops.

Kaiser Wilhelm had already received a similar message even before the outbreak of the war. The Kaiser was fascinated with Spiritualism and was present at a séance when a medium gave him a message from the Other Side. She predicted that the German Royal House would fall in a war to end all wars. When the Kaiser was forced into exile in Holland in 1918 he spent his time studying in his occult library. He blamed the First World War on a conspiracy between Czar Nicholas II, King George V of England and the secret societies.

It is impossible to know the source of Hitler's prophecies about German defeat but he was convinced that the war would end with an Allied victory. In the last month of the war Hitler was caught in a British mustard gas attack. Temporarily blinded he was sent from the front line to recover his health in a small town near Berlin. When he had fully recovered, Hitler was posted to a prisoner-of-war camp on the Austrian border where he carried out guard duties. In 1919 the camp was closed and Hitler returned to Munich where he became attached to the German Military Intelligence Department. His task was to act as an undercover agent spying on the Communist revolutionaries who had engineered a coup in Munich which had briefly given them power. Hitler helped unmask their leaders who were shot by firing squad. He also attended meetings of the German Workers Party, which opposed the Communists, initially as an undercover agent, but he was converted to the Party's policies and rose to become its leader.

The German Workers Party had been founded in 1919 to promote racial superiority, German nationalism and anti-Semitism. It was a socialist political party founded and funded by the Thule Gesselschaft or Thule Society. The Thulists were one of the most important secret societies in Germany, mixing extreme right-wing politics with occultism and Teutonic paganism. The Society had originated with Baron Rudolf von Sebottendorf, a self-styled Saxon aristocrat who was in fact the son of a railway worker. He worked variously as a stoker and electrician on steamships visiting New York, Naples, Australia, Egypt and Constantinople (Istanbul). While visiting Egypt, von Sebottendorf became interested in the occult arts and, while in Turkey, he contacted the Sufis and began to study astrology, alchemy and Rosicrucianism. In 1901 von Sebottendorf was initiated into a Masonic lodge which, like many in the Middle East, had connections with the French Grand Orient. The Turkish lodge also had links with the Society of Union and Progress, founded to promote liberal politics during the repressive regime of the Sultan.

In 1910, while living in Istanbul, von Sebottendorf decided to found his own secret society based on a combination of Sufi mysticism, Freemasonry, alchemy and a right wing political philosophy which was anti-Bolshevik and anti-Semitic. It was at this period that he began to claim aristocratic links, adopting the name of the von Sebottendorfs, an ancient Silesian family who had served with both the Prussian and Habsburg armies. He fought in the Balkan War of 1912 and as a result of wounds he received returned to Germany. In 1916 von Sebottendorf made contact with the German Order and in the next two years played a prominent role recruiting new members. By the end of the war von Sebottendorf had moved to Munich and the German order had adopted the name of the Thule Society. This was to prevent its activities being disturbed by the Communists who were opposed to the German Order's right-wing, pro-monarchist views.

In 1918 the Thule Society had over 250 members in Munich and nearly 1,500 members scattered across the Bavarian countryside. Its membership list included many local dignatories including judges, lawyers, police chiefs, aristocrats, doctors, university lecturers, scientists, military officers, industrialists and businessmen. Among its leading members were Franz Gurtner, the Bavarian Minister of Justice, who later held the same position in the Nazi regime; Pohner, the police commissioner of Munich; and Wilhelm Frick, the assistant police chief who became the Minister of the Interior in the Third Reich. Another leading member of the Thulists was an occultist called Deitrich Eckart who held séances with two White Russian emigrés. Eckart was associated with a White Russian printing house which produced an anti-Communist newspaper specializing in stories alleging that the Jews had financed the Bolshevik revolution.

At the occult séances organized by Eckart the medium was a peasant woman who allegedly manifested ectoplasm from her vagina. This ectoplasmic substance formed into human shapes representing long-dead spirits. While she was in trance the medium spoke in foreign languages and predicted the rise of a messiah who would lead Germany to victory and world domination. Dead members of the Thule Society materialized at these séances, including Prince von Thurn und Taxis who had been murdered in early 1919 by the Communists. The Prince had been a member of the Order of Bavarian Mystics which claimed descent from the Illuminati.

The Thule Society took its name from the mythical hyperborean island which once existed in the north Atlantic between Scandinavia and Greenland. It was believed by occultists that this island had once been part of Atlantis and was the source of the occult wisdom of the Northern Mystery Tradition. Politically, the Thulists were committed to the establishing of a pan-German state based on the Habsburg dynasty which had abdicated in November 1918 when faced with a socialist revolution in Austria. With the Communist uprisings in 1919 in defeated Germany the Thule Society went underground. They organized a terrorist network which supplied arms to the rightist counter-revolutionaries and distributed German nationalist and anti-Semitic literature calling upon the people to rise up against the Bolsheviks who had seized power in several German cities.

As part of their popular movement against the Communists, the Thulists had started the German Workers Party. The idea was to attract the ordinary Germans away from left-wing socialism to a new kind of socialist politics based on nationalism and Aryan racial supremacy. The Communists were well aware of the Thule Society's political activities by this time. In the April 1919 coup, Communist militia raided the Society's headquarters in Munich. Several leading Thulists were taken hostage and later shot dead, including Prince von Thum und Taxis and several titled aristocrats. When the hostages were shot the Thulists organized a citizens' army against the Communists and on 1 May troops loyal to the counter-revolution entered Munich and regained control of the city.

In the pre-war years Hitler had been exposed to the racist and occult theories of Guido von List and was conversant with Nordic and German mythology. It is possible that through this interest Hitler decided to adopt the swastika as the emblem for the German Workers Party. It had already been used by several German nationalist groups, including the German Order and the Thule Society. In fact it was a leading Thulist, Dr Frederick Kohn, who provided Hitler with the final design for the Nazi flag which became the national emblem of the Third Reich.

Hitler was impressed by Guido von List's political philosophy which involved the relegation of the Jews to a slave race who would work for their German masters in a future Aryan-dominated Europe. Where Hitler disagreed with von List, and the Thulists, was in the idea of a new pan-European dynasty centred on the Habsburgs and a revived Holy Roman Empire. Hitler frequently spoke out against the Habsburgs whom he regarded as traitors who had betrayed the German-speaking peoples of Europe. In *Mein Kampf* Hitler had written 'How could one become a faithful subject of the House of Habsburgs whose past and present policy is a betrayal of German origin?'

Von Sebottendorf had resigned as head of the Thule Society by the time Hitler had joined the German Workers Party, but his pro-monarchist views may have been responsible for his failure to revive Thulism during the Third Reich. In the 1920s he had been inducted into the Imperial Constantine Order which was virulently anti-Bolshevik and he acted as a secret agent for this group when he returned to Munich from abroad in 1933. With the rise of National Socialism von Sebottendorf believed Hitler would encourage the rise of the new Thule Society. In fact von Sebottendorf was arrested by the Gestapo in 1934 and interned in a concentration camp. When he was released, von Sebottendorf returned to Istanbul where he claimed he was working for the *Sicherheitsdienst*, the Nazi Intelligence Service. He committed suicide in 1945 when he heard the news of the German surrender.

Hitler was influenced in his attitudes towards the Jews by a publication called *The Protocols of the Elders of Zion*. This document was said to be an account of the World Congress of Jewry held in Basel, Switzerland in 1897, during which a conspiracy was planned by the international Jewish movement and the Freemasons to achieve world domination. Copies of this publication had been imported into Germany from Russia by the Thule Society at the beginning of the First World War. They had used it to suggest that the 1917 Russian Revolution had been financed by the Jews.

The Protocols were used by the German nationalists to prove that the defeat of the Second Reich in 1918 was caused by a global Jewish conspiracy. The report of the Congress had allegedly been smuggled out of Switzerland by a Russian journalist who had placed the documents in the safe keeping of the Rising Sun Masonic lodge in Frankfurt. Before handing over the document he had made several copies which he circulated in rightist circles in Moscow and St Petersburg. In fact *The Protocols* were a forgery created by dissident members of the Czarist secret police. They planned to use the document to undermine the influence on Czar Nicholas II of several leading Freemasons who were urging the monarch to adopt liberal policies. Although *The Protocols* were exposed as a fraud in 1921, their influence was widespread for many years after and they are still regarded by some conspiracy theorists as genuine. In *Mein Kampf* Hitler, obviously influenced by his reading of *The Protocols*, denounced the Jews as agents of an international conspiracy devoted to global domination through the control of the world's financial centres and money markets.

Once he was established in the German Workers Party, Hitler decided to modify the Thulist philosophy to produce a political movement which would have mass appeal. He wanted to use the Party to create a right-wing counter-revolution which would sweep away the Jews, the Communists and the Social Democrats whom he, along with many other Germans, believed had betrayed the country during the war. In common with the Kaiser before him, Hitler believed that the Freemasons had played a part in the defeat of Germany at the hands of the Allies. He interpreted their myths based on King Solomon's temple as evidence that they belonged to the international Jewish plot for world domination.

In 1920 the German Workers Party changed its name to the National Socialist Party and Hitler prepared his grand plan to gain supreme political power in post-war Germany. Assisted by Deitrich Eckart, he transformed National Socialism into a mass political movement. Eckart knew that the Party needed a charismatic leader and he saw in Hitler the messiah predicted by the old peasant woman in her séances. Eckart taught Hitler social manners and introduced him to wealthy Thulists and White Russian emigrés who provided the funds for the embryonic Nazi Party. These people were frightened that a Bolshevik revolution could still sweep through Germany and were eager to finance a new political party which promoted German nationalism. The early meetings of the German Workers Party had been advertised in the Thulist newspaper *Volkisher Beobachter* and this later became the official organ of the Nazi Party. Police protection for Hitler was also provided by the Bavarian police whose members included many leading Thulists.

Hitler's early career was dominated by another occultist called Karl Haushofer. He had been the German military attaché in Tokyo before the war and had been in contact with several Eastern secret societies. During the war Haushofer was a general in the Imperial Army and after the armistice he became a professor of geopolitics at Munich University where Rudolf Hess, later Deputy Fuehrer in the Third Reich, was his assistant. Haushofer's son, who was an astrologer and a student of the prophecies of the medieval French mystic Michel Notre Dame, or Nostradamus, was later to become involved in Hess' disastrous peace mission to Britain in 1941.

Haushofer travelled extensively in the Far East in pursuit of occult knowledge. He believed that the Aryan race had originated in Central Asia and he was later to try and persuade Hitler to extend the Third Reich's political influence to Persia, India and Tibet. While visiting Tibet in 1908, Haushofer met George Ivanovitch Gurdjieff, the extraordinary Russian occultist who is not only believed to have been influential in the foundation of the German Order but is also said to have had contact with the Soviet dictator Josef Stalin when the latter was a student and stayed as a lodger in the Gurdjieff household.

Gurdjieff had been born on the Russian-Turkish border and at an early age was introduced into a secret society known as the Community of Truth Seekers. This was a group of powerful occultists who believed that there had been a single world religion in ancient times which had fragmented into the various religious beliefs and occult doctrines which exist today. The teachings of this once universal religion now only survive in legends, folklore, music and the secret teachings of esoteric fraternities. It was the task of the Truth Seekers to travel the remoter parts of Europe, the Middle East and Asia contacting the secret societies who still preserved the Ancient Wisdom and re-establish the ancient world religion.

During his own travels in Asia, Gurdjieff masqueraded as a carpet salesman and fashion designer who sold ladies' corsets. He was also acting as a spy for the Russian Secret Service against the British in India and Afghanistan. He stayed for ten years in Tibet as the tutor of the Dalai Lama and hatched a plan to convert Czar Nicholas II to Buddhism. While in the East, Gurdjieff was initiated into the Sarmoung Brotherhood which had been founded in Babylon in 2,500 BCE. Shortly before the outbreak of the Great War, Gurdjieff returned to Russia to teach his own occult system based on his Eastern studies. With the rise of the Bolsheviks he was forced to leave and established a spiritual commune in France which attracted writers and intellectuals from all over Western Europe.

It was through his contact with Gurdjieff that Haushofer was first introduced to the legend of the subterranean city of Agarthi. According to occult doctrine Agarthi was a mysterious underground kingdom situated in a remote part of the Far East. The city was constructed over 60,000 years ago by occult adepts who fled the cataclysm which destroyed Atlantis. Agarthi supposedly had huge libraries of rare volumes containing ancient esoteric wisdom. It is said to have been the source of the material in *The Secret Doctrine* written by the founder of the Theosophical Society, Helena Blavatsky.

Considering the relationship between Haushofer and Hess it seems possible that Gurdjieff's assertion that the human race was spiritually and morally asleep and had to be awoken from its dream state by the application of occult techniques may have reached Hitler. Occultists have pointed out that the use of the Nazi slogan 'Germany Awake' could be traced back to Gurdjieff. The concept of the Aryan master race and the creation of supermen who would rule a Nazi dominated world may also link with the legend of Agarthi and its immortal occult adepts. It was the German philosopher Neitzsche who gave us the superman concept but it was occult doctrine which refined the idea in the minds of the early Nazis.

Another source for the master race theory in the early days of the Nazi Party was the occultist Alfred Rosenberg who, while Hitler was in prison from 1922 to 1924, was the acting leader of the National Socialists. Rosenberg and Eckart had been instrumental in importing copies of *The Protocols of the Elders of Zion* into Germany and both men acted in a guru role in relation to Hitler. Rosenberg was convinced that the Aryan race had originated on the lost continent of Atlantis which was the source of all ancient occult beliefs. He claimed that the mythical continent had been destroyed because the Gods condemned Atlantean experiments which mated animals with women to create a hybrid race which was half-animal and half-human and were to be used as slaves. When Atlantis was threatened with cosmic destruction the priesthood received prior warning and some fled to Asia where they established themselves as rulers of the indigenous aboriginal inhabitants. Rosenberg believed the modern Hindu caste system was a pale imitation of the original racial subdivisions imposed by the Atlanteans on their conquered inferiors.

Rosenberg also believed that the fleeing Atlanteans had established colonies in the Middle East, including Persia where they founded the Zoroastrian religion with its dualistic philosophy of the eternal struggle between light and darkness. This religious belief, as we have seen earlier, gave birth to the Manichean heresy which was promoted in medieval Europe by the Cathars until they were exterminated by the Roman Church. This philosophy in an altered form was revived in Germany between the wars by the occultist Rudolf Steiner who was a member of the German Theosophical Society and who was later persecuted by the Nazis for his occult beliefs.

The short career of Alfred Rosenberg as leader of the Nazis marked the beginning of the movement's flirtation with neo-paganism. He asserted that Christianity could not provide the necessary spiritual force needed in the Third Reich because its dogmas were opposed to the pagan beliefs of the ancient Germanic race. When the Nazis came to power Rosenberg said that the crucifix and the Bible would be removed from church altars and replaced by the symbol of the swastika. On each altar would be a copy of *Mein Kampf* and a sword symbolizing the unconquerable will of the German people. When Hitler was released from imprisonment he rejected Rosenberg's idea of a new German religion. He realized that millions of Germans found comfort in the Church and any attempt to outlaw Christianity would be political suicide for the new party. However, after Hitler gained power in 1933, several attempts were made by occultists in the Nazi Party to revive neo-paganism as the spiritual framework of the political ideals of National Socialism.

Hitler initially seems to have supported the idea only in a sublimated form because he believed it would never get the support of the German masses. While he despised Freemasonry as a Jewish invention he used Masonry as the model for the inner circle of the Nazi Party. 'They (the Masons) have developed an esoteric doctrine, not formulated it, but imparted it through the medium of symbols and mysterious rites . . . our Party must be of this order. An Order, the hierarchical Order of a secular priesthood.' In 1934 Hitler progressed this idea a step forward when he declared, 'We shall form an Order, the Brotherhood of the Templars around the Holy Grail of the pure blood.'

It was to be Heinrich Himmler who was to become the creator of Hitler's dream of a new Templar Order with the formation of the *Schutzstaffel* or SS who had originally acted as the Fuehrer's personal bodyguard in the 1920s. Himmler transformed the SS into an élite unit of crack troops, ruthlessly dedicated to the Nazi ideology. They were destined to become feared throughout occupied Europe and were responsible for controlling the network of special concentration camps set up in 1942 to deal with the Jewish 'problem'. Himmler was a disciple of the occult doctrines which were at the root of the racial policies of the Third Reich. He believed that the SS would be the vehicle through which the racial purity of Germany would be re-established by scientific breeding programmes designed to create the master race of supermen.

Himmler drew on many historical precedents when he reformed the SS into a secret society within the German military machine. These precedents included the Jesuits, the Freemasons, the Knights Templars, the Teutonic Knights, the Order of the Garter and the Fellowship of the Round Table. The headquarters of the SS was established in the castle of Wewelsburg which had been modelled on the castle in the Arthurian myth of the Holy Grail. In the castle the SS officer corps were initiated in neo-pagan rites and were given a special ring carved with a skull, runes and the swastika.

A special investigation group staffed by top SS officers was also formed under Himmler's direction. This group was given the task of studying history from a Nazi viewpoint with special emphasis on the secret societies in medieval Europe, including the Templars and the Cathars, and occult symbolism. For some reason Himmler was convinced that the British Secret Service had been infiltrated by the Rosicrucians. This apparently explained their successes during the First World War as their agents had been trained in occult and psychic techniques.

It was the influence of Himmler and his SS troops which was to make

the extermination of the various 'sub-human inferior races' in occupied
Europe such a success from the Nazi viewpoint, although the energy
and resources which were poured into the Final Solution considerably
weakened the overall German war effort and assisted the Allies to defeat
the Nazi evil. Hitler's hatred of the Jews was long standing, as we have
seen, but his attitude toward the gypsies is more difficult to trace, without
reference to the occult beliefs which predominated in the early years of
the National Socialist movement and which affected the political decisions
of the Third Reich.

In the 1920s the Nazis displayed quite a lot of interest in gypsy
culture. They believed that this culture should be preserved because the
gypsies were the descendents of the Indo-European race which had
settled in Asia. Hitler's plan was to settle the gypsy population of
Germany in one area. In 1937 the Gestapo rounded up isolated gypsy
bands and settled them in residential camps outside the cities. In fact
this was the prelude to the mass extermination of the gypsy race who had
suddenly become condemned as 'carriers of disease' and 'tainters of the
pure Aryan race'.

Why did Hitler persecute the gypsies? Possibly because their
swarthy, dark physical characteristics were the opposite of the Nazi
image of the Aryan race as blond, blue-eyed supermen. If, as Nazi racial
experts claimed, the gypsies were related to the Aryans, the whole
master race theory was undermined. Another possible, if more
speculative, reason for their extermination was the Nazi belief that the
gypsy population possessed a storehouse of occult knowledge.
Superstitious Nazi leaders believed that this knowledge could be used to
threaten the Third Reich. For this bizarre reason 400,000 gypsies were
destined to die in the gas chambers. Hitler was terrified of anyone with
occult power who might pose a threat to his rule. In 1937 the Nazis
prohibited several leading occult groups, including the Theosophists,
the followers of Ruldof Steiner, the OTO, the Hermetic Order of the
Golden Dawn and the Order of New Templars.

Hitler's fear of occult opposition was well founded. There were many
practising occultists who had become aware of the Nazis' involvement
in the black arts and were prepared to fight them on the magical and
psychic level. It was well known that extremist political groups of all
types had used the occult movements in the period between the two
wars. Writing in the 1930s from her own personal experience, the
occultist and Golden Dawn member Dion Fortune described, in her
book *Psychic Self Defence* the way revolutionary groups exploited occult

fraternities for political purposes. Fortune cites two cases known to her. In one incident an attempt was made by political extremists to use the headquarters of an occult society as a post box for the collecting of certain letters. This bypassed the normal channels which were being monitored by MI5 (the British Security Service responsible for counter-espionage and counter-subversion). In the second case Fortune herself was asked to give shelter to a political agitator who faced deportation. Although a sum of several thousand pounds was offered for this service the request was refused.

Occult involvement in the 1926 General Strike has also been claimed. According to the Roman Catholic exorcist Dom Robert Petitpierre, he and his colleague Father Gilbert Shaw were convinced that Russian occult adepts were projecting psychic forces at Britain in the 1920s to precipitate industrial unrest. This they hoped would lead to a socialist revolution and the overthrow of the monarchy and the government. Both men were attending a theological college in Essex situated near a prehistoric burial mound. This site was allegedly on a leyline extending from Russia to Mount Snowdon in North Wales and it was being used by the Russian occultists to focus psychic energy.

Several well-known occultists played a role in the psychic opposition to Hitler and the Nazis, including the controversial magician Aleister Crowley. His activities extended from acting as a spy in pre-war Berlin to playing a part in the 1941 peace mission by Rudolf Hess. Crowley however had displayed a distinct lack of patriotism in the First World War when he actively supported the Kaiser. He was living in Switzerland when the war began and had offered his services to the British government but they refused to have anything to do with him. In October 1914 Crowley sailed to New York, and in 1915 he became interested in German nationalism. A chance meeting on an omnibus with a mysterious Irishman named O'Brien led Crowley to denounce his British citizenship, tear up his passport and call on the Irish people to support Germany by rising up against their English oppressors.

While living in the United States Crowley wrote pro-German propaganda for two right-wing publications called *The Fatherland* and *The Internationalist*. He later claimed that he carried out this work as an agent for MI6 (the British Secret Intelligence Service) and had been working for the Allied cause. The Secret Service denied all knowledge of this arrangement and denounced him as a 'small time traitor' who acted from a desire for self advertisement rather than treason. However, as a result of this condemnation, the police did raid his occult temple in

London and seized numerous documents and magical regalia.

After the war it was suggested that Crowley should be prosecuted but he seems to have persuaded the authorities that he was trying to help the Allies by writing tongue-in-cheek articles which in fact ridiculed the Germans. Crowley offered his services as an agent to MI6 after informing them that the head of the OTO, which he had joined in 1912, was a German Intelligence officer. In the 1920s and 1930s Crowley worked on an informal basis for MI6 supplying them with information about the European Communist movement and the links between the German nationalist groups, occult fraternities and the Nazis. It is possible that Crowley's employment by the British Secret Service was well known to the Germans. While he was living in Berlin the bisexual magician shared a home with an Englishman who was a German agent.

The head of the OTO who Crowley suspected of spying was probably Karl Germer who used the magical pseudonym Frater Saturnus. He had fought in the First World War and had been awarded the Iron Cross for unspecified 'special services'. His Intelligence activities had brought him in touch with Theodor Reuss, the founder of the OTO, and Germer was initiated into the secret society. When Reuss died, Germer became the new head of the OTO. In the 1920s Germer was working as the manager of a publishing house in Munich and was responsible for the translating and publishing of several of Crowley's occult books.

Both Germer and Crowley were associated with an occult secret society known as the Fraternitus Saturni, or the Brotherhood of Saturn, from whom Germer derived his magical name in the OTO. This Order had been founded in seventeenth-century Denmark and Sweden and it also had lodges in Poland. Its modern history began in 1921 when a neo-Rosicrucian, Gregory Gregorius, founded the Pansophic lodge of the Order in Berlin. This event was attended by the Grand Master of the German Rosicrucian Order, Aleister Crowley, in his role as British head of the OTO, and the Grand Masters of several other European and American secret societies in the Rosicrucian-Masonic tradition. In 1933 the Brotherhood was outlawed by the Nazis and several of its leaders were thrown into prison. It was, however, re-organized after the end of the war and became a prominent neo-Rosicrucian society in the Germany of the early 1950s.

Germer himself, despite his past work for the Intelligence Service, was arrested by the Gestapo in 1935 because of his connections with Freemasonry. He was tortured in prison before being despatched to a concentration camp but was mysteriously released ten months later.

Germer fled from Germany at the beginning of the war but was arrested by the Belgian police and then deported to France. After a period of imprisonment in an internment camp Germer left France for the United States where he died in 1962.

Crowley's lack of patriotism in the Great War was made up for when hostilities broke out in September 1939. Because Crowley had extensive contacts with the European secret societies his specialist knowledge was used by the SIS for 'Black propaganda' purposes. Crowley had confided to the writer Aldous Huxley in 1938 when they met in Berlin that Hitler was a practising occultist. He also claimed that the German branch of the OTO had helped the Nazis to gain power.

In the Second World War Crowley was involved in the Hess peace mission in May 1941. Crowley had come into contact with MI5 some years before through his friendship with Dennis Wheatley, the popular thriller writer who penned novels about black magic and the occult. In 1943 Wheatley had offered his services to the Ministry of Information at the suggestion of his wife who was in MI5. He was appointed as an officer on the Future Operations Staff and worked until 1944 as one of Winston Churchill's special staff officers. In this position Wheatley had access to the official minutes and reports of the Defence Committee, the War Cabinet, the Chiefs of Staff, the Home Office, the Foreign Office and the Joint Intelligence Committee who were responsible for the activities of MI5, the SIS and the SOE (Special Operations Executive).

In the 1930s Wheatley had become friendly with a high-ranking MI5 officer, Maxwell Knight. Both men had been cadets on HMS *Worcester* at different periods in their naval careers, shared an interest in the occult and had written crime thrillers. In 1933, the year the Nazis came to power, Wheatley's stepson Bill Younger, who was then at Oxford University, was recruited by Knight. His job was to spy on fellow students who were involved in Communist activities or had fascist sympathies. After he left university, Younger became a full-time MI5 agent working in the counter-subversion department. Younger was also interested in the occult and was a friend of Joan Grant who wrote several 'fictional' historical novels based on her past lives.

Dennis Wheatley had been introduced to Crowley by the journalist Tom Driberg who later became a Labour MP. He had also been used by MI5 to infiltrate the British Communist Party. Wheatley used his introduction to Crowley to obtain material for his black novels such as *The Devil Rides Out* published in 1936. On one of his visits to the Wheatleys in 1937, Maxwell Knight met Crowley. He later described the occultist to friends as a well-dressed middle-aged eccentric with the manner of an Oxford don. Knight became very friendly with Crowley and he and Wheatley attended magical ceremonies organized by the magician. The purpose of these visits was to research material for Wheatley's occult novels.

Because of his link with Maxwell Knight, Crowley became entangled in the attempt by the British Secret Service to lure Rudolf Hess to Britain in the early summer of 1941. At the outbreak of the war, Commander Ian Fleming, later to become world famous as the creator of James Bond 007, was working for Naval Intelligence. He knew Knight and was aware of the MI5 officer's interest in the occult and his friendship with Crowley. He was also aware, perhaps through Crowley's Intelligence reports for the SIS, that many of the leading Nazis were engaged in occultism.

Fleming suggested that a trap could be laid which would persuade Hess to fly to Britain. His subsequent capture would provide a superb propaganda coup for the Allied war effort. Fleming used a Swiss astrologer to infiltrate the occult circles in Germany which were frequented by Hess. The Nazi leader was fed the information that an organization known as the Link, which had been active during the 1930s in England supporting the Nazis, was still operating underground in wartime Britain. It retained an influential membership of pro-German activists who were secretly plotting to overthrow the Churchill government. Once this was accomplished the traitors would be capable of negotiating peace terms with Hitler.

Hess was told that the Duke of Hamilton was willing to talk to him personally as the representative of the Link. Hess was further told, in January 1941, by an astrologer working for the SIS, that on 10 May the position of six planets in the Zodiac sign of Taurus coincided with the full moon. This was regarded by Hess as a favourable omen and he chose that date for his ill-fated mission to contact the Link. The Duke of Hamilton was working for the RAF in Scotland and when Hess parachuted into the country and was arrested by the police he asked to see the aristocrat.

Originally Fleming had asked MI5 to induce Crowley to use his wide contacts in the German occult fraternities to trap Hess. Unfortunately British Intelligence knew that Crowley's influence was limited because of his activities as an MI6 agent in pre-war Berlin when he spied on both the Communists and the Nazis. In one of his infamous radio broadcasts, Lord Haw Haw (William Joyce) had claimed satirically that when the Nazis occupied London, Crowley would celebrate a Black Mass in Westminster Abbey. Crowley believed he had become a specific target for the Nazis in the Blitz and moved out of London to a house on Richmond Green in Surrey.

When Hess was captured, Ian Fleming suggested to his boss, Rear Admiral John Godfrey, the director of Naval Intelligence, that Crowley should be allowed to interview Hess about the role of the occult in Nazism. Knight was also keen on this idea but others in MI5, MI6 and the NID (Naval Intelligence Department) were less happy about the idea and it was dropped. In fact the Intelligence Services seem to have badly mishandled the whole Hess operation and any chance to embarrass the Nazis with his capture was quickly lost.

In Germany Hitler's reaction to the affair was swift and violent. He knew nothing about the mission and his first reaction when he heard the news was that Hess had suffered a brainstorm. Hess was dismissed in the official Nazi newspaper as a sick man who had been led astray by his interest in the occult and astrology. Several hundred astrologers, occultists and members of secret societies were rounded up by the Gestapo and questioned to establish if they knew Hess or other leading members of the Nazi Party. In June 1914 the public practice of the occult arts, astrology, fortune telling and psychic powers was banned by the Nazis.

Previous to his savage reaction against occult activities in Germany, it is alleged that Hitler had sanctioned the use of occult groups to raise psychic power to block the radar of RAF aircraft flying over Germany. The idea was that the planes would miss their target, get lost and fly into the searchlights of the German anti-aircraft batteries. It has been rumoured that a similar psychic operation was set up in the United Kingdom by British Intelligence. It involved psychics who worked from secret location in Wales. Their purpose was to deflect the Luftwaffe during their raids on English cities into ambushes set up by the RAF's Fighter Command.

MI6 became interested in the Nazi preoccupation with the occult early in the war. Several occultists were employed by the SIS to combat the Nazis on a psychic level. A Hungarian born astrologer called Louis de Wohl was attached to the Psychological Warfare Department with the rank of major. His job was to examine Hitler's birth chart and send regular reports to the War Office detailing what Hitler's astrologers were advising the German leader to do in the war. It has been said that the SIS employed several other pet astrologers who produced fake predictions which suggested that Germany would lose the war. Faked astrological publications were smuggled into occupied Europe by SIS agents who circulated them widely. They also used the prophecies of the sixteenth-century seer Nostradamus who predicted the rise and fall of a European dictator called Hister or Hitler.

One of the most successful psychics employed by the British Secret Service in the war was known simply by the codename 'Anne'. She had offered the Intelligence Service her occult services, which included the ability to project her mind to remote locations and report what was happening there. At her interview she impressed the assembled Intelligence officers by entering a trance state and projecting her mind to the next room. She described how a group of men were sitting reading *The Times* and circling certain advertisements with blue pencils. This information was checked and found to be correct.

In the following weeks 'Anne' was rigorously tested by the Secret Service who tried to prove that her powers were faked. She astounded the testers by repeating conversations between British officers who were stationed overseas. Eventually the Intelligence officers had to admit that her powers were genuine and they used her gifts on several occasions. 'Anne' achieved her most astonishing coup when she successfully projected her mind to the Nazi High Command's headquarters in Berlin. There she read certain top secret documents and reported their contents back to her British Intelligence colleagues when she had recovered from her trance.

The psychics working for the Secret Service were not the only occultists engaged in anti-Nazi activities. Before the war there had been a revival of witchcraft and it was alleged that a Hungarian occultist had organized witch covens in the Cotswolds to fight the Nazis using psychic powers. This person had contacts with the Intelligence Service and had recruited occult circles in the West Midlands area to use telepathy to combat the Germans.

One of the leading personalities in the witchcraft revival was a retired Customs officer, Gerald Gardner, who had returned from the Far East and settled in the New Forest in Hampshire. Gardner was interested in Spiritualism and the occult and as a result joined a Rosicrucian theatre company operating in Christchurch before the war. This theatre had been founded by disciples of Annie Besant who were co-Masons and had formed a group known as the Corona Fellowship of the Rosy Cross. This was an unofficial offshoot of the Temple of the Rose Cross founded by Besant in 1912. Gardner soon discovered that several of these neo-Rosicrucians were also members of a witch coven and in 1939 he was initiated as a witch by their high priestess, an old lady called Dorothy

Clutterbuck who lived in a large house in the New Forest.

In June 1940 when England faced invasion from the Nazis, Gardner claims that the high priestess of his coven called a huge gathering of witches in the New Forest where the Great Circle was erected. This was a magical ritual only performed in cases of extreme emergency. Previously it had only been raised twice, in 1588 to combat the Spanish Armada, which was defeated not only by Drake and his ships but with the help of a great storm, and in the 1800s when it looked as if Napoleon would cross the Channel. The ritual in the forest involved raising a cone of psychic power and directing it towards the French coast with the command, 'You cannot cross the sea. You cannot cross the sea. You cannot come.' According to Gardner this ritual involved the use of the life force of the gathered covens and as a result several elderly witches died. The ritual was repeated four times and then the Elders said 'We must stop. We must not kill too many of our people.'

At the opposite end of the occult spectrum, although linked by their Rosicrucian affiliations, the theosophical occultist Dion Fortune was also working against the Nazis on the psychic level. She used racial and national archetypes in magical practices to protect Britain from invasion. From the autumn of 1939 to 1942 Dion Fortune produced a series of newsletters which replaced the official journal of her Fratnerity of the Inner Light which could not be produced because of the wartime paper shortage. These newsletters provided the membership of the Inner Light scattered all over the country with a series of meditation exercises which were practised each Sunday.

On each Sunday morning the inner circle of initiates of the Fraternity met at the group's London headquarters in Bayswater. All the other members nationwide linked in with the inner circle in London to form a network of trained minds. In her first newsletter sent out in October 1939 Fortune explained that the idea was to contact the spiritual influences ruling the British race, using the symbol of a cross surmounted by a rose and surrounded by golden rays of light. This particular symbol had been common to the medieval Rosicrucians and to modern occult groups, such as the Hermetic Order of the Golden Dawn which Dion Fortune had joined just after the First World War.

By 1940 the Fraternity of the Inner Light was involved in magical rituals to invoke the guardian angels of the British Isles who were visualized robed and armed patrolling the shores of the country to prevent the German invasion.

There has been considerable speculation concerning the occult beliefs associated with National Socialism and the role played by the Secret Societies in its rise to power. This has led to exaggerated and sensational stories which have confused the real facts of the matter. This confusion was helped by the Allied attitude to the true nature of the Nazi political doctrine after the war. Churchill allegedly suppressed the facts about the Nazis involvement in occultism. He ordered that under no circumstances should the general public be informed of the extent of the occult activities engaged in by the Third Reich. At the Nuremburg trials of the major Nazi war criminals, including Rudolf Hess, the truth about their occult activities and practices was hidden from the world. It was believed that if it had been revealed in open court, many of the war criminals on trial would have been declared insane and would have escaped the death penalty demanded by the Allied prosecutors.

7

SECRETS IN THE VATICAN

In the alternative history of the secret societies the position taken by the Vatican, and whoever occupied the papal throne at any point in that history, has always been a matter of great importance. The relationship between the Pope and the Grand Masters of the secret societies was an explosive one. It could be nothing else. The Church regarded the members of the secret societies as spiritual anarchists who were agents of a Satanic conspiracy against organized religion. The Freemasons and Rosicrucians on the other hand accused the Church of suppressing the true teachings of Jesus of Nazareth. Other secret societies, such as the Illuminati and the Carbonari, were fervently anti-clerical. They plotted the overthrow of the Catholic Church because it opposed the old pagan religions and the Manichean heresy, from which these groups drew their spiritual inspiration, and supported the wealthy landowning class who were oppressing the masses.

Papal support for some of the secret societies had been freely given at first. Chilvalric Orders such as the Knights Templars, who were nominally Christian, were granted special papal favours. Even the Priory of Sion, which we are led to believe promoted the heresy that Jesus survived the crucifixion, was initially granted a charter by Pope Alexander III in the twelfth century. This was the same pontiff who had given the Templars special dispensations. In addition the medieval Church patronized the masonic guilds whose craftsmen built the Gothic cathedrals even though their legendary origins pre-dated Christian belief and were firmly rooted in the pagan Mysteries.

It was only when the Vatican perceived the secret societies to be a political and ideological threat to the Church that the climate of suspicious tolerance began to change. The creation of a 'Church within the Church' by the Templars and rumours of their heretical and pagan practices had reluctantly forced the Vatican to support King Phillip of France's personal crusade to wipe out the Order in the early fourteenth century. The Church had previously acted against the Cathars and other heretics to retain its spiritual monopoly in the face of a growing alternative religion.

In taking this kind of action the Vatican was following an historical tradition, for the early Christian Church had moved to neutralize dissent within its ranks by a series of councils which established the officially recognized tenets and doctrines of Christianity. These councils, principally the infamous Council of Nicea convened by the Roman Emperor Constantine in the fourth century CE, rejected pagan beliefs such as reincarnation which were held by early Christians and presented Jesus as God incarnate rather than a human spiritual teacher. Anyone who disagreed with these decisions was branded a heretic, meaning 'one who chooses', and could expect little tolerance from the new breed of Christian leaders who were in political control of the new Church.

One of the first victims of the intolerance of the early Christian Church was Celtic Christianity which was dissolved by the Council of Whitby in 664 CE. Celtic Christianity had developed its unique character during the Roman occupation of Britain and was heavily influenced by Druidism. According to legend, the first Christian church in this country was built by the uncle of Jesus, Joseph of Arimathea, at Glastonbury in Somerset on the present site of the medieval abbey. Joseph was a wealthy merchant who visited the tin mines of Cornwall for trading purposes. On one of these business trips it is said that Joseph took his young nephew who was initiated into a Druidic college. Glastonbury had been a spiritual centre since prehistoric times and the version of Christianity introduced by Joseph and his disciples intermingled with paganism. A separate branch of the Celtic Church was established in Wales during the fifth century CE by Irish monks who had blended Eastern traditions with the native paganism of Ireland.

In addition to Druidism, the Celtic Church had been influenced by Coptic Christianity. This unorthodox version of the new faith was founded by Clement of Alexandria who had blended the teachings of Jesus with Gnosticism, Judaism and Neo-Platonism. Clement founded his Coptic Church on the Secret Gospel of Mark, written by the evangelist in Alexandria following the death of Jesus. This gospel preserved the inner teachings given by Jesus to his closest disciples who had been initiated into the Christian Mysteries. It is interesting to note that Ormus, the legendary first-century founder of the secret society which became the Priory of Sion, lived in Alexandria and was converted to Christianity by Mark.

Our contemporary knowledge of the Gospel of Mark dates back to 1958 when an American professor of theology, Dr Morton Smith, discovered references to it in a letter by Clement preserved in a desert monastery. According to Smith the inner teachings of Jesus were passed by him to his disciples during an initiation rite which resembled those of the pagan Mysteries. Smith interprets the ritual communion meal practised by early Christians as a pagan rite descended from the Mysteries of Isis and Osiris. It was this esoteric interpretation of Christianity which was accepted by the medieval secret societies in contrast to the censored version offered by the Church.

Before it became an established power structure protected by the might of Imperial Rome early Christianity had operated underground like the pagan Mystery cults and suffered persecution for its subversive beliefs. The Roman hatred of Christians was based on the belief that their teachings were politically subversive and threatened the status quo. By the third century CE, when the Roman Empire had entered a crisis period, Christians had infiltrated into important positions in Roman society despite the fact that they were regarded as dangerous dissidents whose alien ideas posed a danger to the social fabric of the Empire. This persecution coincided with major conflicts within the Church itself concerning the imperial power of the Roman emperors in relation to Christian spirituality. In the first decade of the fourth century a situation arose where several rival emperors fought to occupy the Roman throne. From this internecine struggle emerged one candidate who was to play a decisive role in both the history of the Roman Empire and Christianity during his long reign from 306 to 337 CE. This man was Constantine the Great.

Constantine had been reared on the pagan religious beliefs of the Sol Invicta cult which identified the emperor as the incarnation of the Sun god. This cult was the first attempt in Roman culture to impose a monotheistic structure on the polytheistic pantheon of gods and goddesses worshipped by the ordinary people. It was similar in many ways to the Aton religion of Ancient Egypt created by the heretical pharoah Akhenaton. Initially Constantine was a devout pagan, and it is recorded that while fighting in Gaul (France) he saw a vision of the solar god Apollo who was worshipped in Rome as the supreme incarnation of the divine Sun. However, while marching on Rome, Constantine saw another vision, of a flaming cross in the sky and above it in letters of flame the motto *In hoc signo vinci* or 'In this sign I conquer'. When he won his battle the next day the opportunist Constantine decided the Christian god was a powerful deity who was worthy of his worship.

From that moment Constantine, while not fully accepting Christianity until a dramatic death-bed conversion, became more tolerant of the new religion. The Christian community soon realized that they had a friend occupying the Roman throne and turned this fact to their advantage. Christian leaders identified the new emperor as 'the beloved of God' who 'guides and steers, in imitation of the Lord, all the affairs of the world.' In these words the early Church had clearly marked out the Roman emperor as the representative of God on Earth. It even embraced the symbolism of the pagan solar cult by describing Constantine as 'the light of the Sun (who) illuminates those furthest from him with his rays.'

Constantine in turn increased the political power of the embryonic Church by appointing Christians to key positions in his court, by prohibiting the private practice of magical rituals and by declaring Sunday a public holiday. During his reign paganism still flourished and sacrificial rites were practised as an important aspect of state ritual. Nobody, however, was under any illusion that while Constantine tolerated this state of affairs he secretly favoured Christianity. Any doubts in this direction were finally swept away when in 324 CE the emperor officially declared that Christianity would become the state religion of the Roman Empire.

The sympathetic approach to Christian beliefs pioneered by Constantine was continued by his sons who followed him to the throne but suffered a brief reversal during the short reign of his nephew Julian from 355 to 363 CE. He was a mystical intellectual who had been initiated into the pagan Mysteries of the Greek goddess Hecate as a young man. While pretending to be a devout Christian Julian worked to reverse the advances made by the Christian religion during the previous forty years. He provided a high degree of freedom for all religious beliefs, including Christianity, but was biased towards paganism. His death in the Persian campaign brought a sudden end to the neo-pagan revival in the Empire. Rumours quickly spread that Julian had not been killed by the Persians but assassinated by a Christian member of his own army who objected to the emperor's pagan beliefs.

With the death of Julian the Christian religion quickly re-established itself in Rome and under the Emperor Theodosius (378–395 CE) the worship of the old pagan gods was finally prohibited. This event coincided with attacks on Rome by barbarian tribes which were to mark the end of its Imperial glory. In 452 the dwarfish Attila the Hun appeared at the gates of Rome but was repulsed by the bishop of the city who declared that the temporal power of the Roman emperor had been passed down to him.

In the bloody aftermath of the barbarian invasions and the beginning of the so-called Dark Ages the Roman Church began to establish its political power. In the fifth century the Church recognized the Royal family of the Franks, the Merovingians or 'long haired kings', by baptizing Clovis the first Catholic monarch in Europe. The Church had decided that a strong leader was required to forge European unity in the face of barbarian invasion and ensure the survival of Christianity in the face of pagan opposition. In 751 when the Merovingian throne was usurped by a court chancellor the Vatican swiftly recognized the new regime. The last Merovingian king, Childeric III, was deposed and imprisoned. His flowing hair, which was of spiritual significance to the family, was ritually shorn by the reigning Pope as a symbol of the dynasty's broken power. The Merovingian bloodline however survived by marrying into the family of the dukes of Hapsburg and Lorriane.

By the late eighth century the relationship between the Frankish kings and the bishop of Rome had grown stronger. In 795 Pope Leo III recognized the Frankish monarch Charles the Great of Charlemagne as the patrician of Rome. When Charlemagne saved the Pope from the disgrace of an adultery charge the grateful pontiff crowned him as the new Roman Emperor. The Holy Roman Empire ruled by the Frankish king was the first attempt by the medieval Church to expand its power base from the spiritual realm into the world of international politics. The Vatican's aim was to form a united Europe based on Christian values and chivalry through which it could exert absolute spiritual and temporal power.

With the death of Charlemagne this dream of European unity quickly faded. His grandson was crowned as Roman Emperor in 915 but when he died nine years later the Imperial throne lay empty for two decades. In 936 Otto, the son of Henry the Fowler who had joined the Saxon dynasty in Germany, was elected king by the German aristocracy. He declared his intention to fight the enemies of Christ and drive the pagans out of his land. The Vatican saw in this German warlord the potential for a Roman emperor.

In 951 Otto was crowned as king of Lombardy and became the ruler of northern Italy. Following his defeat of the pagan Magyars in 955 Otto took the title of 'Protector of Europe'. In Rome Pope John XII, a notorious womaniser who turned the Vatican into a brothel during his papacy, appealed to Otto for help to fight his enemies. He rewarded the German king by crowning him Holy Roman Emperor in 962. For the next century the Italian Popes and the German emperors ruled Europe with the latter considered by the Church to represent the temporal power of God on Earth.

The election of Pope Gregory VII in 1073 brought this cosy alliance under stress. The new Pope asserted his belief that the Vatican was the master of the Roman Emperors and the chosen vicar of Christ. He claimed that the crowning of the Holy Roman Emperor by the pontiff demonstrated in public that the political power of the Empire derived from God through his chosen emissary in the Vatican. Emperor Henry IV challenged this view and was promptly excommunicated by the Pope for treason. Faced with local revolts which threatened to topple him from the throne Henry was forced to retract his view and submitted his authority to the Pope.

This ideological battle between the Popes and the Roman Emperors they had created raged for several hundred years. The point where we can discern the beginning of the secret societies' influence in this power struggle was in the reign of Frederick II, crowned as Holy Roman Emperor in 1215. Frederick was a man possessed with a great spiritual vision and he followed in the footsteps of his grandfather Frederick Barbarossa who had defiantly declared, 'We hold our kingdom and our Empire not as a fief of the Pope but by election of the princes from God alone.' Frederick II became king of Sicily and in 1228 left on a crusade to the Holy Land which resulted in him becoming the king of Jerusalem. Frederick was rumoured to have been involved in the practice of the occult including astrology and alchemy. He kept a harem at his court in Sicily, spoke Arabic and had allegedly been inducted into the Moslem faith. This may explain why Pope Gregory IX denounced Frederick as a heretic and the personification of the AntiChrist.

Frederick's political ambitions in the Middle East had brought him into open conflict with the Templars after he negotiated the return of Jerusalem from Moslem hands to the Christian armies. In the treaty Frederick agreed that the Moslems should retain the site of the temple of Solomon which was then a mosque. This angered the Templars who regarded this concession as an insult and betrayal because of the spiritual significance of the temple to the Order. In their view it was essential while the Order survived that Solomon's temple was in the possession of Christian crusaders. Frederick was well aware of their anger and it is said that he fled Jerusalem fearing that the Templars, or their allies the Assassins, were plotting to kill him.

The opposition of Frederick to the Templar Order was determined by the fact that he shared political aspirations with them. The Holy Roman Emperor had founded his own chilvaric Order, known as the Teutonic Knights, as rivals to the Templars. From 1230 to 1239 several battles were fought between the two Orders for supremacy in the Holy Land. As an occultist it is possible that Frederick was opposed to the Templars because he did not share their spiritual beliefs and thought they had strayed from the true path. Frederick knew any attempt to overthrow the Order by force was doomed to failure because of their support in the Vatican at that time. However his opposition to the Order in the Holy Land seriously weakened their political power and the loss of the temple in Jerusalem sapped their morale. These circumstances contributed to the eventual downfall of the Templars.

With the death of Frederick in 1250 the Holy Roman Empire collapsed. For twenty years Europe was devastated by war until in 1273 the concept of the old Empire was revived with the crowning of a new Holy Roman Emperor, Count Rudolf von Habichtsburg or Habsburg, meaning the Castle of Hawks, in Austria. For the next three hundred years, under the patronage of the Vatican, the Habsburgs extended their empire throughout Europe, based on their temporal power and the spiritual power of the Roman Catholic Church.

The successful alliance between the Habsburgs and the Vatican was seriously weakened by the actions of one man, a crusading reformer who used the symbol of the rose and the cross on his personal seal. He was the German monk Martin Luther who in 1517, disgusted by the corrupt practices of the Church, nailed a document to the door of his local church condemning the selling of papal indulgences. Pope Leo X immediately issued a bull against Luther who promptly burnt it in public, leading to his excommunication in 1521. The Reformation, allegedly supported by the Rosicrucians and other secret societies who opposed the Roman Church, swept through Europe. It became a popular movement supported by the ruling classes and this prevented the Vatican from successfully halting its relentless progress through European society.

This period of the Reformation represents a key time in history during which the relationship between the Church and the secret societies changed. In the twelfth and thirteenth centuries the Church had used the powers of the Inquisition to crush the Cathars who had challenged its rule in southern France. In the early fourteenth century it had destroyed the Templars and by the end of that century had begun persecuting the witches who had inherited the debased remnants of the pagan old religions. With the Reformation the Church was faced with an enemy within, whom it could not destroy without bringing down its own edifice. With the Reformation the whole concept of organized religion in Europe was revolutionized overnight. If the Reformation had been helped by the secret societies then it was a masterstroke of genius on their part.

In 1529 the German princes who had supported Luther and his reforming policies protested to Emperor Charles V about restrictions imposed on the new Christian movement. It was from this outcry that the word 'Protestant' came into being and a campaign to reform the Roman Church from within was transformed into an alternative religion which challenged the spiritual authority of the Pope and the material power of his Holy Roman Empire. Support from the Grand Masters of the secret societies was offered to the religious reformers because the Reformation was recognized as a means to weaken the influence of the Catholic Church in European affairs.

The Reformation effectively emasculated the political power of the Church. It laid the foundation of the Puritan movement whose members fled religious persecution in Europe to found a new nation in the Americas based on spiritual principles drawn from Rosicrucian sources. It also provided an atmosphere of open mindedness which was to allow the seeds of the Renaissance to flower, based on the best ideas of the pagan classical world. Indirectly the Reformation gave the impetus for the Scientific Revolution of the seventeenth century, which centred on well-known Rosicrucians such as Sir Francis Bacon and Sir Isaac Newton, and led to the founding of the Royal Society after the English Civil War. In Europe, although the Habsburgs were to rule as Holy Roman Emperors for another 300 years until Francis II relinquished the crown in 1806, the Reformation destroyed any hope of a united Europe controlled by the Roman Church. Above everything else the religious reforms of the sixteenth century marked the beginning of the period when the Roman Church became determined to exterminate the secret societies which had weakened its power base.

The rise of the Rosicrucian Order into public view in the seventeenth century preaching political equality, religious freedom and liberty and the eighteenth-century revival of the Masonic guilds, using the symbolism of medieval craft masonry as spiritual metaphors, posed a further threat to the Roman Church. The Church's authority over ordinary people was based on its claim to exercise power through apostolic succession from Jesus through St Peter. The medieval Church had created a climate of fear by promoting the existence of a Satanic conspiracy which included anyone who dared to resist Christian doctrine. In contrast the secret societies provided an alternative version of spirituality to their followers. Not only did the leaders of these societies allege that the Church had deliberately subverted the teachings of Jesus but they taught there were other sources of spiritual knowledge which were as valid as Christian belief but predated it by thousands of years.

When the Masonic lodges began to spread throughout Europe the Church reacted by conducting a smear campaign which was similar to the one used against the heretics and witches. Anti-Masonic tracts were distributed alleging that unnatural sexual practices including sodomy and flagellation took place in the new Masonic lodges. In 1738 the first papal bull to combat Freemasonry was issued by Pope Clement XII. This bull threatened any Catholic who became a Mason with excommunication, at that time an extremely serious punishment. As a result of this bull some limited police action was taken against Masons in France and elsewhere.

In the 1780s claims that secret societies such as the Illuminati were using Freemasonry as a cover for radicalism and revolution gave the Church fresh charges to level against the Masonic lodges. Many European governments were contemplating action to curb the political excesses of the Masons and they received support from the Vatican in their efforts. However the Reformation and the Age of Reason, with its humanistic and rationalist philosophies, had undermined the Roman Church. The bulls issued by the Popes condemning secret societies only had effect in Catholic countries and because many of the occult fraternities had influential friends in high places the extent of clerical action was very limited.

The climax of the Church's crusade to destroy the influence of Freemasonry came in the nineteenth century. In 1864 Pope Pius X condemned socialism and the secret societies in his *Syllabus of Errors* which he published following an investigation of revolutionary activities in Italy. The Carbonari, who had recruited their membership from Army officers, policemen and landowners, had been active in Italy in the first three decades of the century and, in 1848, revolution had spread like wildfire across many European countries including Italy. Twelve months after the publication of *Errors* the Pope again condemned the secret societies specifically attacking Freemasonry as anti-Christian, Satanic and pagan in origin. In 1884 Pope Leo XIII issued a proclamation identifying Masonry as one of the secret societies working to establish Satan's kingdom on Earth. He also condemned Freemasonry because he claimed it was attempting to 'revive the manners and customs of the pagans.'

The nineteenth-century concept of Masonry as a Satanic plot was finally dispelled following the exposure of the sensational and bizarre confessions of the high priestess of an occult group called the New Reformed Lodge of the Palladium. These confessions were an elaborate hoax perpetuated by a French journalist, Leo Taxil, who in 1885 and 1886 published a series of pamphlets exposing Masonry as a revival of the Cathar heresy. Taxil presented to a gullible public the high priestess of a secret Masonic Order named Diana Vaughan, who was descended from the seventeenth-century alchemist Thomas Vaughan. The lodges of her Order admitted both men and women on equal terms and practised Satanism. Diana claimed to be associated with the Society of Rosicrucians in Anglia, founded by William Wynn Westcott of the Hermetic Order of the Golden Dawn who was secretly the leader of the English Luciferians. Taxil informed his readers that Diana Vaughan had given up 'the Satanic cult of Freemasonry' and had become a convert to the Roman Church.

Diana's memoirs, ghost written by Taxil, became an overnight bestseller. The cover of his anti-Masonic tract Les Mysteres de la Franc Macconerie depicts a group of Freemasons worshipping Baphomet, the idol of the Templars, inside a Masonic temple. In the foreground stands the cloaked figure of an assassin clutching a knife and a female figure with an Arabic sword holding up a decapitated head. These lurid books were eagerly read by the Pope who used them as evidence of the evils of Freemasonry. Taxil's anti-Masonic campaign was so successful that a conference was organized attended by thousands of people eager to hear further revelations. The Pope sent a telegram blessing the event which was read out to loud cheers from the crowd. At the conference delegates called on Taxil to present his star witness but the wily journalist told the assembly she had been forced into hiding after threats to her life from Masonic assassins.

The anti-Masonic crusade continued unabated until 1897 when Taxil finally confessed at a press conference that Diana Vaughan had been a figment of his imagination. He claimed to have written the books to expose the ludicrous excesses of the Roman Catholic Church's attacks on Freemasons. This statement, plus the use of Templar symbolism and connections with the Golden Dawn, suggests the anti-Masonic crusade was a 'dirty tricks' operation used by the secret societies to discredit future attacks on them by the Church. It certainly had that effect although the hapless Taxil was set upon by his outraged journalistic colleagues, who had been duped by his lies, and had to be rescued by the police.

It has often been claimed that the ultimate objective of the secret societies was to infiltrate the Vatican and place their own man on the papal throne. The Illuminist conspiracy had been exposed after all in 1785 when a priest who was a member of the Order died in an accident. He was killed by lightning while on a secret mission for the Order and his body was taken to a nearby convent. A nun preparing the body for burial found a cache of documents sewn into the lining of his cassock. These documents outlined plans for the destruction of the Catholic Church from inside. The authorities promptly outlawed the Order and its leader Adam Weishaupt was banished from Bavaria. Although he died in obscurity some years later, in the immediate period following his banishment he laid the foundation for the completion of his grand plan which many believe is still in operation today.

Certainly one of the main objectives of the Carbonari was to infiltrate the Church at all levels and eventually have one of its own members elected as Pope. Some modern critics of the Roman Church, especially those with right-wing political views who support ultra-traditionalist doctrines such as the Latin mass, have seen in the liberalization of the Church in recent years proof that its hierarchy has been penetrated at the highest level by agents of the secret societies who are working for its eventual downfall.

In his book *The Broken Cross*, Piers Compton, an ex-editor of the Catholic newspaper *The Universe*, has traced the alleged infiltration of the Roman Church by the Illuminati. He cites as evidence the use of the Illuminatist symbol of the eye in the triangle by leading Catholics. It has been used by the Jesuits, it has appeared as the seal of the Philadelphia Eucharistic Congress in 1976 and featured on a special issue of Vatican stamps in 1978. Compton further claims that Pope John XXIII, who died in June 1963, used the symbol on his personal cross.

According to Compton, Pope John (formerly Bishop Angelo Roncalli) was an initiate of a secret society. Roncalli was consecrated as a bishop in 1935 and entered the Vatican Diplomatic Service as the Apostolic Visitor of the Holy See in Sofia, Turkey. It was while he was in Turkey that Roncalli allegedly became a member of a secret society which used the symbol of the rose and the cross. During the papacy of John from 1958 to

1963 the first major reforms in the Catholic Church's theology since the Middle Ages were instigated. These reforms in the eyes of the traditionalist tendency in the Church were a programme of radical change dictated by the Grand Masters of the secret societies to their papal puppet.

In his book Compton claims that several hundred leading Catholic clerics are members of secret societies. He quotes an article in an Italian journal in 1976 which lists over seventy-five Vatican officials who are secret society members. These include Pope Paul VI's private secretary, the director general of Vatican radio, the Archbishop of Florence, the prelate of Milan, the assistant editor of the Vatican newspaper, several Italian bishops and the abbot of the Order of St Benedict. It is presumed that the secret society involved is Freemasonry although at least one name on the list is said to have family connections with the Rosicrucians.

In his exposé of the secret societies and their alleged influence on the Vatican, Compton singles out the nineteenth-century Cardinal Mariano Rompalla (1843–1913) as one of their key agents inside the Church. This Sicilian liberal had radical political views and rose to the position of Secretary of State in the papacy of Leo XIII. When the Pope died in 1903 Rompalla emerged as the leading candidate to follow him. He only failed because the Cardinal of Cracow, acting on behalf of Emperor Josef von Habsburg, exercised a veto. As the rulers of the Holy Roman Empire until 1806 the Habsburgs had retained the right to veto any papal candidate they regarded as unfit to hold office.

Considering the Austrian Emperor's dislike of secret societies and their dabbling in European politics, his action is significant. Following his defeat the cardinal seems to have had very little influence in Vatican affairs. It is said that after his death documents were found among his papers which linked him with both the OTO and Aleister Crowley. Unfortunately the incumbent Pope was so horrified by their contents that he ordered them to be burnt so we will never know what they contained.

With the death of the reforming Pope John in 1963 the Catholic Church entered a turbulent period which saw the Vatican shaken by financial scandal caused by its doubtful relationship with a secret Masonic lodge, the Mafia and right-wing extremists. The new Pope, Giovanni Montini, was the Archbishop of Milan, who was regarded by his critics as a socialist who had attempted to make a pact with the Italian Communist Party after the Second World War. In fact the new Pope's political views were more complex than this flirtation with left-wing politics suggests. Montini certainly had very strong anti-Nazi views which he exercised from 1940 to 1945 as a section head in the Vatican Intelligence Service in occupied Europe.

Archbishop Montini's father was a leading Social Democrat and his family connections allowed his son, as Vatican Secretary of State, to meet leading Communists in 1944 to discuss power sharing with the Socialists and Democrats in post-war Italy. According to a CIA (Central Intelligence Agency) report of the meeting, Montini was hopeful that communications could be established after the war between the Vatican and the Soviet Union despite Pope Pius XI's anti-Communist views.

Montini's political affiliations seem to have changed dramatically after the war. By the early 1950s he had become directly involved with the CIA through its front organization, the American Committee for a United Europe (ACUE), and allegedly worked for the Agency spying on fellow priests with left-wing opinions. The ACUE had been founded in 1949 and its first chairman was William 'Wild Bill' Donovan, a wartime hero of the Office of Strategic Services (OSS) which was a forerunner of the CIA. The secretary of the ACUE was a director of the Council on Foreign Relations (CRF) and a co-ordinator of the later Tri-lateral Commission, both groups regarded by conspiracy theorists as front organizations for the modern activities of the Illuminati in international power politics.

The aim of the ACUE, as its name suggests, was to provide American assistance in the political unification of Europe in the post-war period. This idea had the support of many leading politicians including Churchill who had frequently endorsed a 'united States of Europe' after the war. The ACUE was a product of Cold War mentality and it promoted a policy of anti-Communism. It was secretly funded by the US government and had links with Prince Bernhard of the Netherlands and a former director of the British Special Operations Executive (SOE) which parachuted undercover agents into occupied Europe to perform acts of subversion and sabotage during the war.

When Montini was elected as Pope Paul VI in 1963 his critics noted that the Vatican's previous hard line on Freemasonry notably relaxed. In 1917, coinciding with the First World War and the Bolshevik Revolution, the Vatican had forbidden Catholics to become Freemasons. A Catholic who was found to be a Mason or a member of 'any other secret society which plotted against the state' could be excommunicated. With the papacy of Paul this harsh stricture was relaxed and a Catholic could join a Masonic lodge providing membership did not involve anti-clerical activities. This led in 1975 to a Brazilian archbishop celebrating a special mass to mark the fortieth anniversary of a Masonic lodge.

In 1978 Pope Paul became aware of rumours of an imminent Communist takeover in Italy. It was reported that the Vatican had transferred $5 billion of its financial holdings from Italy to the United States because the Pope had lost confidence in the European democratic system. Paul allegedly believed that Europe was on the verge of a left-wing revolution. Rumours circulated in the Vatican that the Pope was willing to break with tradition and retire so that his chosen successor, a non-Italian European, could be elected and make a deal with the Eastern bloc to preserve the Church in a future socialist Europe.

The Pope's fear of a left-wing takeover was shared by the secret societies and especially by members of a Masonic lodge in Italy whose public exposure was to highlight the clandestine financial and political intrigues within the Vatican and possibly lead to the murder of the next occupant of the papal throne. Propaganda Two, or P2 as it became more popularly known, was an élitist Masonic lodge founded in 1960 by a wealthy businessman, Licio Gelli. He had fought with the Italian Black Shirts in the Spanish Civil War in the 1930s and had fraternized with the Nazis during the 1939–1945 conflict. Despite his right-wing views Gelli had established links with Communist partisans during the hostilities so escaped prosecution as a war criminal. Gelli had connections with various fascist groups in Latin America, the CIA and the Mafia. He regarded his membership of Freemasonry as an important aspect of his political work. In 1976 he told friends 'Freemasonry hates Communism because it is contrary to the idea of the dignity of personal individualism, the destroyer of fundamental rights which are the divine inheritance of all men and the enemy of the Masonic principle to have faith in God.'

The anti-Communist crusade which motivated Gelli and the other members of the P2 Lodge allowed it to become a front for the CIA's subversive activities in Italy during the 1970s. Several leading members of P2 received financial support from the Agency to fight Italian Communism and they channelled funds to other anti-Communist groups overseas. The political philosophy of P2 was centred on the creation of an alternative government which would take power if Italy were ever faced with a Communist uprising or a victory by the Communists in a democratic election. The plan was for P2 to create a 'white coup' by counter-revolutionaries with the outside assistance of the CIA and American troops if required which would establish a right-wing, pro-US regime.

In common with political secret socities of the past, such as the Illuminati and the Thule Society, the P2 Lodge drew its membership, estimated at 2,500, from the highest levels of the social, political and military establishment. They included three Cabinet ministers, the heads of the Italian Secret Service, the chiefs of staff of the Army, Navy, and Defence Ministry, the commanders of the paramilitary and Customs police, eighteen members of Parliament, twenty-one judges, leading businessmen, journalists and political commentators. P2 also had overseas branches in Cuba, South America and the USA, and was described by an official Italian government report as 'a secret sect that combined politics with business with the intention of destroying the constitution of the country.'

According to an article by Jonathan Marshall in the parapolitical journal *Lobster*, P2 also had connections with neo-Templar groups in France. Gelli, as Grand Master of P2, had made contact with Jacques Massie, a Marseilles police inspector who was a member of an extreme right-wing group called Service d'Action Critique (SAC). Massie and five members of his family were gunned down when he allegedly betrayed the secrets of the group to his police colleagues. The members of SAC included prominent political figures, former mercenaries who had fought with the OAS terrorists in Algeria and underworld elements. Massie was involved in smuggling arms from Turkey to both the left-wing Red Brigade and neo-Nazi terrorists in Italy to fund the political activities of SAC.

While he was in Marseilles visiting Massie, the Grand Master of P2 had meetings with representatives of a neo-Templar Order who sympathized with the aims of SAC. Gelli allegedly discussed his plans for the future of Italy with his new friends. In France the modern Templar Orders included top government officials, bankers, Army and police officers and members of the French Secret Service (SDCE) which is the equivalent of the British MI6. The Orders are divided up into several different branches, some of which are associated with Masonic and political groups in France who finance anti-Communism.

One of these neo-Templar groups exposed in the 1960s had wealthy members with Vatican connections. This group was strangely pro-Catholic, pro-monarchist and anti-Communist and one of its leaders, Constantin Melnik, was associated with the French Secret Service, Radio Free Europe (a CIA front organization) and the Rand Corporation (a right-wing 'think tank' financed by the Pentagon). Melnik was of French birth but his parents were White Russians and he claimed his grandfather had been Czar Nicholas II's personal physician.

A further, if unlikely, link between the Vatican, the Romanovs and the secret societies was provided in the 1960s when the deputy head of the Polish Secret Service defected to the United States. Mikael Goliniewski provided the CIA with a flood of sensational revelations concerning the alleged penetration of Western society by Soviet moles. The Agency however became suspicious when the Polish defector changed his name to Alexi Nicholaevitch Romanov and announced he was the secret son of Nicholas II.

Goliniewski was supported in this claim by a right-wing chivalric Order called the Knights of Malta who traced their pedigree back to the crusaders who fought in the Holy Land. According to occult tradition, one of the Grand Masters of the Knights of Malta, Manuel de Fonseca, was an initiate of the Templar tradition in the eighteenth century and had introduced Count Cagliostro into Templarism. The modern Order boasted it had sympathisers inside the Vatican, the Russian Orthodox Church and the White Russian emigré groups in the West who were seeking to re-establish the monarchy in their homeland. This Russian connection derives from 1778 when Napoleon invaded Malta and the Knights were offered sanctuary by Czar Peter I. He is credited with forming a clandestine group of Army officers and Russian Orthodox priests known as the Secret Circle who were fanatically dedicated to the preservation and protection of Mother Russia. The Secret Circle, which had links with the Knights of Malta, survived the Bolshevik Revolution and infiltrated its agents into the Western Intelligence Services with the aim of destroying Communism and restoring a White Russian government in Moscow.

The modern Knights of Malta support the ultra-traditionalist, right-wing faction in the Vatican who opposed the reforms of Pope John and those who followed him. It has campaigned for the return of the old Latin mass and regards the liberals in the Church as enemies of the true faith. In recent years rumours have circulated linking the Knights of Malta with extreme right-wing political groups and the CIA.

Goliniewski had an odd connection with the British Royal family which is of interest. Lord Louis Mountbatten, uncle of Prince Charles, was a leading critic of the Polish defector's claim to be a descendant of the Romanovs. Mountbatten was related, through Queen Victoria, to the Russian Royal family and was also a strong opponent of the Knights of Malta and a critic of their association with the CIA. Mountbatten's name had been raised when Churchill and Roosevelt, who was allegedly a member of an Illuminist-inspired secret society, discussed the reviving of the old Habsburg Empire in the post-war period as part of their grand plan for a united Europe. Churchill believed the revival of a European super-monarchy would act as an antidote to Communist expansion plans in post-war Germany, France, Italy and Austria. Mountbatten was proposed as a suitable candidate for Emperor as was Dr Otto von Habsburg, who is a leading exponent of a pan-European federation.

The exposure of the illegal activities of the P2 Lodge not only revealed a web of right-wing conspirators engaged in subversive acts but also exposed a financial scandal which involved high officials in the Vatican. This scandal came to light with the collapse of the Banco Ambrosiano, whose managing director was Robert Calvi, a staunch Catholic but also a leading personality in the P2 Lodge. In 1971 Calvi had been introduced to the director of the Vatican Bank, Bishop Marcinkus, by another P2 member who was a financial advisor to Pope Paul. The bishop became a director of Banco Ambrosiano whose subsidiaries were actively engaged in laundering illegal funds for the Mafia. Links were quickly established between the Banco Ambrosiano and the Vatican Bank, entangling the Catholic Church in a financial operation which connected it with Freemasonry, right-wing extremists and organized crime.

Calvi's task in P2 was to use his extensive contacts among international bankers to set up an overseas structure which would act as an alternative to the Italian banking system in the event of a Communist government coming to power. Although a devout Catholic, Calvi ruthlessly used his membership of P2 to further his own financial ends. When he apparently committed suicide by hanging himself under Blackfriars Bridge in London it was rumoured that he had been murdered to prevent him revealing the inside secrets of international Freemasonry. This theory was reinforced by the fact that his briefcase containing documents implicating the Vatican with Banco Ambrosiano and P2 vanished after his death.

The P2 scandal came to light after the death of Pope Paul VI in the summer of 1978. A socialist Pope, Albino Luciani, who had been the Patriarch of Venice was elected by the College of Cardinals and took the name John Paul I. He seemed determined to bring a new style of papacy to his role as the vicar of Christ and was quickly dubbed 'the smiling Pope' by the media because of his relaxed manner, sense of humour and informality. John Paul I was not just a good public relations officer for the Church. He was also a sophisticated liberal who advocated artificial birth control and wanted to relax the Catholic hard line on divorce, abortion and homosexuality.

It would also seem that the new pontiff planned to investigate the Church's recent financial affairs, sell off many of its financial holdings to provide money for the poor and reform the Vatican's banking system which had been dominated by the influence of the P2 Lodge. John Paul further shocked many traditionalists by openly referring to God as both the father and the mother in a sermon to the crowds in St Peter's Square. The androgynous nature of God had been discussed by liberal-minded theologians for many years but had always been regarded as a heresy by the Vatican. Within a few days of his election gossip was circulating in the corridors of the Vatican that the new Pope was a heretic, a practising homosexual and a crypto-Communist.

Predictably, John Paul I faced severe opposition from within the Vatican to his campaign to cleanse the corruption which had been allowed to fester in the Church during the previous papacy. Shortly after he was elected the pontiff was presented with a list of the prominent Masons in the Catholic hierarchy. He also became aware of the activities of the P2 lodge and how it had supported and nurtured the ultra-. traditionalist elements in the Vatican in order to create divisions in the Church. The new Pope had powerful enemies and, when he died suddenly in September 1978, there were many people inside the Vatican, and in the shadowy world where criminals, political extremists and renegade members of secret societies plot and conspire, who were secretly relieved. Since his death, rumours have spread that John Paul I was poisoned by assassins who feared his reforming policies and investigations into the links between the Church and the P2 Lodge.

With the death of the smiling Pope, a Polish cardinal was elected as the next pontiff and took the name John Paul II in reverence to his short-lived predecessor. At first the media portrayed the Polish Pope as a liberal in the same mould as his namesake but it soon became clear that he was a traditionalist in matters of Catholic doctrine. In a series of keynote sermons John Paul II reinforced the Church's traditional teachings on birth control, homosexuality and family life. As a possible response to the public uproar over the P2 revelations the Pope also reinforced the Church's historical opposition to Freemasonry. In 1981 the Congregation for the Doctrine of the Faith, which is the modern equivalent of the medieval Inquisition, issued a declaration condemning Freemasonry and confirming that any Catholic who belonged to its lodges would be excommunicated.

However, the new Pope did very little to deal with criticisms of the

Vatican's dealings with the Banco Ambrosiano. In fact in 1987 the Pope defended his long time friend Archbishop Marcinkus when he was accused of fraud by special prosecutors investigating Calvi's mysterious suicide. The prosecutors decided that the archbishop should face fraud charges but the Pope responded by granting Marcinkus sanctuary inside the Vatican where, because the Holy See was an independent state from Italy, the arrest warrant was not valid. This act by the Pope can be interpreted as an attempt to limit the damage to the Church by the Banco Ambrosiano affair and an example of loyal friendship rather than a conspiracy involving secret societies.

The financial investments made by Pope Paul VI in American banks in the 1970s when he feared a Communist coup in Italy were relocated according to Vatican insiders following the assassination attempt on John Paul II by a Turkish gunman in 1981. A disinformation cover story was spread by Western Intelligence Services in the media alleging that it had been an attempt by the KGB, using the Bulgarian Secret Service, to silence the Pope's support for Solidarity in his native Poland. However, insiders pointed out that the would-be assassin had no links with the Eastern bloc and in fact was a member of the Grey Wolves, a right-wing Turkish terrorist group funded by the CIA and Italian neo-fascists.

It has been alleged that the Vatican was warned in advance of a possible plot to kill the Pope. The source for this information was a high-ranking official in the Soviet Embassy in Rome. Because of this tip-off, and information collected by the Vatican Intelligence Service, the Pope was convinced the murder attempt was not a Soviet conspiracy but the work of Western business interests. On the day he was shot John Paul planned to launch an attack condemning the immorality of Western capitalism and demand a return to spiritual values in European and American society.

Despite his traditional views on moral issues there are still some extreme voices within the Vatican who speculate that Pope John Paul II may be under the influence of the secret societies. Since the days of Pope John XXIII there has existed a radical movement within the Church which has sought closer links between Catholicism and other Christian churches with the ultimate aim of reversing the divisions of the Reformation which weakened Christianity. This event would certainly not be welcomed by the secret societies but in the Pope's desire to support this theme the ultra-traditionalists have seen evidence of an anti-Catholic conspiracy.

At the celebrations in honour of St Francis of Assissi in 1986, which stressed the unity of all the world's religions, the Pope participated in a multi-religious prayer for world peace. Traditionalists were horrified to see the pontiff happily share a platform with a Tibetan lama, a Hindu swami, a Native American medicine man, a Jewish rabbi and a Maori high priest. It was noted that the unity of all the world religions and the recognition that they all derived from the same ancient source is the central philosophy of the secret societies.

THE OCCULT AND MODERN POLITICS

The involvement of the P2 Lodge with neo-fascism and the Vatican is only one example, albeit a negative one, of the way in which occultism and the secret societies have influenced modern politics. Exactly how great this influence has been since the end of the First World War, except for the early history of National Socialism in Germany, is a matter of debate. Frequently writers on the subject have fallen into the trap of projecting their own ideological views, both left and right, and personal prejudice into the subject to create sensational scenarios of the sinister motives of groups and individuals who allegedly operate in modern times as agents of the Illuminati and other occult-related secret societies.

Typical of these politically motivated conspiracy theorists was Nesta Webster who wrote a series of bestselling books in the 1920s exposing the so-called Jewish world domination plan. She claimed that the Jews, working through the secret societies and the international banking system, were the *éminences grises* behind the revolutionary movements of the eighteenth and nineteenth centuries. The fact that the Templars revered Solomon's Temple and were international bankers, the allegation that the House of Rothschild financed the Illuminati, and the use of Judaic symbolism in Freemasonry apparently added fuel to Webster's speculative theories of a historical Jewish conspiracy. Webster believed she was the reincarnation of a countess who had been executed in the French Revolution and was convinced it was her duty in this lifetime to expose the secret societies who had plotted the 1789 uprising.

In the 1920s, when anti-Semitism was rife, Webster's theories were widely accepted by the British Establishment, including such well-known politicians as Sir Winston Churchill who quoted extensively from her works in his attacks on the Bolsheviks in Russia. Webster became regarded as an unofficial expert on secret societies and revolutionary

movements by the British government and gave lectures on the subject to
the armed forces and Secret Services. Webster revealed her true political
colours in 1923. Her books had reviled Marxism as the modern cover for
the 'Jewish menace' and in that year she went a step further by joining the
British Fascist Party, which imitated Mussolini's new political
movement in Italy. This organization later developed into the British
Union of Fascists, led by Sir Oswald Mosley, which received
considerable media attention and public support in the 1930s.

Although Webster's researches were heavily prejudiced by her anti-
Semitic views and hatred of Communism the basic theme of her books
was the alleged manipulation of historical events by politically motivated
conspirators using the secret societies and the occult tradition as their
cover. This theme has been taken up by other modern researchers who
recognize the influence of the occult puppet masters in modern politics.
In order to establish how deeply the secret societies have penetrated
international politics it is necessary to understand how the history of the
twentieth century has been moulded by a hidden power group. This
group is not necessarily aligned to either the left or right wings of the
conventional political movements which have taken the public role in
shaping world events in the years since the end of the First World War. It
operates within both capitalism and Communism and has as its ultimate
goal a politico-spiritual vision which transcends both these materialistic
systems which are used to control the masses.

The four years from 1914 to 1918 represent one of the most significant
periods in modern history. They saw the destruction of three of the great
imperial powers which had dominated European politics in the previous
century. In this short period of time the Habsburg, Romanov and
Hohenstauffen dynasties were destroyed. The Great War also saw the
weakening of the foundations of the British Empire and both America
and Russia emerged from the war as potential super-powers of the
future. The war also saw the climax of German nationalism which,
through its messiah Adolf Hitler, spawned a new political force that
twenty years later would be responsible for another major European
conflict. From that terrible holocaust was born the Nuclear Age and the
present suicidal confrontation between the opposing power structures of
West and East who hold the world hostage with the threat of imminent
global destruction.

If we are to accept, as did the leaders of the defeated nations in 1918,
the role played by the secret societies in the First World War, the Russian
Revolution and the rise of National Socialism, it has to be realized that

these influences, both positive and negative, did not wane with the defeat of Germany in 1945 but continued into the post-war period and are still with us today. In general, as far as it can be detected at all by those who are not directly in contact with its working, this influence can be categorized as benign. However, the unpalatable fact must also be faced that in some instances the pursuit and exercise of power in the political arena can have a corrupting effect, especially when it encounters the inherent weaknesses of human nature.

The exposure of the P2 lodge in Italy was a rare example of the workings of a renegade secret society becoming public knowledge through the misdeeds of its leadership. Usually, because of their very nature, the secret societies work behind the scenes and their activities seldom become known to the outside world. Any interpretation of their activities must therefore be confined to an analysis of the outward signs of their influence within the overall pattern of international politics. These signs are occasionally revealed in major historical events or socio-political movements whose impact on mass consciousness is so great that the hidden hands behind them are briefly revealed to general view, albeit in a shadowy and indistinct form.

One classic example is the world government movement which in the decade following the First World War seems to have become the focus for the efforts of the leaders of the respectable secret societies who played no role in the events leading up to the 1914–18 conflict. Their goal seems to have been the elimination of the risk of any future outbreaks of war on a global scale. One of the political figures who played an influential role in the world government movement was President Woodrow Wilson of the USA, who was allegedly a secret member of a Rosicrucian Order. Wilson was a statesman who had an unusually idealistic view of world politics which sometimes led his more realistic critics to denounce him as a naive romantic. His foreign policy reversed past trends by respecting the rights of small nations and promoting non-intervention in the domestic disputes of other countries.

This foreign policy was responsible for Wilson's reluctance to allow the United States to be drawn into the war between Germany and Britain in 1914. He adopted a neutral stance and in fact engaged with Kaiser Wilhelm in protracted negotiations to bring a peace settlement. However, when details of a proposed military alliance between Mexico, Japan, and Germany, which would have involved Mexican troops invading Texas, was revealed, Wilson was reluctantly forced to act. In April 1917 the US Congress approved the President's declaration of war on the Axis powers and American troops were committed to the European conflict.

Influential power groups had already been urging the developed nations while war waged to create a neutral organization dedicated to international co-operation. Wilson was a prominent advocate of this idea which he recognized as a unique historical opportunity to prevent armed conflict between nations and secure a lasting world peace. This concept was also supported by the Great White Brotherhood, the esoteric group of occult adepts who were the hidden influence behind the secret societies. Following the entry of the Americans into the war, popular uprisings in the Austro-Hungarian Empire and public protests in Germany forced the Axis powers to seek a negotiated settlement. In 1918 a peace conference was convened in Paris to discuss terms.

President Wilson had already sent his special advisor, Colonel E.M. House, to begin talks with several of the Allied governments, with the objective of creating an international organization for world peace. Wilson himself travelled to the Paris peace conference where the foundations of a new League of Nations were laid. A covenant was drawn up by the founder members which agreed on a joint policy of collective security. The nations who participated in the formation of the League pledged to act jointly against any aggressor. They also promised to solve international disputes by arbitration, pursue graduated disarmament and establish an international court of justice.

In the 1920s the League of Nations set up its headquarters in Geneva, a city regarded by the secret societies as one of the world's major sacred power centres, and began to pursue the arduous task of promoting world peace and security. Unfortunately the failure of the US Congress to ratify the covenant of American membership weakened the position of the League. In the 1930s the organization's impotence in preventing the Sino-Japanese war, the invasion of Abbysinia (Ethopia) by Italy, and the annexation of Poland by Hitler which led to the Second World War contributed to its eventual demise with the outbreak of hostilities in 1939.

Despite the failure of the United States to become a full member of the League of Nations, Wilson did not abandon his dream of world government on different lines. In 1919 Colonel House travelled again to Paris but this time to have discussions with members of a British quasi-political group called the Round Table which also had branches in North America. In a meeting held in the Majestic Hotel in May 1919 the idea was mooted of an alternative international organization to the League of Nations. This new group would act as the co-ordinating agency for the establishment of a future world government dominated by Britain and the United States.

The idea of the Round Table had been conceived by the nineteenth-century diamond and gold magnate Cecil Rhodes, who gave his name to Rhodesia (Zimbabwe). Rhodes was a fanatical exponent of the world government concept and the idea behind The Round Table was to promote British imperialism worldwide. Conspiracy theorists have identified Rhodes' group as a classic example of a semi-public secret society with internationalist ambitions. It had been founded because Rhodes fervently believed that British values should be extended throughout the world, creating an imperial global power which would render war impossible. He was allegedly a disciple of Professor John Ruskin, the radical Oxford don who taught philosophy and art in the 1870s and who has been claimed as a follower of Adam Weishaupt and his Illuminist doctrines. In his will Rhodes left instructions to Lord Rothschild requesting time to expand the work of the Round Table which he had modelled on the organizational structure of the Jesuits and the Freemasons.

From its inception the Round Table had been influential in shaping British government policy, especially relating to foreign affairs. It is believed to have played an important role in the events leading up to the First World War. With the successful outcome of the 1918 peace conference it seems that the Round Table was anxious to extend its political influence on an international scale. An American branch of the group had already been founded and when Colonel House approached it with his President's grand plan for a world government the Round Table was more than eager to become involved in his idealistic venture.

The new organization which arose from the Paris meeting was on a smaller scale than the League of Nations, reflecting its more modest ambitions, but it shared the same aspirations. In Britain the organization was called the Institute for International Affairs (IIA) while in New York it operated as the Council for Foreign Relations (CFR). The finances for the group came from wealthy international bankers and it quickly recruited prominent American and British political figures who supported its aims. Initially the CFR was regarded by its critics as an élitist, right-wing power group and it was even accused of helping to finance Hitler's rise to power although no evidence has ever been found to support this claim. Following the Second World War however, the CFR has been labelled a promoter of international socialism through the United Nations. Conspiracy theorists claim it was the CFR who supported Henry Wallace's plan to have the Illuminist symbol of the eye in the triangle on the one dollar note. The CFR's apparent contradictory political ideals are said to be typical of modern Illuminati front groups which allegedly use both right and left ideologies to further their cause which transcends conventional politics.

In the eyes of their opponents, the CFR is currently dedicated to destroying the sovereignty of the United States, reversing the democratic process which instigated the 1776 American Revolution, promoting internationalism and the foundation of a world super state embracing both capitalism and Communism in a new political order. The evidence for this seems to be largely based on the neutral stance adopted by the CFR in American politics. It has recruited its membership from both the Democratic and Republican parties, and leading members of the CFR have included Adlai Stevenson, Robert and Edward Kennedy, Hubert Humphrey, John Foster Dulles, Robert McNamara, Henry Kissinger and Nelson Rockefeller. Several men who later became Presidents of the United States were CFR members earlier in their political careers such as Eisenhower, John Kennedy, Richard Nixon and Jimmy Carter.

After the Second World War the CFR turned its attention to supporting the United Nations Organization founded in 1945. The idea for this international organization developed in US State Development policy documents drawn up at the beginning of the war. A study group called the Committee on Post War Problems (CPWP) was set up with the brief to formulate plans for a new international and social organization to replace the old League of Nations. This policy unit was allegedly staffed by CFR agents who were working within the State Department manipulating US government foreign affairs.

The first use of the words 'United Nations' was by Franklin Roosevelt, who is said to have had secret society connections, in the Declaration of United Nations in January 1942. This was a declaration issued by twenty-six nations who had pledged to fight the Axis powers of Germany, Italy and Japan. However it was not until the end of the war that plans to form the United Nations were seriously considered. A conference on International Organizations met in San Francisco from April to June 1945 and deliberated on proposals worked out by China, the USSR, the UK, and the USA during a series of high-level meetings from August to October 1944.

The United Nations officially came into existence in October 1945 with the purpose of securing international peace in the post-war period. As with its predecessor, the League of Nations, the UN found this a difficult task even with the use of an international peace keeping force drawn from the armies of its member states. Since the 1960s the UN has become more concerned with economic and social issues, including education, science, environmental protection, health, the refugee problem, disaster relief, drug abuse, racism and human rights. Although in these areas the UN has had some success it seems unlikely that it will provide the basis for a future world government at this stage in its history.

Conspiracy theorists regard the UN with suspicion because of the alleged involvement of the CFR in its creation. Further suspicion has been cast on the UN by the activities of a shadowy group called the United World Federalists (UWF) which was founded in 1947 by two CFR members. The UWF promotes the setting up of a world governmental structure under the auspices of the United Nations involving countries from both the East and West power blocs. Right wingers who oppose the Soviet influence in the present UN see in this plan an Illuminist conspiracy to create a one world state based on Marxism.

The activities of the CFR have been linked with two other political 'think tanks' which have emerged in the post-war period and whose secret origins and unorthodox political views have labelled them as covers for the secret societies. These organizations are the Bilderberg Group and the Tri-lateral Commission and they have been suspected of being covert power groups engaged in the secret manipulation of international affairs. Because these groups go to extraordinary lengths to avoid publicity, hold their regular meetings in private and guard their important members by taking extreme security measures, the speculation concerning their real motives has become more and more sensationalized over the years.

The Bilderberg Group was founded in May 1954 and its first meeting took place in the Bilderberg Hotel in Osterbeck in Holland, hence the name it adopted. The chairman at the first meeting was Prince Bernhard of the Netherlands who remained in this position until 1976 when he was forced to resign over the financial scandal involving the Lockheed Aircraft Corporation. He was replaced by ex-British Prime Minister, Sir Alec Douglas-Home. There is no official membership list for the group but at its meetings held once or twice a year eighty to a hundred people drawn from the political, financial and media spheres are invited to attend, although few will reveal afterwards the discussions that take place behind closed doors.

What prompted the foundation of the Bilderberg Group? In his book *The Global Manipulators* Robert Eringer links them with the CIA and international Freemasonry. According to Eringer, the first Bilderberg conference was organized by a mysterious personage called Dr Joseph Retinger. He had been involved in secret activities for nearly half a century and was reputed to be the top agent for international Freemasonry. Retinger knew everybody who was anybody in European politics, although it was rumoured that he had been banned from 10 Downing Street when he accused the wife of the then Prime Minister, Lord Asquith, of being a practising lesbian.

During the First World War Retinger was in Mexico working for President Wilson when he uncovered a conspiracy by Texan oilmen to spark a war between the Mexicans and the United States. In the 1920s, despite his Masonic connections, he was involved in special missions for the Vatican and in 1924 he established a secret organization dedicated to European unity. Despite the rise of Nazism he continued his crusade for a united Europe and when war broke out he joined the Polish Free Forces in London. He parachuted into occupied Poland with the British SOE to assist the resistance movement during the Warsaw uprising.

In 1946, at a lecture given to the IIA (the British branch of the CFR) in London, Retinger expanded on his personal vision of a united Europe as a bulwark against post-war Soviet expansionist policies. His morbid fear of Communism led him to join the American Committee for a United Europe (ACUE) which was channelling funds to anti-Communist groups in Europe and included the future Pope Paul VI as its top agent in the Vatican. In his function as a member of ACUE, Retinger approached Prince Bernhard of the Netherlands and suggested that he use his Royal influence to help assemble a group of influential Europeans who shared the two men's anti-Communist views and belief in a united Europe. This new group would act as a select 'think tank' co-ordinating policies designed to combat the alleged Communist menace to Western society. In 1952 Retinger made contact with the CIA and requested the Agency to provide financial and moral support for the venture. Two years later the first meeting of the group was held in Holland with delegates attending from Europe and the USA.

Conspiracy theorists who see the Bilderbergers as an Illuminist front cite the fact that its steering committee consists of the odd number of 39 which is 13 + 13 + 13. In occultism the number thirteen has many mystical meanings and sinister associations. They also point out that Prince Bernhard's wife, Queen Juliana, has been involved in occult practices including Spiritualism and healing. Her daughter, Crown Princess Beatrix, attended a Bilderberg conference in 1965. This meeting was also attended by Prince Phillip and Lord Mountbatten and was held at the Villa d'Este on Lake Como in Italy. Como was, of course, the ancient headquarters of the Order of the Comacine who were the forerunners of the medieval Freemasons.

The Bilderberg Group was originally founded as an anti-Communist organization with a predominantly right-wing membership. However, in 1976, fifteen representatives from the Soviet Union attended one of its conferences in the Arizona desert. This move was interpreted by observers as a shift in focus by the Group from a united Europe opposing the Eastern bloc to the idealistic concept of world government promoted by internationalists within the secret societies. This change of emphasis coincided with the new policy of *détente* followed by CFR member Jimmy Carter when he became President.

Another mysterious power group associated with the CFR and the Bilderbergers is the Trilateral Commission which dabbles in international politics and supports the world government movement. The Trilateralists were the brainchild of certain American politicians who in the early 1970s became concerned that the traditional links between the United States were becoming weakened. Their plan was to create a new community of nations centred on North America but including Western Europe and Japan, which they identified as a future super power. The groundplan for this community was to begin with a policy group composed of industrialists and politicians from each geopolitical sphere. While on paper the Trilateralists are confined to co-operation between the United States, Japan and Europe the high number of CFR members who belong to it suggest that its inner doctrine is based on world government.

The director of the Trilateral Commission in the 1970s was Zbigniew Brzezinski who was a special advisor on national security in the Carter administration and a member of the CFR. He was quoted as saying, 'The world is not likely to unite behind a common ideology or a super government. The only practical hope is that it will now respond to a common concern for its own survival. The active promotion of such trilateral co-operation must now become the central priority of US policy.'

Both the Bilderbergers and the Trilateralists act as shadow governments promoting internationalist policies of European unity and world government. They act as a form of political Freemasonry offering world leaders and national insiders the chance to meet in secret to exchange information and discuss undisclosed social changes which can be put into practice in their respective countries. Individual members of these groups deliberately play down the real significance of these meetings but, despite this, world leaders take out valuable time from their work schedules to attend them. It is, of course, mere speculation to recognize in the workings of these covert power groups any resemblance to the Invisible College of the sixteenth-century Rosicrucians writ large on the modern stage of international politics.

Originally, Utopian, liberterian concepts were promoted by the medieval Freemasons and Rosicrucians. The occult adepts who were operating at the highest levels in those secret societies were genuinely concerned with the progress of humanity on both the material and spiritual level. They supported the political concept of an equalized society where everyone had the right to worship God in whatever form he or she believed in, and to follow the politics of their choice, providing they were based on democracy and freedom of thought and action. At a time when millions were enslaved to the medieval feudal system, the secret societies taught that all men and women were free individuals.

The secret societies advocated the reform of social conditions which imprisoned the soul, universal education for the masses and civil liberty. They believed the advantages of the new scientific research and the gifts of artistic creation were not the hidden treasure of a few but should be available to everyone. The secret societies believed that if knowledge were made more widespread a natural social progress would lead to the evolution of the individual from the common herd which was their long-term objective. The foundation of special organizations, such as the Royal Society, social movements and religious groups, was only a staging post for the grand plan of uniting religion, science and the arts into a universal philosophy for the enlightenment of the human race.

A very important aspect of the work of the secret societies has always been the ultimate unification of the world religions. This aim was based on the restoration of the pre-Christian Mystery Tradition, which had been persecuted by the early Church and forced to go underground in medieval Europe, and the recognition that all religions had originated in a universal spirituality referred to as the Perennial Philosophy, the Primordial Tradition or the Ancient Wisdom. The mystical beliefs of the secret societies were, and indeed are, based on the Hermetic maxim 'As above-so below' which teaches that the natural world is a material reflection of the spiritual. It forms the esoteric basis for the Ancient

Egyptian Mysteries, Gnosticism, Esoteric Christianity, the Cabbala, the Hermetic tradition, alchemy and societies such as the Templars, Freemasons and Rosicrucians. The occult doctrines of geomancy, alchemy, astrology and sexual magic taught by these secret societies were used as symbolic metaphors illustrating the progression of the individual from material darkness to the spiritual light of understanding.

We have traced how the political philosophy of the secret societies developed in the twentieth century but how did these esoteric teachings express themselves in the mass consciousness? Secret societies such as the Rosicrucians have very seldom exposed their inner activities to the public gaze, preferring to work within established occult organizations which, because of their élitist structure, have concealed their real work from the gaze and criticism of the profane. In rare instances these esoteric teachings have been presented by an initiate to the public in a way which has made them accessible to the average person. A classic example of this was the foundation of the Theosophical Society in 1875 by Madame Helena Blavatsky. The formation of this group seems to have been a deliberate act by the Great White Brotherhood to establish the occult tradition in materialistic European society and to unite the spiritual beliefs of East and West.

Another initiate of the secret societies who was instrumental in the spread of their esoteric teachings in the early part of the twentieth century was Rudolf Steiner (1861–1925). He had been a member of the German Theosophical Society and had connections with various Masonic and Rosicrucian groups. He spent some years as the secretary of the German Theosophical Society and had extensive contacts with Annie Besant, the left-wing activist who had replaced Madame Blavatsky as the leader of the TS. In 1909 Steiner separated from the Theosophical Society, declaring that he was opposed to the policy which had become popular in Theosophical circles in regard to the emergence of a new Messiah. Steiner's work was preeminently Christ-centered, and he strongly held that Christ incarnated only once as described in the New Testament. Because of the new direction the Theosophical Society was taking, Steiner resigned to form a new occult group called the Anthroposophical Society.

Steiner began to tour Europe lecturing on his theories about the spiritual value of art and alternative education which seem to have been deeply rooted in Rosicrucian tradition even though he had given them a modern gloss. In common with the medieval Masons, Steiner believed that the new spiritual impulse he felt flowing through the world had to be expressed through the medium of radical architecture. This led him to design an ultra-modern building at Basle in Switzerland to house the headquarters of his new occult fraternity. His unconventional ideas on educating children based on self-expression and artistic skills were crystallized in the founding of special Steiner schools which still flourish today.

At the end of the First World War Steiner was briefly involved in politics when, being sympathetic to the world government concept, he advocated a solution to the problems of central Europe based on ideas of liberty, fraternity, equality and freedom which seem to have been based on Masonic and Rosicrucian teachings. He also promoted a vision of human development and evolution which drew its inspiration from neo-Manichean doctrines based on the eternal struggle between the powers of darkness and the forces of light. These teachings however were largely eclipsed by his ideas in the fields of organic farming, alternative medicine, the spirituality of art and the education of young children, where he brought together the latest scientific research with ancient occult techniques to provide a unique solution to many social problems.

It is significant that many of Steiner's ideas have been accepted and adopted by followers of the modern New Age movement which arose in the early 1970s but had its spiritual roots in the counter-culture of the 1960s. Today it has become fashionable to regard the Sixties as a wasted period of permissive self-indulgence which spawned our present social problems of drug abuse, political extremism and sexual immorality. Such a view is a simplistic one which ignores the fact that the period represents one of the most important influxes of spiritual energy ever experienced by Westernized society.

On one level it was a time of change and social upheaval when young people threw aside the moral shackles imposed by convention and elected to follow a radically different lifestyle to that of their parents. This new way of living embraced self-sufficiency, vegetarian diets, psychedelic drugs, astrology, radical politics, pacifism, free love, rock music, bizarre clothes and a spiritual devotion to exotic forms of religion based on Eastern mysticism and Western paganism.

It is difficult because of the fragmented nature of the counter-culture to identify clearly the esoteric sources which were at work behind the scenes or to pinpoint any actual involvement by the inheritors of the Rosicrucian and Masonic traditions. However the Sixties movement brought into public consciousness many of the symbols and beliefs of the occult tradition which became generally accepted as a natural part of daily life. The concepts, philosophies and ideals which arose from this important historical period were deeply influenced by more traditional esoteric beliefs and they were later to be taken on board by the New Age movement of the 1970s and 1980s.

Central to the beliefs of the new spirituality is the imminent dawning of the Aquarian Age. According to occult tradition every 2,000 years the world enters a new Zodiacal Age. The Piscean Age began with the birth of Jesus and was dominated by Christianity as the most influential world religion. The beginning of a new Zodiacal Age provides us with a unique chance to accept the eternal truths of the Ancient Wisdom in a new form. This changeover period between the Piscean and the Aquarian Ages is an important one because it is the first time in recorded history that our species has had the ability to commit global genocide and to destroy the planet by either a nuclear holocast or an ecological disaster.

This changeover period is, as we can see from the daily events recorded in the mass media, a time of confusion, apprehension and extremism on a planetary scale. Dark forces are manifesting in the world, symbolized by international terrorism, famine, ultra-materialism, dictatorship and religious fanaticism. Such manifestations are to be expected because, according to occult belief, the new waves of spiritual energy which flow through the planet at these changeover periods meet with resistance from the old energies which are the psychic leftovers from the dying age.

The Aquarian impulse which motivated the Sixties generation encompassed an idealistic, if romantic, vision of a Utopian society based on love and peace. War would be eliminated by common consent and all countries would unite in a non-political planetary brotherhood of nations. In this idealistic society every individual would have the right to worship whatever God (or gods) they chose and there would be complete freedom and equality between the sexes. It was a dream which would have been instantly recognized by sixteenth-century Rosicrucians such as Sir Francis Bacon and the Grand Masters of the Masonic lodges who influenced the American and French Revolutions.

In the counter-culture the hybrid forms of mysticism which arose as a side effect of the search for individual freedom and developed into the New Age movement drew from historical sources which can be identified with the secret societies. The late 1960s and early 1970s saw a tremendous revival of interest in occultism, Spiritualism, paganism, astrology and magical practices which was a reaction to the failure of orthodox religion to provide spiritual sustenance for the new educated class. Like Gnosticism, the New Age movement attempted – and still attempts – to synthesize Eastern and Western forms of religion and offer the individual seeker the ability to communicate with God without the interference of a priestly middle man.

The New Age movement and the occult revival, while claiming to be presenting a new style of spirituality, still relies on the traditional philosophies of past occultists such as Blavatsky, Besant, Steiner, Alice Bailey and Aleister Crowley to provide its theological framework. Rare texts of medieval magic have been unearthed and reprinted in cheap editions while interest in ley lines, stone circles, Celtic mythology and ancient Egyptian religion flourish in neo-pagan revivals supported by numerous magical groups and witch covens.

One of the most important aspects of the New Age movement is its holistic approach to spirituality. It embraces such varied subjects as ecology and 'Green' politics, alternative medicine, hi-tech science, Eastern religion, quantum physics and feminism in an attempt to look at society in a unified way. In common with the Rosicrucian-Masonic tradition the New Agers have realized that if society is to be transformed then a common ground must be found between religion, science and art, and spiritual concepts and principles applied to these disciplines. The 'one planet' ideal of the New Age groups which has been adopted by the Green political movement has many similarities with the secret societies' aspirations towards world government. In fact many of the Theosophically derived occult fraternities and New Age groups are strong advocates of the ideal of a global government.

The New Age concern for sexual equality and the importance of the feminine principle is another aspect of Aquarian spirituality which links it with the aims of the secret societies. In the last 2,000 years our planetary culture has been dominated and stifled by the forces of patriarchy which, in both a religious and political sense, have formed a primary restriction on the progressive work carried out by those who follow the tenets of the Ancient Wisdom. We have seen in our historical investigation of the secret societies that one of the common beliefs shared by the pagan Mystery cults, the Gnostics, the Cathars, the troubadours, the Templars, the Freemasons and the Rosicrucians was a reverance for the feminine principle. This reverence has always been a key focus for adherents to the secret tradition and is the key to understanding the occult symbols they used to reveal their spiritual truths to initiates and to the outside world.

The Aquarian Age, whose spiritual movement is at present undisciplined and immature, is destined according to the inner teachings of the secret societies to provide a new balancing of the male and female energies. This will in turn create a better relationship between humanity and Mother Earth and usher in a period of increased spiritual awareness. The various spiritual ideals expressed in New Age teachings are gradually filtering through to society creating subtle changes in the way ordinary people look at their planet and fellow human beings. On a mundane level the opening of health stores, the trend towards alternative medicine, the practice of meditation by tired businessmen, widespread support for ecological action groups like Greenpeace and Friends of the Earth, the interest in Eastern religions, Christian mysticism and Western paganism, and the widesrpead practice of occult techniques like astrology are all examples of the social and spiritual changes which can be expected to accelerate as we enter the Aquarian Age around the year 2025.

While the New Age movement has updated the occult tradition and presented it in a way which has mass appeal it has sometimes produced a simplistic and superficial version of the Ancient Wisdom. By contrast, traditional Rosicrucianism (as the inherited tradition of the pre-Christian Mysteries) has been widely represented in modern times by several semi-secret groups who claim descent from the original fraternity of the Middle Ages. These groups include the Rosicrucian Fellowship, the Fraternity of the Rosy Cross, the Ancient and Mystical Order of the Rosy Cross (AMORC) and, most recently, the Lectorium Rosicucianum.

These neo-Rosicrucian fraternities all claim genuine connections with the medieval Order of the Rosy Cross and are linked together by either common membership or affiliation. The Rosicrucian Fellowship was founded by a German-American of Danish extraction, Max Heindel (1865–1919), who had been a leading member of the German Theosophical Society. While living in Europe Heindel claimed he was initiated in a secret Rosicrucian temple in Bohemia (Czechoslovakia) and given instructions to form a new branch of the Order in the United States. Because he was a practising astrologer Heindel introduced elements of astrological symbolism into his neo-Rosicrucian tradition.

The Fraternity of the Rosy Cross claimed descent from P.B. Randolph who was involved in sex magic and had been connected with the OTO. The FRC itself was linked with groups which had in turn derived their inspiration from continental occult fraternities which mixed Rosicrucian and Masonic beliefs, including the Kabbalistic Order of the Rosy Cross, founded in France in 1889. The AMORC has a high public profile and places regular advertisements in popular newspapers and magazines, offering a correspondence course to its new members. It has over 50,000 members in the United States and from its worldwide headquarters in San José, California it operates lodges in Britain, France, Australia, Germany, Switzerland and South Africa. Its teachings involve the occult use of colour and light, alchemy, the perfection of the physical body, the development of will, the nature of matter and the mysteries of time and space. In common with the traditions of medieval Rosicrucianism, AMORC advocates a synthesis of science and religion.

In contrast to the above groups the Dutch based Lectorium Rosicrucinum sidesteps the medieval Rosicrucians and claims to trace its ideology back directly to the pre-Christian pagan Mystery schools. Formed in Holland in the 1920s it holds public meetings in European capital cities to introduce its neo-Gnostic teachings to interested parties. It would appear to draw some of its beliefs from the Cathar heresy and is a unique phenomenon among modern neo-Rosicrucian fraternities.

Even less orthodox survivals of the Rosicrucian tradition exist today which have emerged from the occult revival of recent years and the influence of several different groups who claim to preserve the traditional workings of the Hermetic Order of the Golden Dawn and other nineteenth-century magical and occult societies. In addition several rival organizations exist in Europe and the United States claiming to be the genuine OTO and there are new occult groups following Crowley's teachings. These include the Nu-Isis Lodge, the Knights of the Solar Cross and the Order of Maat. Although there is little evidence to suggest that any of these branches or imitators of the OTO are involved in political activities, Crowley's personal brand of anarcho-liberterianism, summed up by the slogan 'Nothing is forbidden. Everything is permitted', which has been described by his critics as magical fascism, has attracted a new generation of would-be magicians and occultists.

The Templar tradition is also represented in many different forms in modern times by chilvaric Orders and Masonic fraternities which claim descent from the original knights but can usually be traced back to the eighteenth-century revival of Templarism. There were new revivals of Templarism in France during the nineteenth century which were linked with Freemasonry. One branch of this Templar tradition exerted its influence during the days of the wartime Vichy government when Masonry was forbidden in line with the Nazi policy on secret societies. In this period the neo-Templars became involved with synarchism, a new political movement which combined bureaucratic socialism, pacifism and the technological control of society. It seems to have received support as an anti-Vichy and anti-Nazi movement from foreign

Intelligence agencies, including MI6. In common with the original Templars, and most wartime Allied politicians, it was committed to a united Europe after the War. As we have seen however in the 1960s and 1970s, Templarism in France seems to have been associated with right-wing politics and forged international links with politically motivated Masonic groups such as the P2 Lodge in Italy.

The most recent of the modern neo-Templars groups in France is the oddly named *L'Ordre Internationale Chevalvesque Tradition Solaire* or International Order of Chivalry, Solar Tradition. It was founded by a Templar Order in 1984 with the task of reviving genuine Templarism in the modern world in preparation for the coming Aquarian Age. The impetus for this resurgence of Templar activity came in 1952 when representatives of the Order met secretly at an old country house in Switzerland which had once been owned by the Knights of Malta.

According to its manifesto published in 1987 the OICTS encourages the ancient civilizing ideals of chivalry, campaigns for spiritual unity, fosters the fraternity of all races, integrates spirituality into everyday life, and works to improve the quality of life by the adoption of spiritual principles. The new Order has established itself in North America because it believes that continent has an important role to play in the Aquarian Age. It seems to operate a theology based on esoteric Christianity, the Grail Mysteries and a respect for the feminine principle. For this reason women are admitted to the Order on equal terms to men which is a direct departure from the medieval Templar tradition.

In the modern occult groups who claim to be following the traditions of the medieval secret societies, and these include the neo-Templars, esoteric Masonic lodges and such shadowy organizations as the Priory of Sion, several common themes come together. Politically they include a unified Europe, based on spiritual principles. At present the EEC with its overweight bureaucracy and food surpluses seems a transitory shadow of the great plan envisioned for Europe in the twenty-first century by those who are working on an esoteric level behind the scenes of international politics.

The occult conspiracy which has been outlined in these pages is in reality a historical review of attempts by initiates of the secret tradition to progress the evolutionary development of the human race in the social and spiritual spheres. As it will have become apparent these attempts were often perverted and frustrated by those lesser souls whose only concern was with the vain glories of the material world, the acquiring of personal power, the suppression of knowledge for selfish ends and the control of the masses for political purposes.

Many renegade elements have attempted to use the secret societies as a cover for their own power games and some of these have worn the masks of initiates. The legitimate efforts by the secret societies and occult fraternities to advance social progress and eradicate ignorance have often been grossly misrepresented by prejudiced observers who had their own reasons for wanting these efforts to end in failure. In our study of the hidden events which have shaped history we have not ignored these negative aspects. They provide an invaluable, if depressing, insight into these human minds who work for the downfall of civilization. However, the reader can be assured that even in the crisis torn 1980s initiates of the Great White Brotherhood are still working behind the scenes, even if their existence is not recognized or is even denied by those who have no knowledge of their activities and little awareness of the spiritual reality beyond the physical world.

CHRONOLOGY

The following is not intended to be an exhaustive chronology of the influence of the occult tradition and the secret societies on world history. It does highlight key events which can be traced to these sources since ancient times.

40,000 BCE

Early establishment of Mystery schools, as depicted in the Lascaux cave paintings.

30,000 BCE

According to some occult traditions this period saw the colonization of Asia and Australasia by the inhabitants of the lost continent of Lemuria or Mu Goddess worship and matriarchal cultures established worldwide.

10,000 BCE

Evidence suggestive of early contact between extraterrestrials and Stone Age tribes in Tibet.

9,000–8,000 BCE

Estimated date of the destruction of Atlantis, according to some occult traditions. The Atlantean priesthood flee to establish colonies in the British Isles, Western Europe, North Africa and South America. Rise of the Northern Mystery Tradition centred on the island of Thule and the Aryan culture. Invention of the runic alphabet.

5,000 BCE

First primitive cities established in the Middle East. Agriculture begins with domestication of animals such as sheep and goats. Possible contact between extraterrestrials and early Sumerian culture.

5,000–3,000 BCE

Formation of the two lands in pre-dynastic Egypt ruled by outsiders (Isis and Osiris). The Egyptian pantheon of gods established including Horus, Thoth, Set, Ra, Ptah and Hathor. Pharoahs regarded as the divine representatives of the Gods.

3,000–2,000 BCE

Building of burial mounds and chambered tombs in Western Europe and the Mediterranean area; the Sphinx and the Great Pyramids of Giza and Cheops of Egypt, and the ziggurat (Towers of Babel) in Ur. Sarmoung Brotherhood founded in Babylon.

2,000–1,000 BCE

Reign of Thothmes III in Egypt (c. 1480). Foundation of the Rosicrucian Order. Reign of Akhenaton (c. 1370 BCE) who establishes the mystical Brotherhood of Aton dedicated to the worship of the Sun as a symbol of the Supreme Creator. Erection of Stonehenge and other megalithic stone circles in the British Isles. Reign of Ankhenaton's son Tutankhamun who re-establishes the old pantheon of Egyptian gods and goddesses. Moses leads Children of Israel out of slavery in Egypt during the reign of Rameses II to the promised land of Canaan.

1,000–500 BCE

Foundation of the Dionysian Artificers. The building of Solomon's temple (c. 950). Establishment of the city states of Greece and the Olympic pantheon of gods to replace earlier Nature worship. First temples erected in Mexico, Peru and southwest North America. Celts invade Western Europe. Decline of Goddess worship and rise of patriarchal sky gods personified by priest-kings. Rome founded (750).

500 BCE–001 CE

Celtic culture established in Britain. The foundation of Druidic wisdom colleges in Gaul (France) and the British Isles. Odin recognized as major god of the Northern Mysteries replacing the Mother Goddess and is credited with inventing the runes. Buddha, Lao Tze, Confucius, Pythagoras, Plato and Zoroaster preach their new religions and philosophies. Maya culture in South America. Establishment of Eleusinian mystery cults. Rise of the Essene sect in Palestine and Judea. Birth of Jesus of Nazareth.

001–400 CE

Jesus possibly travels to India, Tibet and Britain to be initiated into the esoteric traditions of East and West. Crucified for his radical political and religious ideas (c. 33). Joseph of Arimanthea establishes first Celtic Church at Glastonbury (c. 37). Invasion of Britain by Roman legions and suppression of the Druids (40–60). Paul travels to Asia Minor and Greece preaching his version of the gospel (50). Jewish revolt against Roman rule led by Zealots (66). Essenes suppressed and Dead Sea Scrolls hidden in caves. Temple in Jerusalem destroyed by Romans (70). New testament written. The Nazarenes break away from Judaism to found the Christian

Church (c. 80). Ormus is converted to Esoteric Christianity by Mark. Mithraism and the Mysteries of Isis compete with Christianity in the Roman Empire. Mani, a Persian high priest of Zoroastrianism, is crucified (276). Emperor Constantine declares Christianity the official religion of the Roman Empire. The Council of Nicea defines heresy, condemns paganism and lays the theological foundation for the Catholic or Universal Church (325). Constantine's successor Julian the Apostate (361-363) briefly re-establishes the pagan old religion. Emperor Theodosius outlaws the worship of the pagan gods in Rome and closes the pagan temples (378). Invasion of Rome, Greece and Europe by the barbarians led by the dwarf Atilla the Hun (395-480). Withdrawal of the Roman legions from Britain (395). Foundation of the Order of Comacine by ex-members of the Roman College of Architects.

500-1,000 CE

Mohammed founds Islam (dies 632). Celtic Church outlawed by Council of Whitby (664). Foundation of first Sufi secret societies (c. 700). First written translation of Emerald Tablet of Hermes Trismegistus. Charlemagne founds alleged first Rosicrucian lodge in Toulouse (898). Foundation of the Cathars, Druzes and Yezedi (900). Heretical Catholic monks found first Rosicrucian college (1,000).

1000-1400 CE

Foundation of the Order of the Devoted of Assassins by Hasan-i-Sabbah (1034-1124) and the Order of St John (1050). First Crusade to the Holy Land (1095). Capture of the city of Jerusalem by Godfrey de Bouillan, founder of the Priory of Sion (1099). Assassins infiltrate Thuggee cult in India. Foundation of the Order of the Knights of the Temple of Solomon in Jerusalem (1118). Charter granted to the Priory of Sion by Pope Alexander II (1178). Crusade launched against Cathars (1208). Inquisition created to fight heresy (1215). Massacre of the Cathars at Montsegur in Southern France (1241). Troubadours practising their cult of courtly love. Occult schools teaching the Cabbala and alchemy established in Spain by the Moors. Count Rudolf von Habsburg crowned as Holy Roman Emperor (1273). Knights Templars arrested by King Phillip of France on charges of devil worship, heresy and sexual perversion (1307). Templar Order disbanded by papal decree (1313). Last official Grand Master of the Templars, Jacques de Molay, burnt at the stake and the Order goes underground (1314).

1400-1600 CE

Alleged life of Christian Rosenkreutz (1379-1482). Foundation of the Order of the Garter by Edward III (1348). First publication of the *Corpus Hermeticum* by the Medici family in Italy (1460). Publication of *Malleus Malifiracum* and the papal bull of Pope Innocent which began the medieval witch hunting hysteria (1484 and 1486). Martin Luther begins Reformation (1521). Henry Agrippa refers to the Templars as Gnostics and worshippers of the phallic god Priapus (1530). Life of Dr John Dee (1527–1608). Foundation of the British Secret Service by Sir Francis Walsingham. Birth of Johann Valenti Andrea (1586). Life of Sir Francis Bacon (1561–1626). Defeat of the Spanish Armada, with magical help from the New Forest witches (1588).

1600–1700 CE

Foundation of the Virginia Company by James I (1606). The Romanovs become Czars of Russia (1613). Publication of Rosicrucian manifesto (1614). Life of Elias Ashmole (1617–1692). Voyage of *The Mayflower* to New England and the publication of Sir Francis Bacon's novel *The New Atlantis* (1620). Establishment of the pagan community of Merrymount in Massachusetts by Thomas Morton. English Civil War begins (1642). First English Masonic guild accepts non-stonemasons into its meetings (1646?). Charles I convicted of treason and beheaded (1649). Oliver Cromwell allegedly makes pact with the Devil in order to retain power. Introduction of Freemasonry to American colonies by Dutch settlers (1658). Order of Pietists founded in Pennsylvania (1694).

1700–1800 CE

Birth of the Comte de Saint-Germain (1710). Masonic Grand Lodge of England and Druid Order founded (1717). First Masonic lodge founded in France (1721). Benjamin Franklin initiated as Mason (1731). Chevalier Alexander Ramsey informs French Masons they are heirs to the Templar tradition (1736). Roman Church condemns Masonry (1738). Birth of Count Cagliostro. Comte de Saint-Germain involved in Jacobite plot to restore Stuart dynasty to the English throne (1743). Society of Flagellants and Skopski founded in Russia (1750). George Washington initiated as a Mason (1752). Sir Francis Dashwood founds the Hell Fire Club. Franklin visits England to discuss the future of American colonies with Dashwood (1758). Foundation of the Rite of the Strict Observance by Baron von Hund based on the Templar tradition. Frederick of Prussia founds Order of the Architects of Africa and uses the title Illuminati to describe his neo-Masonic lodges (1768). Franklin elected Grand Master of the Nine Sisters lodge in Paris (1770). Grand Orient founded in France (1771). Boston Tea Party (1773). Washington appointed Commander-in-Chief of the new American Army (1775). Order of Perfectibilists or Illuminati founded. American Revolution (1776). Czar Peter I founds the Secret Circle (1778). Supposed death of the Comte de Saint-Germain (1784). Grand Masonic Congress allegedly plots French Revolution. Cagliostro involved in Diamond Necklace Affair. Illuminati banned in Bavaria and goes underground (1785). French Revolution (1789). Illuminist conspiracy to overthrow the Habsburgs (1794).

1800–1900 CE

Count Grabinka founds secret society in St Petersburg based on Martinism and Rosicrucianism (1803). French republican plot to assassinate Napoleon

Bonaparte by placing a bomb under his coach, led by occultist Fabre d'Olivet. Emperor Napoleon takes control of French Masonry (1805). Revived Templar Order in France celebrates the martyrdom of de Molay with public requiem (1808). Foundation of the Order of the Sublime Perfects (1809). Eliphas Levi (1810–1875) reveals the secret symbolism of the Templar idol Baphomet. Czar Alexander I and Emperor Francis von Habsburg unite to defeat Italian revolution incited by secret societies. John Quincy Adams, initiate of the Dragon Society, is elected US President (1820). Czar Alexander outlaws Masonry in Russia (1822). Decembrist secret society attempts coup when Alexander – allegedly – dies (1825). Anti-Masonic Party founded in USA to combat secret societies in American politics (1828). Wagner joins the *Vaterlandsverein*, a secret society dedicated to the formation of a pan-European federation of nations. Masonic convention at Strasbourg allegedly plots second French Revolution (1848). Napoleon III condemns Grand Orient for dabbling in radical politics (1850). Paschal Randolph founds Hermetic Brotherhood of the Light (1858). Abraham Lincoln is assassinated (1865). Klu Klux Klan founded (1866). Society of Rosicrucians in Anglia founded (1867). Foundation of the Theosophical Society by Madame Blavatsky on instructions of the Great White Brotherhood. Birth of Aleister Crowley (1875). Mysterious suicide of ArchDuke Rudolf von Habsburg at a hunting lodge at Mayerling (1889). Foundation of the Hermetic Order of the Golden Dawn (1888). Assassination of Empress Elizabeth Von Habsburg by anarchist (1898).

1900–1987 CE

Foundation of the Ordo Templi Orientis (1900). International Order of Co-Freemasonry founded (1902). Publication of *The Protocols of the Wise Men of Zion* in Russia (1905). Foundation of the Ancient and Mystical Order of the Rosae Crucis (1909). Black Hand Society founded (1911). Aleister Crowley accepted as head of the British branch of the OTO. Order of the Temple of the Rosy Cross founded (1912). Assassination of Archduke Franz Ferdinand and Archduchess Sophia von Habsburg. Attempted murder of Rasputin. First World War begins (1914). Kaiser Wilhelm abdicates. Habsburg dynasty is overthrown. Bolshevik Revolution in Russia (1917-18). Foundation of German Workers Party by Thule Society (1919). Hitler joins GWP and changes its name to National Socialist Party (1920). Crowley employed by MI6. Cardinal Roncalli, later Pope John XXIII, allegedly joins Rosicrucian Order. Hitler becomes first chancellor of the Third Reich (1933). Roosevelt places Illuminist symbol of eye in triangle on dollar bill (1935). Nazi invasion of England prevented by New Forest witches (1940). Rudolf Hess lured to Britain on peace mission by fake astrological data (1941). Order of the Temple revived in France (1952). First Bilderberg meeting (1954). Foundation of P2 Lodge (1960). Death of Pope Paul VI, election and alleged murder of Pope John Paul I, and election of Pope John Paul II (1978). Exposure of P2 conspiracy. Attempt to assassinate John Paul II (1981). L'Ordre Internationale Chevelresque Tradition Solaire founded on instructions of the revived Order of the Temple in France (1984).

BIBLIOGRAPHIC NOTES

In any book which deals with controversial subjects and an alternative version of history, the issue of references will always be a contentious one. Some of the material in this book is based upon my own interpretation of historical events in the light of more than twenty five years of research into occultism, parapolitics and secret societies. Other information was provided by insider sources who do not wish to be indentified. The following list of biographical references is provided for those readers who wish to follow up my primary sources for most of the available esoteric material in the book.

CHAPTER ONE
THE ANCIENT MYSTERIES

Dionysian Artificers
Costa, Hippolyte, *The Dionysian Artificers*. London: Sherwood, Nelly & Jones, 1820.
Hall, M.P., *Masonic Orders of Fraternity*. Los Angeles: Philosophical Research Society, 1950.
Steers, Albert, *Cyclopedia of Fraternities*. London: Hamilton Publishing Co., 1899.

Freemasonry
Hall, M.P., *Freemasonry of the Ancient Egyptians*. Los Angeles: Philosophical Research Society, 1971.
Heckleton, Charles, *The Secret Societies of all Ages & Countries*. London: George Redway, 1897.
Knight, Stephen, *The Brotherhood*. London: Granada, 1983.
Ward, J.S.M., *Freemasonry of the Ancient Gods*. London: Simpkin, Marshall & Kent, 1926.
Ward, J.S.M., *Who Was Hiram Abiff?* London: The Baskerville Press, 1925.

Goddess Worship
Black, Barbara, *The Book of Lilith*. York Beach, Maine: Nicholas Hay, 1986.
Hall, M. P., *Secret Teachings of All Ages*. Los Angeles: Philosophical Research Society, 1961.
Patai, Raphael, *The Hebrew Goddess*. Hoboken, New Jersey: Ktav Publishing House, 1967.

Rosicrucian Order
Lewis, H. Spencer, *Rosicrucian Questions & Answers*. San Jose: AMORC, 1929.

Temple Symbolism
Horne, Alexander, *King Solomon's Temple in the Masonic Tradition*. Aquarian Press, 1972.
Wood, David, *Genesis: The First Book of Revelation*. Tunbridge Wells, Kent, England: The Baton Press, 1986.

Other
Harrison, Michael, *The Roots of Witchcraft*. London: Frederick Muller, 1973.
Pagels, Eliane, *The Gnostic Gospels*. New York: Random House Inc., 1979.
Pennick, Nigel, *Sacred Geometry*. London: Turnstone Press, 1980.
Spence, Lewis, *The Myths of Ancient Egypt*. London: George Harrap, MCMXV.

CHAPTER TWO
THE CURSE OF THE TEMPLARS

Cathars
Keightley, T., *Secret Societies of the Middle Ages*. London: C. Cox & Co., 1848.

Death of Jesus
Baignet, Michael, *Holy Blood, Holy Grail*. New York: Dell Publishing Co., Inc., 1982.
Leigh, Richard and Henry Lincoln, *The Messanic Legacy*. London: Jonathan Cape, 1986.

Islam and Christianity
Billings, Michael, *The Cross & The Crescent*. London: BBC Publications, 1987.

Islamic Sects
Burman, Edward, *The Assassins*. Wellingborough, England: Aquarian Press/Crucible, 1987.
Daraul, Arkon, *Secret Societies*. London: Frederick Muller, 1961.

Knights Templar
Burman, Edward, *The Templars: Knights of God*. Wellingborough, England: Crucible, 1986.
Howarth, Stephen, *The Knight Templars*. London: William Collins, 1982.
Levi, Eliphas, *Transcendental Magic*. London: Rider & Co.

Mystery Cults
Begg, Ean, *The Cult of the Black Virgin*. London: Arkana, 1985.
Godwin, Jocelyn, *Mystery Religions of the Ancient World*. London: Thames & Hudson, 1981.

Priory of Sion
Baignet, Leigh & Lincoln, *Holy Blood, Holy Grail*. New York: Dell Publishing Co., Inc., 1982.

Sufism
Bennett, J.D., *The Masters of Wisdom*. London: Turnstone Press, 1977.

Shah, Idries, *The Way of the Sufi*. London: Cape, 1961.

Other
Boyce, Mary, *Zoroastrians*. London: Routledge & Kegan Paul, 1979.
Jones, Hans, *The Gnostic Religion*. Boston: Beacon Press, 1958.
Walker, Benjamin, *Gnosticism*. Wellingborough, England: Aquarian Press, 1983.

CHAPTER THREE
THE ROSICRUCIAN CONNECTION

Johann Valentin Andrea
Hall, M.P., *Orders of Universal Reformation*. Los Angeles: Philosophical Research Society, 1949.

Elias Ashmole
McIntosh, Christopher, *The Rosicrucians*. Wellingborough, England: Crucible, 1987.

Compte Cagliostro
Wilgus, Neal, The Illuminoids. Albuquerque: Sun Books, 1978.

John Dee
Deacon, Richard, *A History of British Secret Service*. London: Frederick Muller.
Fell, Charlotte, *John Dee*. London: Constable & Co., 1909.
French, Peter, *John Dee*. London: Routledge & Kegan Paul, 1972.

Comte de Mirabeau
Birch, Una, *Secret Societies of the French Revolution*. London: John Lane & Co.

Jacques de Molay
Partner, Dr. Peter, *The Murdered Magicians*. Oxford: Oxford University Press, 1981.

Comte de Saint-Germain
Hall, M.P., *Secret Teachings of all Ages*. Los Angeles: Philosophical Research Society, 1961.

Hermeticism
Scott, Walter, *Hermetica*. Boston: Shambhala Publications, 1985.

Knights Templar
Partner, Dr. Peter, *The Murdered Magicians*. Oxford: Oxford University Press, 1981.

Masonic Lodge Neuf Soeurs
Burch, Una, *Secret Societies of the French Revolution*. London: John Lane & Co.

Masonry
Frost, Thomas, *The Secret Societies of the European Revolution*. London: Tinsley Bros., 1876.

Andrew Ramsey
McIntosh, C., *The Rosicrucians*. Wellingborough, England: Crucible, 1987.

Rosicrucianism
Lewis, H. Spencer, *Rosicrucian Questions & Answers*. San Jose: AMORC, 1929.

McIntosh, Christopher, *The Rosicrucians*. Wellingborough, England: Crucible, 1987.

Royal Society
Hall, M.P., *Orders of Universal Reformation*. Los Angeles: Philosophical Research Society, 1949.

Templar Revival in Germany
Partner, Dr. Peter, *The Murdered Magicians*. Oxford: Oxford University Press, 1981.

Adam Weishaupt
Roberts, J.M., *The Mythology of the Secret Societies*. London: Secker & Warburg, 1972.

CHAPTER FOUR
THE AMERICAN DREAM

American Flag
Hall, M.P., *Secret Teachings of All Ages*. Los Angeles: Philosophical Research Society, 1961.

Sir Francis Bacon
Dawkins, Peter, *The Great Vision*. Stratford-upon-Avon: Francis Bacon Research Trust, 1982.
Hall, M.P., *America's Assignment with Destiny*. Los Angeles: Philosophical Research Society, 1950.

John Wilkes Booth
Wilgus, Neal, *The Illuminoids*. Albuquerque: Sun Books, 1978.

Christopher Columbus
Hall, M.P., *America's Assignment with Destiny*. Los Angeles: Philosophical Research Society, 1951.

Sir Francis Dashwood
Colquhoun, Ithell, *The Sword of Wisdom*. Channel Islands: Neville Spearman, 1975.
Towers, Eric Dashwood, *The Man & the Myth*. Wellingborough, England: Crucible, 1986.

Benjamin Franklin
Towers, Eric Dashwood, *The Man & the Myth*. Wellingborough, England: Crucible, 1987.
Hall, M.P., *America's Assignment with Destiny*. Los Angeles: Philosophical Research Society, 1950.

Great Seal
Raymond, E., *The Great Seal of America*. Thousand Oaks, California: Artison Sales, 1979.

Great White Brotherhood
Tomas, Andrew, *Shamballa: Oasis of Light*. London: Sphere Books, 1977.

Hermetic Brotherhood of the Light
McIntosh, Christopher, *The Rosicrucians*. Wellingborough, England: Crucible, 1987.

The Holy Grail and The Aquarian Age
Tomas, Andrew, *Shamballa: Oasis of Light*. London: Sphere Books, 1977.

Johannes Kilpius and The Pietists
Hall, M.P., *America's Assignment with Destiny*. Los Angeles: Philosophical Research Society, 1950.

Masonry
Hall, M.P., *America's Assignment with Destiny*. Los Angeles: Philosophical Research Society, 1951.

Ordo Templi Orientis
McIntosh, Christopher, *The Rosicrucians*. Wellingborough, England: Crucible, 1987.

Other
Mannix, D., *The Hellfire Club*. London: Four Square Books, 1961.

CHAPTER FIVE
GERMAN NATIONALISM & THE BOLSHEVIK REVOLUTION

Disraeli
Roberts, J.M., *The Mythology of the Secret Societies*. London: Secker & Warburg, 1972.

Dr. Gerard Encausse
Jonge de, Alex, *The Life & Times of Grigorii Rasputin*. London: William Collins, 1982.

Hapsburgs
Marek, George, *The Eagles Die*. London: Hart Davis & McGibbon, 1974.

Bulwer Lytton
Jennings, Hargraves, *The Rosicrucians & Their Rites & Mysteries*. Privately Printed, 1887.
McIntosh, Christopher, *The Rosicrucians*. Wellingborough, England: Crucible, 1987.

Order of New Templars
Goodwick-Clarke, Nicholas, *The Occult Roots of Nazism*. Wellingborough, England: Aquarian Press, 1985.

Ordo Templi Orientis
King, Francis, *Sexuality, Magic & Perversion*. London: New English Library, 1971.

Racial Supremacy
Goodwick-Clarke, Nicholas, *The Occult Roots of Nazism*. Wellingborough, England: Aquarian Press, 1985.

Sarajevo
Brook, Shepherd, George, *Victims of Sarajevo*. London: Hamill Press, 1984.
Vivian, Herbert, *Secret Societies*. London: Thornton Butterworth, 1927.

Secret Societies
Troyat, Henri, *Alexander of Russia*. London: New English Library, 1982.

Socialist League
King, Francis, *Sexuality, Magic & Perversion*. London: New English Library, 1971.
Other
Bruce, Lincoln, *The Romanovs*. London: Weidenfield & Nicholson, 1981.

CHAPTER SIX
NAZISM & THE OCCULT TRADITION

Aleister Crowley
Deacon, Richard, *A History of British Secret Service*. London: Frederick Muller, 1969.

Gurdjieff
Bancroft, Anne, *Modern Mystics & Sages*. London: Granada, 1978.

Kaiser Wilhelm
Aronson, Theo, *The Kaisers*. London: Cassell, 1971.

Psychic Warfare
Gardner, Gerald, *Witchcraft Today*. London: Rider & Co., 1952.
Glass, Justine, *Witchcraft, the Sixth Sense & Us*. London: Neville Spearman, 1965.
Hutton, J.B., *Women in Espionage*. London: MacMillan, 1971.
McCormick, Donald, *Murder by Witchcraft*. London: John Long, 1968.
Wuiff, Wilhelm, *Zodiac & Swastika*. London: Coward, McCann & Geoghegon, 1972.

Society of Union and Progress
Goodwick-Clarke, Nicholas, *The Occult Roots of Nazism*. Wellingborough, England: Aquarian Press, 1985.

Other
Fortune, Dion, *Psychic Self Defence*. Wellingborough, England: Aquarian Press, 1963.
King, Francis, *Satan and Swastika*. London: Granada, 1976.
Masters, Anthony, *The Man Who Was M: Maxwell Knight*. London: Basil Blackwater, 1984.
Petitpierre, Dom Robert, *Exorcising Devils*. London: Robert Hale, 1976.
Pool, James & Suzanne, *Who Financed Hitler?* London: MacDonald & Jane, 1979.
Wheatly, Dennis, *Gunmen, Gallants & Ghosts*. London: Arrow Books, 1963.

CHAPTER SEVEN
SECRETS IN THE VATICAN

Frederick II
Burman, Edward, *The Templars*. Wellingborough, England: Crucible, 1987.

Gospel of Mark
Smith, Dr. Morton, *The Secret Gospel*. London: Victor Gollanz, 1974.

Illuminist Conspiracy
Webster, Nesta, *Secret Societies & Subversive Movements*. London: Boswell, 1924.

Priory of Sion
Baignet, Leigh & Lincoln, *Holy Blood, Holy Grail*. New York: Dell Publishing Co., Inc., 1982.

Propaganda Two
Marshall, Jonathan, "Brief Notes on the Political Importance of Secret Societies." Hull, England: *Lobster*, Issues 5 & 6, 1984.
Yallop, David, *In God's Name*. London: Cape, 1984.

The Vatican
Comptom, Peirs, *The Broken Cross*. Channel Islands: Neville Spearman, 1981.

CHAPTER EIGHT
THE OCCULT & MODERN POLITICS

Bilderberg Group
Eringer, Robert, *The Global Manipulators*. Bristol, England: Pentacle Books, 1980.

Heindel
McIntosh, Christopher, *The Rosicrucians*. Wellingborough, England: Crucible, 1987.

International Order of Chivalry, Solar Tradition
Delaforge, Gaeton, *The Templar Tradition in the Aquarian Age*. Putney, Vermont: Threshold Books, 1987.

Organizations for World Peace and World Government
Wilgus, Neal, *The Illuminoids*. Albuquerque: Sun Books, 1978.

Rudolf Steiner
Bancroft, Anne, *Modern Mystics & Sages*. London: Granada, 1978.

Other
Webster, Nesta, *Secret Societies & Subversive Movements*. London: Boswell, 1924.

INDEX